Medieval Pets

Medieval Pets

Kathleen Walker-Meikle

THE BOYDELL PRESS

First published 2012
The Boydell Press, Woodbridge
Paperback edition 2020

ISBN 978 1 84383 758 9 hardback
ISBN 978 1 78327 569 4 paperback

The Boydell Press is an imprint of Boydell & Brewer Ltd
PO Box 9, Woodbridge, Suffolk IP12 3DF, UK
and of Boydell & Brewer Inc.
668 Mount Hope Ave, Rochester, NY 14620-2731, USA
website: www.boydellandbrewer.com

A catalogue record for this book is available
from the British Library

Designed and typeset in Lucida Blackletter and Adobe Jenson by
David Roberts, Pershore, Worcestershire

Contents

$\mathcal{L}$ist of $\mathcal{I}$llustrations

✦ ✦
✦

This book has been produced with the generous assistance of
a grant from Isobel Thornley's Bequest
to the University of London
and
a grant from the Scouloudi Foundation
in association with the Institute of Historical Resarch.

Preface

ANIMALS abounded in all walks of medieval life. Humans hunted them, ate them, milked them, sheared them, skinned them, rode them, ploughed with them, and used them to draw wagons; they imbued them with symbolism, and put those symbols to work in contexts ranging from Bible exegesis to heraldry. However, this book examines *pets*: animals chosen by humans simply to perform the task of being companions.

Pet keeping is one of the most remarkable relationships between humans and animals. The pet is often allowed into restricted spaces, enjoys close physical proximity with its owner (whether carried around or allowed to sleep on beds), is often fed luxury food and indulged with specialist goods, such as cages or collars. It is frequently treated with greater kindness and care than that accorded to most of the owner's fellow humans. Unlike a fine horse or a falcon, which might also be treasured, nothing is asked of the pet except to provide companionship and amusement.

There has not previously been a broad overview of pets in Western Europe during the Middle Ages. Pets and their upkeep are mentioned occasionally in the secondary literature, but little space has been devoted to the practice of pet keeping itself. In the following pages I aim to shed light on that practice and draw attention to the evidence for its prevalence in the medieval period, drawing on a range of historical, literary and iconographic sources.

✦ ✦
✦

Acknowledgements

For guidance, encouragement, never-ending enthusiasm, and for suggesting working on pets in the first place, I must thank David d'Avray. Sophie Page read initial drafts, suggested sources, and had great confidence in the project. Thanks to a Marie Curie Social History of Europe and the Mediterranean fellowship, I was able to spend four months in Italy and dig deep in the Gonzaga archive, with the kind assistance of the staff at the Archivio di Stato di Mantova. Staff in other manuscript rooms, in particular the British Library and Bodleian Library, were very considerate in locating material. Thanks are also due to the Wellcome and Warburg libraries for their assistance. Regarding iconography, the Koninklijke Bibliotheek, the Museum Meermanno, Det Kongelig Bibliotekthe, and the Bibliothèque royale de Belgique were particularly helpful.

Miri Rubin and Peter Edwards reviewed an early version with sympathy. Many thanks to David Walker for photographs, Ivan Polancec for papal references, Mike Parker, Gherardo Ortalli, Sam Worby, Nigel Ramsey, Richard Thomas, Brigitte Resl, Catherine Rider, Martina Giese, John A. W. Lock, Alice Choyke, Krisztina Arany, Irina Metzler, Catherine Rider, Malcolm Jones, Paul D. A. Harvey, Briony Aitchison, Aleks Pluskowski, Desiree Scott, and Peter Biller, for all their help.

Thanks are also due to Caroline Palmer at Boydell & Brewer and David Roberts for final editing.

Unmeasured gratitude is due to Reider Payne, who read drafts with great care, humour, and a keen eye for detail. Finally, I dedicate this book to my parents, Alistair Walker and Isobel Meikle, who read drafts with tolerance and gave me their unwavering support.

Otto catelle
Delicium meum
Hic deditus

1
The Medieval Pet

What is a pet?

PETS are animals kept by humans for companionship. An animal only becomes a pet because its human owner chooses to keep it as one. There are no pets in nature. A 'pet' is thus an artificial, man-made category.

Although I use the English word 'pet' throughout this book, there was no comparable term in the medieval period. In most sources, both in Latin and the vernacular, the pet is identified by a term defining its exact species, such as dog (*canis*) or cat (*muriceps*). The English term 'pet' in the sense of a companion animal did not come into use until the sixteenth century, and even then only in Scotland and the north of England. The *Oxford English Dictionary* records the earliest use in reference to a pet animal in 1539 – 'for the keeping of certane Pettis' – these animals were parrots and monkeys, among others.[1]

The *Oxford English Dictionary* defines a pet as 'An animal (typically one which is domestic or tame) kept for pleasure or companionship', which perhaps does not fully capture the medieval concept. In *Man and the Natural World: Changing Attitudes in England, 1500–1800*, Keith Thomas defines a pet as an animal that was kept indoors, was not eaten and was given a name; these useful criteria may also be applied to the medieval pet.[2]

Pets blur the boundaries between animal and human status. They may be pampered and treated like members of the household. They are allowed indoors into human space, and can be fed and treated with as much care as that accorded to humans.

Pets are the objects of emotional attachment on the part of their owners, but emotional attachment alone is not a sufficient criterion to determine whether an animal is a pet, for in the medieval period other animals could be the objects of such attachment. Owners could have close relationships with animals used in outdoor recreational activities, such as birds used in falconry, or with animals that were technically utilitarian, notably horses, and might lavish care and affection on them.[3] For this reason, I have focused on animals kept indoors. Some medieval pets may well slip through this net, but it explains why the overwhelming majority of pets encountered in this book belonged to women, clerics and scholars, all of whom shared an indoor lifestyle. Thus pets can be gender markers, though the distinction is not always clear cut, and one ought not discount secular men who kept them.

A pet does not have to be small, but this was a useful quality for an animal kept indoors and often carried around. Many terms for pet dogs emphasize their small size: *catulus* or *caniculus* in Latin, *chienet* in Old French, *hündchen* in Middle German, *whelp* or *small hound* in Middle English, *cagnolo* or *cagnolino* in Italian and *perillo* or *blanchet* in Castilian.[4]

Medieval pets, by having no function other than to offer companionship, do not fall into the categories assigned to domestic animals: to be eaten, skinned, milked, or work for humans (be that anything from pastoral work to hunting). They had no particular legal status, as noted by William Lambard in *Eirenarcha* (1588), a manual for justices of the peace, because: 'to take dogs of any kind, apes, parats, singing birds or such like, (though they be in the house) is no Felonie: because these latter be but for pleasure only, and are not of any value'.[5]

The contrast between the spoiled and beloved pet and other domestic animals is laid bare in Marie de France's fable of *The Ass Who Wanted to Play with his Master*:

> There was a rich man, as I've read,
> Who kept a small dog [*chenet petit*].
> He frolicked with him constantly;
> This, the man's donkey chanced to see.
> The ass knew, deep within his breast,
> The dog was loved by all the rest
> Because he was his master's treasure
> And often served to give him pleasure …

The ass, believing that it exceeds the little dog in size and virtue, decides to copy the behaviour of the pet dog and thus win favour. One day, on seeing its master and pet dog playing, the ass decides to put his plan in action. He brays loudly and strikes the master with his hooves, imitating the way the little dog jumps around. The ass ends up knocking the master to the ground and is severely beaten for his pains. The fable ends with the ass returning to his stable, having learned the moral that those of lowly birth should not aspire higher.[6]

Medieval theology conventionally taught that pets, like all animals, lack spiritual souls. However, Adelard of Bath (1080–1152) argued in his *Quaestiones naturales* that animals do have souls, since they have sensation and the judgement to desire or avoid things, and judgement could only exist in the soul and not the body.[7] The idea that animals have non-immortal souls was greatly expanded by Thomas Aquinas (1225–74).

For Aquinas, like Aristotle, animals' souls are not immortal.[8] He followed Augustine, who held that animal souls are not rational, so that they disappear when animals die. Nevertheless, the issue of whether pets had souls does not seem to have diminished the affection lavished on them, nor the grief evoked at their passing.

Who kept pets?

M EDIEVAL pets were often symbolic of the possession of luxurious worldly goods, and the manner in which they were kept might demonstrate their owners' desire to emphasize their elevated social positions and show off their material assets. Nevertheless, we should be careful neither to give a purely economic explanation for the association between pet keeping and the upper classes, nor generalize pet keeping as a mere extravagance for those whose basic needs are fulfilled.[9]

Medieval pets differed from other animals on which care was lavished, notably fine horses, hunting hounds and hawks. All these required specialized attention by trained caretakers and resided in purpose-built accommodation (stables, kennels or mews). Pets, on the other hand, rarely ventured outside, and when they did, that was often under supervision, usually to frolic in enclosed gardens or to be carried if going further afield.

In the High and Late Middle Ages men and women could be identified by the animals they kept. Women and clerics (both the secular clergy and those in religious orders) constituted the vast majority of pet keepers. Although some secular men did keep pets, they generally preferred animals that reflected the qualities they wished to be seen as possessing: strength, loyalty, and fierceness. No purpose or innate qualities for a pet kept by a lady or cleric are technically required, other than to act as a companion. Loyalty is replaced by loving devotion; aggressiveness and strength are replaced by the capacity to distract and amuse. Like its owner, the pet had no need to 'fight' in the world. Since so many women and clerics owned pets, they became identity markers for these groups, in both public and private spheres. By being part of its owner's everyday life, sharing in many activities, the pet became part of the owner's persona. Extensive evidence for the connection between pet ownership and identity comes from images representing the owners with a pet.

The medieval pet, like its owners, did not belong to the 'outdoors' world, which was the province of secular married men. The 'outdoors' lifestyle embraced fighting and hunting, and was thus one in which, theoretically, women and clerics should not participate. They were expected instead to inhabit a nominal 'enclosed' space. Although many clerics, including bishops, travelling papal legates, wandering friars and students, did go out into the world, these excursions do not constitute an 'outdoors' lifestyle. Similarly, although some clerics disregarded the canonical prohibition on hunting, the very existence of a prohibition emphasizes that hunting was part of a lifestyle that they ought not share.[10] Many secular women did hunt, but their activities were circumscribed: they might be permitted to use only certain birds, such as the small sparrow hawk, and operated under close supervision.

Another indicator of the different spheres of action of both the owner and the pet is the conspicuous difference in size between the animals belonging to secular men on the one hand, and women and clerics on the other. The diminutive size of such animals excluded most functions other than being a companion, although certain species performed other roles, for example cats ridding the household of vermin.

There is a logic to the ambiguity of the gender categories, as clerics represented, as it were, a third gender by virtue of their functional celibacy. Since marriage and fighting, signs of masculinity, were barred to clerics, they functioned as another category of gendered identity.[11]

In Old Irish legal texts, pet dogs are associated with high-status women. The *Crith Gablach* declares that a lord should have a hunting hound, while his wife should have a pet dog. Another legal text refers to cats that are kept indoors by women and allowed to sleep in special baskets or on a pillow on the bed. In the Irish texts the usual term for a pet dog is *messán*, a diminutive of the word *mess*, a favourite. In addition, the text links pet dogs to particular occupations: a physician, a harpist, a queen and a hospitaller (*briugu*).[12] That all these male professions which 'allowed pets' are all of the non-fighting variety illustrates the link between pet keeping and gender.

However, these conventions were not rigid. Pet keeping abounds in accounts of royalty of both genders. Alfonso X 'The Wise' of Castile (1221–84) kept a pet weasel and even wrote a *cantiga* on his beloved animal: 'the little beast who so loved the king'.[13] In urban areas, men and women alike kept pets. There is a late fourteenth-century *exemplum* that chastises an advocate for excessive affection for his pet dogs. The lawyer loves only his dogs and sleeps alone on his bed with them. He is found dead by his wife and clients: the dogs, once he is dead and no longer able to provide for them, prove unfaithful, and are discovered eating the corpse.[14] This theme of the foolishness of excessive devotion to one's pets has parallels in *exempla* directed against pet-keeping women. An illustration in an early thirteenth-century *Chirugia* manuscript depicts a surgeon holding a pair of balances with a small dog on his lap; in an early fifteenth-century

Italian *exemplum* doctors visit their patients accompanied by a pet monkey.[15]

By the fifteenth century pet keeping was almost *de rigueur* among scholars and those with scholarly pretensions. Pets appear as a motif in representations of lay scholars, in iconography, verse and letters. Although it would be over-simple to suggest that art and literature merely mimic life, nevertheless the evidence suggests that pets formed a regular part of scholarly domestic life, and were not merely an artistic and literary motif.

It is often assumed that pet keeping as a widespread social phenomenon emerges only in the early modern period. While it is true that most of the medieval sources are concentrated on the higher strata of society, depicting pets as a popular pastime among the nobility and merchant classes, that evidence should not interpreted as meaning pet keeping was confined to those classes.[16]

Types of pets

ALTHOUGH any animal could become a pet, certain species were more commonly kept for that purpose. The most popular choices were small dogs; other favoured species were cats, monkeys, singing and talking birds, squirrels, ferrets and rabbits.[17]

Dogs[18]

The defining feature of pet dogs was usually small size, rather than any favoured breed. The only specific lapdog breed mentioned in the sources is the small snub-nosed long-haired (usually white) Melitaean, which appears profusely in the iconography of noble ladies. The term 'Melitaean' stems from Classical Antiquity, when this dog was presumed to have come from the island of Malta. The early Christian writer Clement of Alexandria (150?–215?) provides an early antecedent to medieval criticism of spoilt pets when he complained about women who 'overlook the chaste widow, who is of far higher value than a Melitaean puppy'.[19] However, there are no sources for a direct breeding line from Antiquity to the Middle Ages, by which time the term might be used to refer to any pet dog, normally one that was long-haired and had white fur. In late medieval iconography Melitaean dogs generally appear to be part of the bichon landrace,[20] but this is arguable, as images of dogs are rarely accompanied by a written description, and most sources referring to pet dogs limit themselves to adjectives concerning the animal's size, colour and fur length. To add confusion, small spaniels were often called Melitaeans as well. The small dogs portrayed in the series of late fifteenth-century

'La Dame à la licorne' tapestries at the Musée national du Moyen Âge in Paris are prime examples of the 'Melitaean' type. In the tapestry 'A mon seul désir', a long-haired white dog sits facing the audience on a brocade cushion on a bench next to the lady, while in the tapestry 'Le Goût', a long-haired white dog stands on the train of the lady's dress, looking up at her.[21] In an illuminated initial from a fifteenth-century Italian choirbook, now in the Victoria and Albert Museum, one of these dogs plays with a chained pet monkey in the company of King David (fig. 10).

Among the hunting breeds that were popular as pets we can include a variety of spaniels, often of a smallish size, and small scent hounds such as the *bracke*.[22] Contrary to the general rule that favoured small size, greyhounds were also popular as pets. White appears the most common coat colour in iconography, but this might simply be an artistic convention. Dogs came in all colours, including brown, dappled, black, spotted, and red. Their coats could be smooth or curly, and their nose shapes could be snub, round or pointed. An example of this assortment can be seen in an early sixteenth-century manuscript in the British Library showing the genealogy of the royal houses of Spain and Portugal. In the illuminations a spectrum of small pets appears in close proximity to their owners. For example, on one folio Doña Inhega holds a smooth-haired white dog, while on another Doña Constança pats a curly fine-coated brown one; Doña Ermesenda has a grey long-haired dog on her lap, and Doña Isabel holds a tiny brown one in her arms.[23]

Regarding types of dogs, we must remember that they were generally classified according to function, and breeds were considerably less closely defined than they are now. John Caius, in his seminal work on English dogs *De canibus Britannicis* (1570), divides all dogs into: 'a gentle kind, serving the game', 'a homely kind, apt for sundry necessary uses' and 'a currishe kind, meet for many toys'.[24] With respect to game dogs, he distinguishes between those destined for hunting and those for fowling. Among the hunting dogs he lists the 'Harier, the Terrar, the Bloudhounde, the Gasehounde, the Grehounde, the Leuiner or Lyemmer, the Tumbler' and the non-barking 'Theeuishe Dogge'; among the fowling dogs, the often multi-spotted 'Spaniell, the Setter, the water Spaniell or Finder', and the 'Fisher'.

After the two categories of game dogs, all 'gentle', Caius moves on to pets dogs: 'our Englishe Dogges of the thirde gentle kinde', the 'delicate, neate, and pretty kind of dogges called the Spaniel gentle, or the comforter' (*Melitaeus or Fotor*). After claiming that these dogs came originally from Malta, he describes their nature, a frivolous and idle one, destined purely for companionship:

These dogges are litle, pretty, proper, and fyne, and sought for to satisfie the delicatenesse of daintie dames, and wanton womens wills, instrumentes of folly for them to play and dally withall, to tryfle away the treasure of time, to withdraw their mindes from more commendable exercises, and to content their corrupted concupiscences with vaine disport (A selly shift to shunne yrcksome ydlnesse.)

After a long discourse on their uselessness and spoiled nature, Caius attempts to find the 'vertue which remaineth in the Spainell gentle otherwise called the comforter'. He falls back onto the traditional belief that little dogs, if pressed to the stomach: 'are good to asswage the sicknesse of the stomacke being oftentimes thervnto applyed as a plaster preseruatiue, or borne in the bosom of the diseased and weake person, which effect is performed by theyr moderate heate.' He concludes by declaring that the general term for such pet dogs is *Canis delicatus* and they are 'a chamber companion', 'a pleasant playfellow' and 'a pretty worme'.

Among the remaining English dogs, Caius discusses working dogs, which include the 'mastiue or Bandogge', the 'Dogge keeper' (a guard dog), the 'Butchers Dogge', the '*Molossus*', the 'Dogge messinger' who 'carrieth letters from place to place, wrapped up cunningly in his lether collar', the 'Mooner' (a dog who barks at the moon), the 'water drawer' (turns well wheels), the 'Tynckers Curre' (which carries the tinker's buckets on its back), and 'defending dogges'. Caius finishes with the lowliest sort of dogs, of 'mungrell and rascall sort': the 'Warner' (which just barks), the 'Turnespete' (which turns the spit in kitchens) and the 'Daunser' (a performing dog that dances to music). The difference between the 'pleasaunt playfellow' lapdog and the 'mungrell and rascall sort' is laid bare in Shakespeare's *Two Gentlemen of Verona*, when Proteus wishes to send a 'little jewel' of a dog to Silvia. The lapdog is lost by his servant Launce, who substitutes his own dog, Crab, a 'cur', with disastrous results.[25]

The pet breeds Caius describes are not mentioned in most treatises on dogs, nearly all of which deal only with game dogs. For example, Edward, Duke of York's fifteenth-century hunting treatise *The Master of Game* (a translation of Gaston Phébus's celebrated *Livre de chasse* with some additional material) describes the different types of hounds, distinguishing between running hounds, greyhounds, alauntes, spaniels and mastiffs. All are game dogs, apart from the mastiff, whose 'office is to keep his master's beasts and his master's house'.[26] Pet dogs, which had no 'office', apart from offering the hard-to-define commodity of companionship, had no place in the world of the hunt, so naturally they are not mentioned.

Fig. 1 Tobias, with his dog at his feet, cures his father Tobit of blindness.
(Jacob van Maerlant's Rhimebible, Utrecht, 1332)

Although during Classical Antiquity the dog was usually treated as a symbol of fidelity,[27] nearly all biblical references to dogs are negative. The exception is in the Book of Tobit, which relates how Tobias is accompanied by his faithful pet dog in his search to find a cure for his father's blindness.[28] The dog plays no part in the narrative, but is an ubiquitous character in the medieval iconography of the story. See fig. 1 (Tobias curing father's blindness) and plate V (Tobias and Sarah's wedding night).

For the twelfth-century Hildegard of Bingen, dogs had a special affinity with humans, owing to the love and loyalty that they bore for their owner. She ascribes to all dogs an ability for prognostication. Dogs are able not only to recognize whether a person is treacherous or a thief, and growl and gnash their teeth accordingly, but can foretell happy future events by being cheerful and wagging their tails, and, conversely, predict evil ones by howling. Hildegard also wrote that the Devil hates dogs because of their loyalty to humans.[29]

Dogs in the medieval bestiary 'know their name and love their master' and 'cannot live without human company'. The bestiary tells of one King Garamentes who was rescued by his dogs when captured by enemies, how Jason's dog's refused food on the death of his master, and how a dog in Ancient Rome tried to rescue the corpse of his dead master from the Tiber.

Bestiary lore also insists that due to their devotion, dogs can uncover the murderers of their masters, a theme which reoccurs in *chansons de geste*.[30] (Fig. 2 shows a bestiary image of a dog attacking his master's murderer and pining next to the master's dead body.) *The Goodman of Paris* (1392–4), a text on household management written by an older husband for the benefit of his young wife, recounts the traditional tale of a dog fighting his master's murderer, adding some contemporary details (names, dates and places) for verisimilitude. After the murder in 1371 of Aubry de Montdidier, his dog showed particular hatred for a man called Macaire. Charles V of France (r. 1364–80) ordered a trial by combat between Macaire and the dog. The dog won the duel; Macaire confessed to the crime and was hanged. The text relates that traces of the lists of the duel could still be seen in the fields on the island of Notre-Dame in Paris. The story of the murderer Macaire and the dog appears in many other sources, including Gaston Phébus's fourteenth-century *Livre de chasse*, where it appears among many other tales of canine loyalty.

The author of *The Goodman of Paris* also claims to have even seen with his own eyes a case of canine loyalty unto death. When the French took the town of Niort after the battle of Chiset in 1373, he saw there an old dog lying day and night on a grave where its master, slain by the English, had been buried. The Duke of Berry, on witnessing the dog's refusal to leave the grave was greatly moved and arranged for the animal to receive a pension of ten francs for life, which was delivered to a neighbour to feed it until it died.

The Goodman of Paris emphasizes the loyalty of commonplace dogs, not just exceptional ones like the dog of Niort, which a loving and loyal wife should attempt to emulate:

> Of domestic animals you shall see how that a greyhound or mastiff or little dog, whether it be on the road, or at table, or in bed, ever keepeth him close to the person from whom he taketh his food and leaveth all the others and is distant and shy with them; and if the dog is afar off, he always has his heart and his eye upon his master; even if his master whip him and throw stones at him, the dog followeth, wagging his tail and lying down before his master to appease him,

Fig. 2 A dog attacks his master's murderer and mourns over the body
(Bestiary, France, *c.* 1450)

and through rivers, through woods, through thieves and through
battles followeth him.[31]

Despite this digression on canine loyalty, it should be noticed that all
the examples of the fidelity of dogs, up to death, are associated with dogs
belonging to lay men. The loyal dogs of women and clerics rarely figure in
such tales, and their role as affectionate companions appears to have been
paramount.

Dogs are the medieval pet *par excellence*, and were seen as having
greater virtue than animals such as cats or monkeys. In honour of
their admirable qualities, above all loyalty, the twelfth-century scholar
Alexander Neckham places them first among all domestic animals in his
De naturis rerum.[32]

Cats

Cats were popular medieval pets. Their role, though, was more ambiguous
than that of dogs, as in many households they were kept as mousers as
well as pets.[33] Since they would forage for their own food or eat leftovers,
they are hard to trace in accounts. In the twelfth-century accounts of a
lease of a manor of St Paul's, there are mentions of one 'elderly cat' and of
two 'young cats'. For the manor of Cuxham in 1293–4 there is an entry for
cheese bought for a cat ('I caseum comm' per catum'); although this cat
may have been a mouser as well, the fact that it was being fed special food
and not left to fend for itself may point to its being a companion animal.[34]

The thirteenth-century scholar Bartholomeus Anglicus in his *De
proprietatibus rebus* wrote that cats came in different colours: white, red,
black, and 'some spotted like a leopard'. Nevertheless, it appears from the

iconography that the majority of medieval cats were grey with stripes. Bartholemus continued by describing them as having large mouths, sharp teeth and long soft tongues. When young, they jumped on everything put before them and would chase and play with a straw led in front of them. In contrast, when elderly they were heavy and always sleepy.[35]

His contemporary, Albertus Magnus (*c.* 1200–1280), in his *De animalibus*, speaks of how the cat:

> Takes delight in cleanliness and for this reason imitates the washing of a face by licking its front paws and then, by licking it, smoothes all of its fur ... This animal loves to be lightly stroked by human hands and is playful, especially when it is young. When it sees its own image in a mirror it plays with that and if, perchance, it should see itself from above in the water of a well, it wants to play, falls in, and drowns since it is harmed by being made very wet and dies unless it is dried out quickly. It especially likes warm places and can be kept home more easily if its ears are clipped since it cannot tolerate the night dew dripping into its ears. It is both wild and domesticated. The wild ones are all grey in colour, but the domestic ones have various colours. They have whiskers around their mouth and if these are cut off they loose their boldness.[36]

Another thirteenth-century encyclopaedist, Thomas de Cantimpré, added the characteristic of purring when describing cats: 'They delight in being stroked by the hand of a person and they express their joy with their own form of singing.'[37]

In marked contrast to what she has to say of dogs, which are characterized by their loyalty, Hildegard of Bingen describes cats as unfaithful, since they will only stay with whoever feeds them.[38]

There are traces of medieval cats not only in medieval sources but on the sources themselves. Manuscripts left open might tempt muddy or dusty paws. There are folios littered with paw-prints in two twelfth-century English manuscripts (British Library Royal MS 6 C X, f. 19v and Burney MS 326, f. 104v) and several smudged pawprints on a page of a fifteenth-century *Sophologium* (Magdalen College Oxford Arch.B.III.1.5). The smudged ones might indicate signs of a struggle to get the cat off the page! A copy of Astesanus of Asti's *Summa de casibus conscientiae* (printed in 1472–3), now in University of Otago Library, has three inky cat paw prints on one page (250), which were probably created when the printed pages were laid out to dry. In the same vein there are three distinct cat paw prints in a medieval floor tile in St. Peter's church, Wormleighton (Warwickshire), attesting a feline witness while the clay was still wet.

Other evidence of feline interraction with text is attested in a early fifteenth-century manuscript written in Deventer, Netherlands, (Cologne, Historisches Archiv, G.B. Quarto, 249, f. 68r). The scribe wrote a furious colophon cursing the cat to explain the empty space on the page, after finding that a cat had urinated on it at some point in the night before, encouraging other cats to follow suite. He added a drawing of a cat to complete his written testimony[39]

In Chaucer's *The Manciple's Tale*, the wildness of the domestic cat is underlined and compared to a wife, both being captives and lustful. While an owner might spoil a cat with milk and meat, and give it silk bedding, it is still wild at heart and could easily leave such luxuries behind in order to catch a mouse:

> Lat take a cat, and fostre hym wel with milk
> And tendre flessh, and make his couche of silk,
> And lat hym seen a mou go by the wal,
> Anon he weyveth milk and flessh and al,
> And every deyntee that is in that hous,
> Swich appetit hath he to ete a mous.
> Lo, heere hath lust his dominacioun
> And appetit fleemeth discrecioun[40]

The Wife of Bath relates how one of her former husbands used to say to her:

> Thou seydest this, that I was lyk a cat;
> For whoso wolde senge a cattes skyn,
> Thanne wolde the cat wel dwellen in his in;
> And if the cattes skyn be slyk and gay,
> She wol nat dwelle in house half a day,
> But forth she wole, er any day be dawed,
> To shewe hir skyn, and goon a-caterwawed.[41]

Just as the Wife of Bath is accused by her husband of being a cat, she in turn calls him 'as dronken as a mouse', emphasizing her predatory nature. And the female cat, according to Aristotle, was believed to be a very lustful beast. The reference to singeing a cat's fur relates to the belief that it would make the animal keep to the house.[42] Jacques de Vitry has an *exemplum* concerning a beautiful cat that likes to go wandering until its master burns its tail and pulls out its hairs, after which it is too ashamed to leave the house.[43]

In the Middle Ages the cat had many negative connotations. It was commonly associated with the Devil. In the early fourteenth century Arnold of Liège compared a cat playing with a mouse to the Devil toying with a human soul.[44] They were also linked with heresy. The twelfth-century French theologian Alan de Lille claimed that the very name of the Cathars came from cats, and that they worshipped a black cat, the Devil in disguise, and would kiss its bottom during their services. One of the charges against the Knights Templar in 1309 was an accusation that they worshipped a cat.[45]

The phenomenon of animal familiars in early-modern witchcraft trials in England is beyond the scope of this book, although many of the alleged familiars appear to have been the pets of the accused. Not only cats, but dogs, toads and bats (among other creatures) were identified as familiars. In one of the earliest trials, in 1324 Dame Alice Kytler from Kilkenny, Ireland, was accused of practising *malificia* along with poisoning her husbands, and it was alleged that an incubus visited her in the shape of large furry black cat. In one of the earliest cases of a cat familiar at an English witch trial, in 1556 one Elizabeth Francis in Chelmsford was accused of keeping company with a large white spotted cat she had called Satan, her alleged familiar, and which had its own sleeping basket.[46] The cat's association with magic, heresy and witchcraft relates in part to its peculiar status as being both domesticated and wild.

Monkeys, birds and other animals

Monkeys were an expensive high-status pet. In Latin texts they are called *simia*, a term that covers both long-tailed monkeys and the tailless Barbary ape. The most popular types kept as pets were imported tailed monkeys.[47] They were widely available in Western Europe from the twelfth century, when Hugh of Saint-Victor chastised clerics for keeping them as pets 'even though the ape is a most vile, filthy, and detestable animal'.[48] They were a popular image in iconography; apart from their presence in affluent domestic interiors as pets, they were used as a symbol of men's folly and vanity.[49] Monkeys take on the worst qualities of men, and in literature are full of greed, malice and devilment.[50] A fable on household pets relates how the monkey encourages the pet dog (or cat) to pull roasting chestnuts out of a fire. The deed done, the monkey eats the chestnuts, leaving the dog or cat hungry, with burnt paws.[51]

All these animals were Old World monkeys and apes, but in the early sixteenth century New World monkeys also came to be adopted as pets. This can be seen in a painting dating from *c.* 1532–6 by Hans Holbein the Younger, in which a young man poses with a pet marmoset.[52]

The thirteenth-century encyclopaedist Thomas de Cantimpré discusses the diet of monkeys. He claims their favourite food is apples and nuts, but if they find a nut with a bitter rind, they will not bother to extract the kernel, but instead will merely discard the nut.[53]

Albertus Magnus discusses monkeys in his *De animalibus*, and describes them playing with other pets. However, they should not be thought of as completely tame, and they could resort to violence:

> [On monkeys] The one that is found most often bears a similarity to humans in the shape of its head and ears and its hands, feet, and reproductive parts. It also has breasts on chest as does a woman, but it is hairy. ... it is imitative of humans and mimics human actions. ... The monkey is a tricky animal with bad habits. However much it might be tamed, it is always wild and imitates the bad rather than the good human traits. It is playful with the small offspring of humans and dogs, but it sometimes strangles unguarded boys, sometimes hurling them off a height. It collects vermin on heads and clothing and eats them. It remembers a wrong for a long time ... When it has been tamed and is living in a house and it gives birth, it shows its offspring to the people as if they were beautiful and pleasing.[54]

Bartholomeus Anglicus also describes monkeys eating vermin off people's heads. A monkey could be tamed by tying it to a heavy block, to stop it running about.[55] It could be disciplined, and trained to turn somersaults and similar tricks. Depictions of domesticated apes invariably show them with a collar and chain, as seen in a twelfth-century walrus ivory draughts piece (fig. 4).

Other popular pet animals included squirrels, which were usually kept on collars and leashes (fig. 8), ferrets (or weasels), and rabbits. Although rabbits were farmed for their meat and kept in warrens, this did not preclude them from being chosen as pets, particularly by nuns.[56] On rare occasions, beasts of burden could become pets, though not using such an animal for work or for food was uneconomical.

More unusually, Charles VIII of France (r. 1483–98) had a marmot as a pet.[57] But possibly the most eccentric collection of pets was that of the Italian artist Giovanni Antonio Bazzi (known as Il Sodoma, 1477–1549), who kept a variety of animals such as badgers, squirrels, monkeys, doves and miniature donkeys in his house, which, his biographer Vasari tells us, resembled a veritable Noah's ark.[58] The artist even immortalized his pets in a self-portrait forming part of the fresco cycle of the life of St Benedict in the cloisters of the Benedictine monastery of Monte Oliveto Maggiore,

Tuscany. He is depicted with two pet badgers, one of which wears a red leather collar with silver studs (plate IX).

Various species of singing and talking birds were kept as pets in cages, including thrushes, nightingales, blackbirds, turtle doves, starlings, skylarks, magpies and finches.[59] One of the pleasures of keeping birds was teaching them to talk: the fourteenth-century Dominican preacher John Bromyard writes of 'caged birds that learn to sing or talk as they hear men speak in English or French'.[60]

The most exotic bird kept as a pet was the parrot. The only species known in Europe in the Middle Ages was the green Indian rose-ringed parakeet (*Psittacula krameri*) described in the satirical poem *Speke Parrot* by John Skelton (1460–1529):

> My feathyrs fresshe as ys the emerawde grene,
> Abowte my necke a cerculett lyke the ryche rubye.[61]

Parrots appear profusely in the sources from the late thirteenth century onwards, although their presence, albeit as rare pets, is attested earlier on. Two parrots, sitting on a pine tree, are carved on a misericord in Wells Cathedral (*c.* 1330–40); a large green parrot preens itself in the *bas-de-page* of a folio of a late thirteenth-century French manuscript, while another parrot sits in the margin of a contemporary English manuscript.[62] Elizabeth de Burgh, Duchess of Clarence, owned two parrots over a decade later.[63] A parrot even sports a gold collar in a fifteenth-century English bestiary (plate III).

Notable parrots in literature include the parrot go-between in Arnaut de Carcasses's thirteenth-century *Las novas del papagay*; King Arthur's loquacious parrot in the romance *Le Chevalier du Papegau*; a similar talkative parrot appears in the Middle High German romance *Wigalois*; and a parrot narrator comforts Marguerite of Austria in Jean Lemaire de Belges's *Les Épîtres de l'amant vert*, a work which in turn influenced the Scottish poet Sir David Lindsay's *Papyngo*, in which a parrot narrator 'writes' two satirical epistles, and Skelton's *Speke Parrot*, another parrot narrator with a sharp taste in political satire (in particular against Cardinal Wolsey).[64]

It was believed that by their nature, parrots automatically said 'Ave', although they could be trained to speak other words. As 'Ave' was the greeting of the archangel Gabriel to the Virgin Mary, they were seen as a symbol of purity, and associated with the Virgin. This accounts for their presence in imagery of the Virgin Mary, as seen in a French book of hours, *c.* 1500, in which the Virgin holds the Christ child, who has a parrot sitting on his wrist.[65] Pliny the Elder's writings on parrots formed part of medieval parrot lore, relating to such matters as the incredible hardness of its beak and how it could be trained to speak by being disciplined with an iron bar.[66]

Names of pets[67]

MEDIEVAL animals, including pets, could have names that were either generic or individual. The generic name is usually derived from a human name and applied to the entire animal species. Generic names for birds in English included Mag (from Margaret) for pies, Robin for redbreasts, and Philip for sparrows. This generic name might also be used as the name for an individual pet – for example, the deceased and much-lamented pet sparrow in John Skelton's poem *The Boke of Phyllyp Sparowe*.[68] In French generic names for animals which could be pets include Robert for a monkey, Fouquet for a squirrel, Pierre for a parrot, Rochard for a jay, Pierrot for a sparrow, Margos for a magpie and Colas for a crow.[69]

In English the generic name for a tomcat was Gyb (the shortened form of the male name Gilbert), and was a popular name for individual pet cats. Its earliest use is on a late fourteenth-century seal of one Gilbert Stone which depicts a cat with a mouse and the legend 'GRET: WEL: GIBBE: OURE: CAT'.[70] The cat who eats Jane Scrope's sparrow Philip in Skelton's poem is called Gyb.[71] There is 'gib our cat' in the early sixteenth-century play *Gammer Gurton's Needle*,[72] 'Gyb, the catte' in John Lydgate's early fifteenth-century *Aesop*, and 'Gybbe, owre grey catt' in the late fifteenth-century poem *Leve Lystynes*.[73] In Shakespeare's *Henry IV Part I*, Act 1, scene 2, Falstaff declaims, 'I am as melancholy as a gib cat or a lugged bear.' The late fifteenth-century Scottish poet Robert Henryson uses the name Gib for a cat in his version of the Town Mouse and the Country Mouse (*The Taill of the Uponlandis Mous and the Burges Mous*), along with the Scots name Baudrons, which was also used in Scotland as a generic cat name:

> Where when the two mice are on a table-topy:
> scantlie had thay drunkin anis or twyse
> Quhen in come Gib Hunter, oure cat.[74]

The English translation of the French poem *Le Roman de la rose* renders the proper name of the cat, Tibers, as 'Gibbe our cat'. Tibers/Tibert was the corresponding generic name for a domestic cat in French. Tibert the Cat is also one of the companions of Reynard the Fox in the Reynard animal fables.[75]

In contrast to the frequently used generic species names derived from human names, individual names – that is particular names just for one specific animal – are rare in the sources. When they do appear, they are usually descriptive or fanciful in nature, though occasionally they are normal human names. Among individual names for cats, there is 'Mite', which is drawn and named in a thirteenth-century account book from Beaulieu Abbey,[76] and Belaud, the beloved grey cat of the sixteenth-century French poet Joachim du Bellay. Individual cat names that refer to the animal's physical appearance appear in Old Irish legal texts, including Méone (little meow'), Cruibne ('little paws'), Bréone (little flame, probably an orange cat) and Glas nenta ('nettle grey').[77] Pangur Bán, the cat immortalized in a ninth-century poem by an Irish monk was likely a white cat, as the name is a reference to fuller's earth.[78]

Individual dog names could derive from physical attributes, such as Sturdy, a dog belonging to Nicholas Litlyngton, a fourteenth-century abbot of Westminster,[79] or Whitefoot, the dog of a fifteenth-century English family.[80] A Berkshire manorial court ordered John Barker to get rid of his brindled dog called Hardy.[81] Anne Boleyn owned a dog called Purkoy (originally belonging to Lady Lisle), a name derived from the French 'Pourquoi' due to the animal's inquisitive expression.[82]

Dogs could have names derived from their breed, such as Terri, a little dog with its name engraved on the collar on the brass (*c.* 1400) of Alice, wife of Sir John Cassy, in Deerhurst church, Gloucestershire.[83] In Chaucer's *The Nun's Priest Tale*, one line names three dogs: 'Ran Colle oure dogge, and Talbot and Gerland'.[84] Colle is a reference to the herding collie landrace, and a talbot was a large white hunting dog, although the name was often used as a generic name for many large dogs. Gerland was not based on any dog breed, but was a personal name.

The dog on the effigy (1448) of Sir Brian de Stapleton, at Ingham, Norfolk, is called Jakke, while a dog on a tomb of a member of the de Reynes family, in Clifton Reynes, Buckinghamshire, has the name Bo etched on its collar.[85] Parceval is the name of the hound at the feet of the French knight Jehan de Seure (d. 1391) and Dyamant is the name on the collar of his lady's dog on their effigies at Ozouer-le-Repos, Seine-et-Marne.[86]

A list of a thousand and a hundred names suitable for hunting dogs is appended to a manuscript of *The Master of Game*, referred to above, listing different names for hounds, brachets, terriers and greyhounds. Although meant to help masters of hounds pick names, some might have been in usage among dogs kept as pets. Among the names are Troy, Blawnche, Nosewise, Swepestake, Smylfeste, Trynket, Amiable, Nameles, Clenche,

Bragge, Holdfast, Crab, Ringwood and Absolom. Manuscripts of Gaston Phébus list hounds named Bauderon, Baudellette, Bloquiau, Briffault, Cliquau, Fillette, Huielle, Huiiau, Loquebaut, Mirre and Ostine.[87]

Another list of dog names survives from the records of a shooting-festival in Zurich in 1504, which lists the names of the participants and their dogs, some eighty animals in all. The most popular name was Fürst(li) (Prince). Dogs with exotic, Classical and names from romance included Artus, Melesinn, Venus, Fortuna, Turgk and Soldan. The dogs called Sattin and Dammast must have had smooth and shiny coats. There are even dogs called after their owner's occupation. Stosel (Pestle) is an apothecary's dog, Hemmerli (Little Hammer) is a locksmith's and Speichli (Little Spoke) belonged to a wagoner.[88]

Other fanciful names include Hapeguay, the pet of Louise of Savoy who died in 1502,[89] and those of the pet dogs from the Mantuan court in the fifteenth and sixteenth centuries, which included Mamia, Aura, Zaphyro, Famia, Bellina, Rubino, Viola and Orsina. A court cat at Mantua received the more prosaic human name of Martino. Court pets included dogs called Mignone, Violina and Courte. The most renowned pet dog in romance is Isolde's lapdog Petitcreiu. Pet dogs belonging to scholars in the fifteenth and sixteenth centuries include Zabot, Lachne, Bembino, Balbina, Borgettus, Saphyrus, Mopsus, Mopsulus, Mamselle, and Monsieur.

Pet names could be humorous, like the sire of Leon Battista Alberti's dog, who was called Megastomo (Big Mouth),[90] or even satirical, such as the little lapdog Gardiner who belonged to Katherine, Duchess of Suffolk, one of Queen Katherine Parr's maids of honour, and named after Stephen Gardiner, Bishop of Winchester.[91]

Criticism of pets and their owners

THE treatment of pets as spoiled equals may explain much contemporary criticism. Medieval critics objected to ostentatious pet keeping, viewing it as both as an extravagance and a distraction from one's duties and obligations, in particular charity to the poor. This may explain why pets are markedly absent from tales or depictions of 'famous and virtuous women', such as those written by Giovanni Boccaccio and Christine de Pisan. Such morally elevated ladies would have had no time for frivolous pets. It is ironic, then, that the *authors* of these texts appear with their pets in images of themselves.[92] In a fifteenth-century manuscript of her works, Christine de Pisan writes in her study accompanied by a small white dog with a red leather collar covered in bells.[93] A similar image appears in a manuscript produced by the Cité des Dames workshop, in which Christine writes while a medium-haired small dog sits on the tiles in front of her.[94] In another fifteenth-century manuscript the poet Boccaccio is seated on a bed with a tabby cat nearby as he converses with an apparition of Petrarch. In the depiction of the same scene in a mid-fifteenth-century French manuscript of Boccaccio's *De casu virorum et foeminarum illustrium*, the poet is accompanied by a dog wearing a blue collar. Elsewhere in the same manuscript, Boccaccio addresses Manutius and followers with an attentive dog at his feet, now wearing a red collar.[95]

If a virtuous lady had to keep pets she should not spoil them. She should keep their numbers to a minimum and she not be distracted from her devotions or charitable duties. *The Goodman of Paris* declares that it is the duty of a good wife to take care of her 'chamber animals such as little dogs and birds', stressing how she should enlist the aid of her housekeeper in making sure that the pets were well cared for.[96]

Much of the criticism comes from sermon literature. The previously mentioned John Bromyard had much to say on the subject of lapdogs. These he regarded as useless over-fed sycophantic accessories of the rich, in the same category as *histriones* (actors) and prostitutes, receiving fine food and presents on demand, while the poor went hungry.[97] In the entry 'Servire' (to serve) in his *Summa praedicantium* (Compendium for Preachers), Bromyard presented over-feeding in terms of an over-emotional attachment to an animal: 'if glutted, they refuse, and there is great wailing over them'. It was also a rejection of one's duty to the poor.[98] Thus spoilt pets, like their owners, became uncaring and uncharitable creatures. Bromyard's wrath was also directed towards the clergy for loving and protecting people who had brought them dogs, among other fine gifts. In the entry for 'Furtum' (theft), Bromyard vents his wrath on lay people who are concerned only with horses, dogs and apes.[99] When criticizing the practice of votive offerings given at the shrines of saints or the Virgin Mary, the fourteenth-century poet Franco Sachetti used a pet cat in his prime example: 'And I, the writer, once saw an individual who had lost a cat make a vow that if he found it again, he would offer a wax model of it to Our Lady of Orto San Michele; and so he did.'[100]

Despite the dangers pets posed to spiritual wellbeing, it was recognized, at a social level, that women and even clerics, might 'need' them for reasons of companionship, and as a remedy against loneliness and melancholy. Some medical texts even recommended clutching a small pet dog to the chest to ward off stomach pains.[101] A fifteenth-century manual on angling and hunting attributed to Juliana Berners, the abbess of Sopwell, even allotted a practical function to pets, alluding to 'smale ladies popis that beere away the flees and dyueris smale fawtiers'.[102] Robert Coquina, Bishop of Durham (1274–83), kept a pair of monkeys 'to ease the burden of his worries'.[103] Provisions were even made for ladies in captivity to keep pets. The accounts of Joan of Navarre, queen of Henry IV of England, mention payments made in 1420 (when she was imprisoned for witchcraft) for the purchase of a cage for her 'jau' (a jay or parrot).[104] The early sixteenth-century traveller Olaus Magnus visited Iceland and noted the small white dogs kept by women and the clergy there and defended their use by members of the clergy:

> In Iceland, however, a true land of ice surrounded by the Ocean, though dogs of various kinds live there and of any breed you could desire, yet among the pets of distinguished ladies and prelates are very white dogs with thick fur, as though they were formed of a mass of tangled wool. The blessed Chrysostom allowed bishops and prelates to keep such dogs for their solace, as puppies, that is, but not greyhounds, or bulldogs, alias hellhounds, for these never cheer those who watch them, but dull the sensibilities with their offensive exhibition.[105]

There were many *de facto* compromises on pet keeping. Permission was given for ladies' pets to stay in spaces such as the royal court that were strictly off-limits to all other animals. This is apparent in the ordinances made at Eltham in 1526, in the seventeenth year of Henry VIII's reign. The italics are mine:

> The King's Highness alsoe straightly forbiddeth and inhibiteth, that no person whatsoever he be, presume to keep any grey-hounds, mastives, hounds, or other dogges, in the court *other then som few small spaniells for ladyes or others*, nor bring or leade any into the same, except it be by the King's or the Queen's commandment; but the said grey-hounds and dogges to be kept in kennells, and other meete places, out of court, as it is convenient, soe as, the premises dewly observed, the house may be sweete, wholesome, cleane, and well furnished, as to a prince's honour and estate doth apperteine.[106]

Saints and animals

NUMEROUS medieval hagiographies relate how a saint befriends and tames an animal, which becomes his or her companion. It is an attribute of saintliness to render the wild domestic, and to be kind towards all of Creation, while asserting man's dominance over the animal kingdom. Among the Desert Fathers, St Macarius befriended a hyena, Abbot Helanus persuaded a crocodile to carry him across the Nile, and Abbot Bes preached to crocodiles and hippopotamuses to persuade them to cease violence. Abbot Gerasimus removed a thorn from a lion's paw, and the beast became his constant companion and helper. This tale was later ascribed to St Jerome, who is usually portrayed in the company of a lion. Lions seem to have been a feature in the Egyptian desert, as St Mary of Egypt also befriended one. In Northumbria, St Cuthbert was dried by solicitous otters after he had been out sea-bathing, and St Godric of Finchale was constantly taking care of sick animals and releasing birds and beasts caught in traps. In Ireland, St Ciaran's shoes were stolen by a fox but promptly recovered by a badger; the two animals (once the fox had sought repentance) thereafter lived with the saint.[107] An early fifteenth-century Spanish book of exemplary tales includes a story involving a holy man called Florentius who has a bear provided by God for companionship (and to help with shepherding duties). Some jealous monks of a nearby monastery kill the bear. Florentius, in his grief, cries out: 'I hope to Almighty God that those who killed my bear, it doing them no harm, will receive in this life vengeance for their wickedness before men and the vengeance of God!' The monks, now cursed, are afflicted with elephantiasis, their members promptly putrefy, and soon they all die. Florentius forever after feels guilty for their deaths, and suffers remorse for his hasty curses, in elevating the life of an animal over a human.[108]

St Francis of Assisi is perhaps the foremost medieval saint connected with animals, his many animal encounters include taming the wolf of Gubbio and preaching to the birds. St Francis' attitude towards animals is not unconventional, but instead, like all the saints mentioned above, a traditional expression of sanctity.[109] A saint loves animals because they are all part of God's creation, not because he feels great affection for the individual animal in question. Pets were not part of the equation, no matter how many injured rabbits and birds St Claire of Assisi might pick up and tend for. In fact the Franciscans banned members of their order from keeping pets for pleasure, and thus clearly distinguished between loving Creation and maintaining a particular animal as a companion.

Many saints thus have an animal companion, but it is usually a 'wild' animal or at least an animal of domestic husbandry. The twelfth-century St Hugh of Lincoln had a swan which he treated as a pet; it followed him everywhere. It appears in his iconography, such as the altar piece of the saint from Thuison-les-Abbeville, *c.* 1480, where a swan wearing a gold collar stands next to him.[110] St Dominic (1170–1221) appears with a dog in his iconography but it is not a pet; instead it is a representation of the

Fig. 3 St Bernard of Clairvaux holding a crozier and a book, with a dog at his feet
(Hours of Philip of Burgundy, Oudenaarde, *c.* 1450–60)

animal his mother is supposed to have dreamed of when pregnant. In her dream the black and white dog held a flaming torch, which it used to set the world afire. The order he founded would guard against heresy like watchdogs, as attested in the pun on the name of the Dominicans: *domini canes* (dogs of the Lord).[111] A similar story appears in the life of St Bernard of Clairvaux, whose mother dreams of carrying a barking white dog. A holy man reassures her that she is bearing a preacher who will bark against the Church's enemies.[112] But in both these cases the dog is merely an attribute of the saint, and plays no part in his life. (Fig. 3 shows an example of the dog in the saint's iconography.)

The most notable case of a saint with a dog-companion is that of St Roch, the fourteenth-century patron saint of plague. The *Legenda Aurea* tells how he is expelled from a town, and wanders through a forest without any sustenance. However, a hound appears with a loaf of bread to feed the famished saint, licks his buboes, and becomes his companion. The hound belongs to a nobleman called Gothard. Being a great favourite, the animal is accustomed to removing bread from its master's table without censure. Gothard notices how his dog keeps leaving the table with a loaf of bread and not eating it so:

> At the next dinner he set a delicate loaf on the board, which anon the hound by his new manner took away and bare it to Rocke. And Gotard followed after and came to the lodge of S. Rocke, and there beheld how familiarly the hound delivered the bread to S. Rocke.[113]

Nearly all iconography of the saint depicts him with a plague bubo and his faithful dog, which invariably holds a loaf of bread in its mouth (plate I).[114]

A peculiar case of saintliness and dogs is narrated by the thirteenth-century preacher Étienne de Bourbon, who discovered, in the diocese of Lyons, that women had been taking their children to a shrine in the forest dedicated to one St Guinefort, protector of children. Stephen finds that Guinfort is a dog, revered as a martyr by the locals to whom they pray when ill or in need. The story told was that a lord and a lady had a baby, and left it alone in the house. A giant serpent appeared and came near the baby's cradle. Thereupon Guinfort, the family's greyhound, attacked the serpent and ripped it to shreds. During the mêlée, the baby's cradle was knocked over. When the inhabitants returned, they discovered the cradle empty and the dog's jaws covered in blood, and quickly jumped to the wrong conclusion. The knight killed the dog, but then discovered the baby safely asleep and the remains of the snake. They buried the dog and planted trees besides the grave, which later would become the shrine.[115]

But saints and pets in general do not mix, in marked contrast to earthly clerics, who throughout this book will be shown as great pet keepers.

2

Getting (and Losing) a Pet

How to get a pet

A MEDIEVAL pet might be acquired by receiving it as a gift, by purchasing it, or breeding it. There were also less conventional methods, including theft. A court case in 1294 in Chalgrave, England, details how one 'William Yngeleys complains against John Saly and Christina his sister because they detain a certain cat to William's damage, which damage he would not have willingly born for 6d'.[1] In a thirteenth-century *exemplum* the Bishop of Paris is forced to arbitrate between two clerics, who both claim a dog as their own, with the first accusing the second of stealing it. The first cleric teaches the dog to walk on its forelegs, but the second steals the dog, renames it and teaches it to walk on its hind legs. The bishop decides to award the dog to the thief, since the dog obeys him, responds to the name he gave it, but ignores the rightful owner.[2]

Pets as gifts

THE most common method to obtain a pet was as a gift. However, it can be difficult to pinpoint which animals exchanged formally as gifts went on to be treated as pets by their new owners; for example, a greyhound might be given with the intention of being used for hunting but might then become a pet. If we confine our attention to animals kept solely as companion pets (lapdogs, caged birds, monkeys) we see that the exchange of pets among the wealthy was defined by gender and status conventions, and generally limited to women and clerics.

Depending on the status of the recipient, the pet could be an expensive import. The accounts of Eleanor of Castile, Edward I's queen, record that the Princess of Salerno had sent a gift of parrots in June 1289; later entries record expenses relating to these birds, with payments made to servants for their upkeep.[3] Similarly, in 1419 Henry IV's queen, Joan of Navarre, sent a 'papegeay' (parrot) to her daughter-in-law, the Duchess of Brittany.[4] Parrots were expensive exotica: the gift of such an animal reflected the high status of both parties.

Giving pet animals to noble women was a common and socially acceptable practice. They would be viewed as perfect gifts that would be appreciated by the recipients. In 1413 the Duke of Burgundy gave four

Fig. 4 Draughts piece depicting a chained monkey
(walrus ivory, Cologne, late 12th century)

little monkeys to Isabeau of Bavaria, Queen of France.[5] The same queen would be given a kitten by a group of children in 1416, possibly at a public event.[6] Marie de Clèves, mother of Louis XII, received three little dogs from the French knight Jean Remon in 1475;[7] Elizabeth of York received a parrot from a William ap Howell in 1502.[8]

Conversely, if a woman gave a secular man an animal, it was hardly ever a species that was recognized purely as a companion. We find in the accounts of Queen Eleanor that in 1290 she received parrots from the Princess of Salerno and gave seventeen stag-hounds to the King of France.[9] Secular men did not give one another animals regarded as pets; instead the gift had to be one that reflected the 'right' animal for their gender. They might be animals destined for the hunt, notably hounds, falconry birds and horses, illustrated by the fine falcon sent by Floris V, Count of Holland, across the Channel in 1290 to Edward I.[10] Or they could be exotic animals, symbolic of princely power, to be kept in a menagerie. In 1254 Louis IX of France sent Henry III of England an elephant which came to be kept in the royal menagerie in the Tower of London along with leopards, lions and a polar bear given by the Norwegian king, Håkon IV.[11]

One of the tales in the *De nugis curialium* of the twelfth-century writer Walter Map tells of an animal exchange with dire results. In the story the ancient English king Herla is given a little hunting dog by his pygmy host. The pygmy instructs Herla to hold the little dog in his arms, in the manner of a pampered lapdog. The entire exchange turns out to be cursed, and Herla and his men are forever condemned to wander as they cannot dismount until the little dog leaps from Herla's arms, which never happens.[12]

Pets could even be given reluctantly, under duress. Lady Lisle, the wife of Arthur Plantagenet, Viscount Lisle, and proud owner of a small dog called Purkoy, was told to relinquish her pet to Anne Boleyn despite her affection for it. John Husse, a member of the king's household, wrote to Lady Lisle on 7 January 1534 to insist on the exchange: 'There is no remedy, your ladyship must needs depart with your little Purquoy, the which I know well shall grieve your ladyship not a little.' Lady Lisle bowed to pressure and gave up her dog to the queen. Purkoy must have arrived in the queen's household by 20 January as Sir Francis Bryan wrote to Lord Lisle telling him to thank his wife regarding 'her little dog, which was so proper and so well liked by the Queen that it remained not above an hour in my hands but that her Grace took it from me'.[13]

Clerics often received pets from a variety of personages, including other clerics, supplicants and parishioners. John Bromyard preached extensively on the high clergy, who adored gifts of pets and were pleased when people gave them dogs, birds, fruits and other gifts instead of their souls.[14]

In addition, pets as gifts between lovers are a common motif in romance, best exemplified by the little magical dog (*Feenhündchen*) given by Tristan to Isolde in Gottfried von Strassburg's thirteenth-century *Tristan*.[15]

Purchasing a pet

SOURCES relating to the direct purchase of pets are scarce, possibly because few pets cost a great deal, and the sum was not worth recording. The accounts for 1265 of Eleanor de Montfort, Countess of Leicester, detail the buying and feeding of many animals, from horses to hounds, but only two entries appear to refer to her pet purchases.[16] The first was a cat in February 1265, while at Odiham; the entry appears in the same line as the purchase of milk for her pet chamber dogs. A second entry in July of the same year details payment for another cat in Dover; this animal was also destined for her private quarters ('ad cameram') and was probably kept as a pet, although no doubt both cats also caught mice.

The economic value of cats, unless they were imported exotic varieties, was generally low. The cats bought by Eleanor de Montfort cost a few pennies at most, and cat skins were among the cheapest of furs.[17] A rather unusual exception to this appears in the early medieval Irish law text *Catślechtae* (cat-sections), where a cat is valued at three cows if it could purr and hunt mice. A cat that could only purr was valued at one and a

Fig. 5 A grey cat (Bestiary, France, *c.* 1450)

half cows. A kitten was worth one-ninth of its mother's value until it was weaned.[18] In Old Irish law texts, pet dogs are usually given the same value as hunting dogs, a value of two *séts*. One of the functions of a woman's pet dog in these texts is to guard against the fairies (*túaithgeinti*) while she is in labour. Thus, if someone kills her pet dog during this period, he must pay *séts* and hire a priest to read scripture at her bedside, in compensation for the animal. In addition, the hospitaller's (*briugu*) dog is worth one-third of his owner's honour price, as long as it accompanies him and watches by his pillow.[19]

The tenth-century Welsh laws of Hywel Dda, King of Deheubarth, put feline value in proportion to age. A kitten was valued at one penny from the night it was born until it opened its eyes. Once it opened its eyes but still had not killed any mice it was worth two pence, and once it had started to hunt, it was valued at four pence. The *Blegywryd Redaction* added a peculiar ritual for valuing a royal cat: 'The value of a cat which guards a king's barn, if killed or stolen: her head is set down on a clean level floor, and her tail is raised up, and wheat grains are poured over her until they hide the end of her tail. That will be her value.' Hywel's laws regarding dogs set the animal's value on the status of its owner. A king's pet dog was worth a pound; an *uchelwr*'s (noble) pet dog, a pound; a free man's pet dog, 120 pence, and an *aillt*'s (unfree person) pet dog, four pence. Although wild animals, such as badgers or foxes, had no value under Welsh law if they were kept as pets, their value depended on who owned them. A wild animal kept as a pet by a king was valued at a pound; that of an *uchelwr*, 120 pence and that of a free man, four pence.[20]

Specialist pet sellers might be found in large urban areas. In Paris from the twelfth or thirteenth century a 'guild' of bird sellers was located in front of the portal of Saint-Geneviève la Petite. The first mention of Parisian bird sellers appears in the thirteenth-century dictionary of Jean de Garlande, who wrote of tradesmen near Notre-Dame selling both edible birds to city residents, and caged birds such as nightingales, parrots, sparrows and starlings.[21] By 1292 there were five master bird sellers in Paris, and there are entries in the city tax records for 1292 and 1313 for those 'qui fait cages', indicating a specialization of craftsmen to make cages, termed *cagettes*, *gayolles*, *geôles* and *gloriettes*, for pet birds.[22]

In 1483 Louis XI, when he was near death, began to purchase pets and exotic animals *en masse* to stop rumours of his illness and assure all that he was in perfect health. Horses, mules, jackals, elks and reindeer were all bought without regard to cost: 'At great expense he sent for dogs from every quarter; mastiffs from Spain, small greyhound bitches, greyhounds and spaniels from Brittany, small shaggy dogs from Valence, all of which he bought more dearly than people usually like to sell them.'[23]

Most medieval cats were of low value. However, from the fifteenth century cats from Syria were widely imported via Venice to Western Europe. These animals, brown with black stripes, were praised as expensive exotica, since most of the native cats were grey with stripes.[24] Tabby cats were still exotic in the seventeenth century, when the antiquary John Aubrey noted that William Laud, Archbishop of Canterbury: 'was a great lover of Cats'. He was presented with some Cyprus-catts, i.e. our Tabby-catts, which were sold, at first for 5 pounds a piece: this was about 1637 or 1638. I doe well remember that the common English Catt, was white with some blewish piednesse: sc, a gallipot blew. The race or breed of them are now almost lost.'[25] In the Gonzaga archives in Mantua there is a long correspondence between Isabella d'Este, Marchesa of Mantua (1474–1539), and her agents in Venice regarding the purchase of cats imported from Syria. These were of the tabby striped coat pattern, which were rare in Europe at the time and in great demand. The entire tortuous correspondence underlines the difficulties that could arise when purchasing exotic pets, complete with failures, missing animals, theft and reluctant sellers.

In 1496 Isabella sent a letter to Antonio Salimbeni, a Mantuan in Venice, asking him to find her three or four Syrian cats, as she had a problem with rats in her chamber.[26] Two years later Isabella was still on the look-out for cats and in September 1498 received a letter from a Brother Paulino in the monastery of San Antonio in Venice. He had heard of the marchesa's desire for two Syrian cats and assured her that he would do his best to fulfil this request.[27] A month later Tolommeo Spagnolo, a Mantuan courtier visiting Venice, recounted how he saw 'a most beautiful Syrian cat' sitting in a window wearing a little collar adorned with bells. This was a rather unusual accessory for a cat, and more common on pet dogs. Spagnolo found the owner, 'the oldest woman I have ever seen', who refused to part with her pet, despite his offer of money and mention of Isabella's name. He even tried to negotiate with the lady's son, but similarly he declined to give up his mother's cat. Frustrated, Spagnolo concluded that the pair were both asses. However, his letter is a clear demonstration of the devotion of pet owners to their animals in the face of monetary inducements.[28]

Spagnolo also mentioned how he had visited the monastery of San Nicolò with one Giovanni Gonzaga. The latter had stolen a 'Syrian or Persian' cat from the 'poor brothers' but unfortunately later lost it. Isabella was still expecting a cat, and in a letter written a day after Spagnolo wrote of his fruitless attempts, she reminded him to bring a 'little Syrian cat' on his return as this would please her.[29] In 1501 she was expecting a cat from Alvise Marcello, another correspondent in Venice. Marcello gave the cat to Francesco Trevisano, another Mantuan in Venice, to deliver to the marchesa. Unfortunately, the cat escaped from the balcony of Trevisano's Venetian home and was lost. Trevisano wrote a long letter to Isabella, explaining the cat's fate. To avoid the 'scandal and words', a distinct loss of face, which would happen when this 'inconvenience' reached Marcello's ears, Trevisano appealed to Isabella, asking her to pretend that she had actually received the cat that he had lost.[30] Isabella complied, and wrote to Marcello, assuring him that Trevisano had delivered the animal.[31]

Syrian cats also figure in the correspondence between Isabella d'Este and her Venetian instrument maker, Lorenzo da Pavia. In November 1498 Lorenzo informed Isabella that he had sent the very best Syrian kitten he could find, although he would try to find a still prettier one.[32] Unfortunately the kitten died before it arrived in Venice. Isabella had to write to Lorenzo asking him to seek out another one, a 'pretty one with lots of spots'.[33] Another correspondent in Venice, Antimacho, assured Isabella that they were still questing such a cat for her.[34] In March 1499 Lorenzo was successful and managed to send Isabella 'a most beautiful female Syrian cat from Damascus who was very charming', adding in his letter that it had taken great effort to find such a beautiful animal.[35] In 1501, still aware of Isabella's predilection for these animals, Lorenzo mentioned that his brother had returned from Damascus with a Syrian cat, although lamenting that it was not the prettier of the two the brother had purchased, as one was stolen on the galley as he returned home.[36] Two years later, he again sent Isabella a young Syrian cat which his brother had brought back from another trip to Damascus.[37] In 1508 Isabella asked for the brother to bring back male and female Syrian cats from his next trip.[38]

Breeding pets

THE practice of breeding pets from one's own animals was done informally, and there is little documentary evidence about it. However, it is probably safe to assume that animals were exchanged regularly between owners for breeding without such problems or the need for formal written requests. A plaintive letter in the Gonzaga archive contains a request for the return of a cat that had been taken away from Jacobo Antonio Stella, a tenant house in Castelgoffredo. It had been sent to Mantua to be bred with a cat belonging to Isabella d'Este.[39] The author wished the family pet to be returned as soon as possible, perhaps fearing that the marchesa would take a liking to the cat and keep it, among her numerous imported Syrian cats.

In the correspondence between Margherita di Domenico Bandini in Florence to her husband Francesco di Marco Datini in Prato, between 1395 and 1402, there are numerous references to their cats. These include the struggles to find a suitable mate for their female cat to breed kittens (Margherita could not locate one in Florence and dispatched the cat to Francesco in Prato), sending cats by coach between the two cities, being given them as pets, and the perils of the cats trying to escape from the house (numerous attempts were made to tie them up).[40]

Regarding the breeding of more pets from one's dogs, the practice appears in the always illuminating Mantua archives. A letter sent in 1511 by Gian Giacomo Calandra, Isabella d'Este's secretary, to Isabella's eleven-year old son Federico Gonzaga in Rome explained how Fanina, one of his mother's little dogs, had given birth. Isabella had decided that the last puppy was to be reserved for Federico when he returned. Calandra described the puppy as 'the most loveliest and appealing in the world', of a reddish colour, with patches of white around the neck, tail and feet. He explained that the little dog had been named Zephyro in allusion to Aura,

Isabella's favourite pet dog, both being Greek names of winds. Calandra assured Federico that he would have a well-trained and sweet 'beautiful little dog' ['bel cagnolo'] who 'is the prettiest of all'.[41] The birth of puppies to the family pets was a noteworthy item of news; in a letter a year later, Calandra informed Federico that Mamia, another of his mother's little dogs, had just given birth to puppies and that 'Mamia is pregnant by your Zephyro.'[42]

Deaths of pets and owners' grief

WHAT happened when pets died? Were there any rituals when burying them? Although animal bones have been found in excavations of medieval domestic sites all over Europe it is difficult to determine whether any of these belong to pets. The remains of dog might belong to a guard dog, a hunting dog, a pet dog, or an urban feral scavenger dog. Richard Thomas has analysed animal remains from England and discusses the near impossibility of identifying function purely using archaeological data. He suggests that the presence of animal remains without butchery marks or those which show signs of healed bones might be possible indicators of a pet.[43]

Determining status from the burial of the animal is also difficult. Animals were sometimes carefully buried (though again it is not easy to be certain) or just put out with the household waste. The latter case may seem an undignified end for a cherished companion, but it may have been that once dead, the corpse of the animal was not important and a specialized burial was deemed unnecessary. For example, excavations in Verona, Italy, found a large quantity of cat bones, mainly from the thirteenth century, which suggested that cat corpses were generally thrown onto a few waste pits. The cats might have had various functions, from being pets, mousers, to being skinned for their pelts (although there are no butchery or flesh stripping marks).[44] A rather isolated case of relatively strong archaeological evidence for a pet dog comes from an excavation in Perth, Scotland. Catherine Smith concludes that the remains of an elderly small dog may have been those of a pet, since it had been cared for in its old age and had been buried in a pit rather than on a midden with other rubbish.[45] When the remains are those of an exotic animal we may more legitimately presume that it was a pet. Parrot bones have been discovered in seventeenth-century deposits under what is now Castle Mall, Norwich, while the remains of a small Barbary ape were found during the excavation of a stone tenement house in Southampton belonging to Richard of Southwick, burgess of the town (d. c. 1290).[46]

Fig. 6 A man plays with a dog (Book of Hours, Utrecht, *c.* 1460)

While archaeological evidence for dead pets is scarce, material abounds regarding the reaction of their owners on the death of their pets. When Anne Boleyn's beloved little dog Purkoy died from a fall, fearing the queen's grief, no one dared inform her of the animal's misadventure; it was left to the king to tell her the sad news.[47] Louise of Savoy, mother of François I of France, would record in her journal the death on 24 October 1502 of her little dog Hapeguay, 'who loved his mistress and was very loyal'.[48]

The reaction could even involve resorting to the law, as seen in the manor rolls of Wakefield for 1286, which recount a suit brought by a woman called Moll de Mora against a William Wodemouse for abuse of a maintenance contract, theft of goods and the murder of her dog.[49] But grief was a common response. Thierry, abbot of Saint-Thrond (d. *c.* 1107), composed a long elegy on the death of his elderly lapdog Pitulus, who is described as a little dog ('scarcely equal to a Pannonian mouse in his whole body'), with black and white fur. Thierry asks, 'What was his function?' and answers, 'That his large master should love a small dog – that was his duty, to play before his master.' He speaks of an owner's grief when addressing the dead dog: 'Such you were, beloved dog, to be laughed at and grieved over; you were laughter when you were alive, but look at the grief when you have died!'[50] Although his elegy is based on a classical animal elegy, the *Culex*, attributed to Virgil, Thierry's deep sentiment of loss and personalization of the dead animal makes the poem more than mere imitation.

There are notable literary works which deal with the death of nuns' pets. Although many adopt a humorous tone, nevertheless it is taken for granted that owners would feel grief at the death of their pets. John Skelton's elegy *The Boke of Phyllyp Sparowe* is centred on the killing of the pet sparrow Philip by Gyb the cat. The bird belonged to a Jane Scrope, from the Benedictine nunnery of Carrow, near Norwich. Skelton's elegy has echoes of Catullus's sparrow poems (*Carmina* II and III) and the service for the dead:

> For the sowle of Philip Sparowe,
> That was late slayn at Carowe,
> Among the Nones Blake,
> For that swete soules sake,
> And for all sparowes soules,
> Set in our bederolles,
> Pater noster qui,
> With an Ave Mari,

Later lines express Jane Scrope's sorrow at the death of her pet:

> I wept and I wayled,
> The tearys downe hayled;
> But nothinge it avayled
> To call Phylyp agayne,
> Whom Gyb our cat hath slayne.[51]

In a similar vein, Cuono of Saint-Nabor's *The Peacock and the Owl*, c. 1000, deals with the death of an albino peacock, while one of the eleventh-century Cambridge Songs speaks of a pet donkey, belonging to an Alfrâd of Homburg, which to the great distress of the nuns is killed by a wolf.[52]

The death of a beloved animal could even later play a part in the owner's own funerary rites. When the tomb of Ralph Neville, 1st Earl of Westmorland, in St Mary's, Staindrop, was opened, a greyhound was found buried next to the earl.[53]

There are numerous documents in the Gonzaga archive that deal with the death of court pets.[54] In life they were lavished with attention; their deaths provoked extensive private and public displays of grief, comparable to the death of a child. In 1462 Rubino, the dog of Ludovico II Gonzaga, Marchese of Mantua, fell ill while his master was away. Despite the ministrations of a doctor, the dog, clearly in pain, continued to worsen, and died. Ludovico, away from the scene, requested that if Rubino died before his return, the dog was to be buried in a casket and that in due course he would arrange a tombstone, complete with epitaph. His little dog Bellina would also receive a Latin epitaph written in her memory after she died in labour.[55]

Later, under Isabella d'Este's tenure, when a cat called Martino died in 1510, it was greatly mourned. The courtier Mario Equicola (1479–1525) took care of the burial, and delivered a sermon at the grave.[56] The Marchese's secretary, Battista Scalona, sent a letter of the proceedings in Mantua to Isabella's son, Federico Gonzaga, in Rome. Scalona acidly commented that such deeds were above the 'pious office' of the marchesa's secretary Calandra. Epitaphs were composed for the deceased, and Scalona mentioned that he had presented three epitaphs to Isabella. Two pet dogs, Isabella's Aura and Federico's Ribolin, were present at the funeral.[57]

It is interesting that the practice of an elaborate burial for a court pet is not seen as out of the ordinary. There is an appropriation of human funeral rituals (the sermon, the tomb, etc.) along with the presence of acquaintances of the deceased, which in this case takes the form of other pets being taken to the funeral to 'mourn'. Equally, the concern of courtiers to please Isabella with epitaphs on the dead animal may not have been a purely altruistic endeavour, but a way to gain favour by assuaging their patron's grief, along with exhibiting skill in composing such elegies.

Isabella d'Este's particular fondness was for little dogs. The author Mateo Bandello (1480?–1562) used the marchesa's pets as a way of telling that Isabella d'Este herself was nearby, as she always appeared with them. In one story, light conversation among the courtiers and ladies-in-waiting comes to an end when they rise to attention as 'The sound of little dogs barking was heard, a sign that madama [Isabella] was coming in.'[58]

But among all her pets, the little dog Aura was most beloved and the death of the pet caused great grief. The following section details the exchange of letters regarding this case. On 30 August 1511 her secretary Calandra wrote to Federico Gonzaga regarding the unfortunate death of his mother's dog:

> My illustrious lord, there was a great misfortune here yesterday. When her Excellency wanted to set off, Aura and Mamia (the two little dogs of her ladyship) started chasing each other as there was enmity between them for the love of Alfonso's dog. Finding herself on a high outcrop of earth, about twenty-two arms-length high, poor beautiful Aura fell from that outcrop onto the forecourt, and died at once. It is not possible to speak of Madama's grief; there is so much of it. Anyone who knows the love she bore the dog can well imagine it. And much was deserved as Aura was the prettiest and most

agreeable little dog that ever there was. Her ladyship was seen crying that evening at dinner, and she couldn't talk about it without sighing. Isabella cried as if her mother had died and it was not possible to console her. I cannot deny that I too have shed some tears. Madama [Isabella] quickly had a lead casket produced and put the dog in it. And I believe she will keep it there until she can put it in a beautiful tomb in the new Hungarian house, for which her Excellency will lay the first stone with her own hand at the twentieth hour by astrological calculation. In the meantime, epitaphs will be written for the noble Aura. Your Zaphyro has lost a friendly companion. My lord, there was very bad weather the night following the unhappy day of the cruel death of Aura.[59]

Calandra's descriptions of the elaborate funeral and the composition of epitaphs echo Scalona's account of Martino's funeral a year earlier. Calandra furnishes details concerning the burial of the dog in a lead casket, the construction of a tomb, and the ceremony (the same ritual enacted when Ludovico II's Rubino had died). Isabella's grief was displayed both publicly, as shown by the funeral and the request for compositions of epitaphs, and privately, as she mourned the animal in her rooms. There is a great deal of anthropomorphism in the letter, for example Aura's death is blamed on a fight caused by jealousy, and regret is expressed that Federico's little dog Zaphyro has lost a 'companion'.[60]

The first letter of condolence arrived on 25 September from Bernardino Prospero, Isabella's informant in Ferrara (her home city). He wrote that Mario Equicola, Isabella's tutor, had told him of the death of 'the sweet little dog of your ladyship'. His reaction, on hearing the sad news, was to compose two epitaphs, even though he claimed, in a self-deprecating fashion, that they were not of the very best quality. Bernardino added that the Ferrarese scholar Alessandro Guarini (1435–1513) and another scholar would be sending other epitaphs to Mantua as soon as possible, and these would be of a better quality.[61] Only after offering his condolences and a pledge to send more epitaphs did Bernardino Prospero mention other events, such as the plague affecting Ferrara.[62]

Isabella's reply was swift. Within a few days she replied to Bernardino, excusing her tardiness and thanking him for the elegies, which were 'most pleasing', asked him to thank the composers in her name, and declared that she would be delighted if they could send some more.[63] Other elegies were sent to Isabella by Antonio dall'Organo in Ferrara; she thanked the author in a letter of January 1512, telling him she found the verses charming in 'honouring our little dog'.[64]

The next letter to arrive in Mantua regarding Aura was sent from Rome on 25 January 1512 by her son, Federico Gonzaga.[65] As with all other correspondence where the dog's death is mentioned, it is the first matter of business. Federico informed his mother that he had received some verses in praise of 'the little dog Aura of your ladyship' by Fillippo Beroaldo (1472–1518), a poet and the keeper of the Vatican Library.[66] In the letter, Federico added that Beroaldo had written the poems to please her since doing 'pleasing' things was a way of showing her that he was a great 'servitor'.[67]

There is no evidence that there was a formal literary competition on the subject of Aura, although many scholars or courtiers must have written their contributions with the knowledge that others were also attempting to ingratiate themselves by composing elegies for the marchesa. Since so many writers were involved, the decision to devise Latin and Italian elegies for this specific dog may have become quite a popular pastime. But it should not be thought that these elegies were merely intended as literary exercises, nor should they be read as purely parody. Isabella's grief for this animal was well known, and her correspondence underlines that these compositions were intended to assuage grief.[68]

Federico wrote another letter on 16 March. Unlike the previous one, this is a short missive written in his own hand, rather than that of his tutor. Even though Aura had been dead for several months, Federico still believed that Isabella would be pleased with even more elegies, and he said that he would send them to Mantua.[69] Isabella was delighted by Federico's letter, and in her reply spoke of her great pleasure in reading a letter in her son's hand, and praised him for sending the poems. She had found all the elegies 'beautiful' and 'elegant', especially the one written by Blosio Paladio (1470–1550), a famed humanist in Rome.[70] The next letter from Rome came from Gadio Stazio, Federico's tutor, in April 1512. After informing Isabella of her son Federico's progress, he mentioned a dinner he had attended with Fillippo Beroaldo, Marco Cavallo and Pietro Bembo, all of whom had written epigrams for the 'little angel of your Excellency'.[71] The scholar-poet and cardinal Pietro Bembo (1470–1547) would have had experience in these matters, as among his compositions is a small elegy to his own dog, Bembino.[72]

It appears that Isabella, later that year, while still grieving for Aura, was also able to devote time to pet cats. In late July her son Federico sent three kittens, hoping they would please her.[73] In mid-August her secretary Calandra wrote about the success of this gift, as Isabella greatly favoured one of these cats. Calandra praised Federico for sending such a beautiful and delicate animal which had 'no other home than in the arms and breast of her Excellency'. The kitten stayed in Isabella's room and amused her. She was very grateful for the cat's company, and Calandra commented with amazement on how happy the little cat had made her, a measure of the grief for Aura that had lasted for months. Isabella lavished this kitten with affection; Calandra noted how she could not stop kissing it and praising it with the 'sweetest little words in the world'. A specially made little bed, probably a sort of basket, was made for it.[74] Calandra may be exaggerating when he claims that her love for Aura was nothing like this; instead it seems that Isabella finally decided to devote her attention to another pet, which perhaps was a more effective remedy for grief than the numerous elegies. In his next letter Federico wrote that he was greatly pleased to hear how well Isabella liked the kittens.[75] Additionally, although Aura had died nearly a year before this letter, Isabella's grief at the loss of her pet is still noted as normal and expected behaviour. As in all Calandra's descriptive letters, Isabella's deep affection for her pets is vividly represented.

In the matter of keeping pets Isabella appears to have influenced her son Federico, who would continue to keep little dogs as pets for the rest of his life. We have already encounterd Zephyro, the little dog he kept in his early teens. At the age of twenty-six, as Marchese of Mantua, he commissioned a tomb from the architect and painter Giulio Romano for a little dog that had died while whelping. Federico wanted a 'beautiful marble tomb with an epitaph', and asked Giulio Romano to send two possible designs.[76] The epitaph can be found in Ulisse Aldrovandi's monumental *De quadripedibus digitatis viviparis*. Aldrovandi devotes an entire page to canine epitaphs on tombs in the Gonzaga palace in Mantua, though unfortunately he does not give an epitaph for Aura, so it not possible to determine which one was finally chosen for her tomb from the many sent to Isabella d'Este for approval. The epitaph for Federico's little dog Viola laments the death of this playful and loyal animal while giving birth, and insists that the dog now resides in heaven.[77] In the Palazzo Te at Mantua, also designed by Giulio Romano, there is an anonymous canine tomb, which might be Viola's. Viola, or perhaps her successor, appears in a portrait of Federico Gonzaga by Titian, completed in 1529. This portrait is a rarity in sixteenth-century male portraiture, and has more in keeping with female portraiture where the sitter is accompanied by a lapdog. It shows a small white long-haired dog of the Melitaean type sitting on a cushion on a table; Federico has one hand on the dog, which in turn places a paw on his waist.[78]

Tombs in gardens for pets appear not to have been merely a courtly affectation. The Italian scholar Antonio Tebaldeo had an epitaph for his dog Borgettus incised on a tombstone in his garden, and nearly a century later, the Flemish scholar Justus Lipsius would erect tombs in his garden for his dogs.[79] Burying the pet in one's garden kept the memory of the lost pet close to home and naturally, by being a secular space, would avoid any criticisms attached to official burial spaces. The mummified body of a cat still resides at Petrarch's final home in Arquà, accompanied by a plaque bearing an elegy by the early seventeenth-century poet Antonio Quarenghi; it is usually presumed to be a by-product of the sixteenth-century interest in Petrarch and visits by tourists to his house.[80] Further descriptions of the owner's grief and funerary rites will be examined in the discussion of vernacular and Latin elegies and epitaphs in Chapter 6.

✦ ✦
✦

3

Pet Welfare

How do you keep a pet?

A FTER obtaining a pet, the new owner had to feed and take care of the animal. Francesco Petrarch (1304–74) was the prototype of a pet-keeping scholar, and his letters provide an overview of the nature of pet ownership. He had several dogs. The first mention of a dog appears in a letter of 1338 to Giocomo Colonna. At that time Petrarch was living in Vaucluse, and he defends his reasons for living in so isolated in a spot, affirming that he had no companions apart from his faithful dog and servants.[1]

A few years later his patron, Cardinal Giovanni Colonna, sent him a dog from Avignon to be 'a companion and source of comfort', and in 1347 Petrarch composed a long letter in verse describing how the animal was settling down. Previously it had been used to fine food, running through elegant halls and sleeping on a 'purple bed'. Petrarch maintains that its new surroundings delight the animal, which is very content with its new life as its new owner's 'source of comfort and companion'. The dog has become accustomed to eating bread and water, the plain simple food Petrarch provides, living in his small home in Vaucluse, running in the countryside and swimming in nearby pools of water. The exercise has even cured the dog of mange, which Petrarch claims was brought on by the unhealthy airs of Avignon. He buys the dog a chain, which contrasts greatly with the accessories the dog arrived with: a collar with a disk and a belt made of red fabric with the heraldic embroidery of the Colonna family, white columns on red. Petrarch comments that the dog has come down in social station, from being owned by a cardinal to being the pet of a minor cleric and poet, an interesting reflection on the status of the animal being connected to its owner's position. The dog even kindly chases away any villagers who come to annoy the scholar with their petty concerns and stays as a constant companion (*comes assiduus*), informing his master that he had slept too long by whimpering and scratching on the door.

The letter offers a wealth of detail on living with a pet dog. Petrarch describes how the animal is always happy to see him and follows him on his walks. If he decides to rest for a while when out strolling, the dog lies down with him, and barks at any interloper. It protects him with its large body. Although the dog can be aggressive to strangers, it is all friendliness with Petrarch's friends, dropping its ears submissively and cheerfully wagging its tail.

Despite being a very large dog, probably of a hunting breed, Petrarch declares that his pet is not at all good for hunting. He describes it running around in the woods, with a high pitched bark (like that of a 'singing child'). Its pursuit of the local wild geese is described as a game, not done in anger. It refuses to harm weak animals and is as 'gentle as lamb' towards sheep, goats and kids, and frightened of hares. In fact it had only ever barked at the safely caged lions in the papal menagerie,[2] but ignored the local fauna of Vaucluse.[3]

Petrarch also appears to have received dogs from friends. Matteo Longo, Bishop of Liège, left a dog in Vaucluse before Petrarch arrived. In 1351 Petrarch wrote to him, praising his new pet; he elaborates on the loyalty of all dogs, illustrating this with stories from Classical Antiquity.[4]

Dogs appear through Petrarch's voluminous correspondence. In a letter to Francesco Nelli in 1352, while spending the summer at the Sorge Fountain, he describes his simple lifestyle, living with 'only one dog and two servants'.[5] The phrase 'with only one dog' occurs in other letters and seems to be connected with the notion of solitude, where one can be alone, lost in one's thoughts or troubles. In a letter of 1353 to his brother Gherardo, a Carthusian monk, he recalls the time when his brother was the sole survivor after the monastery had been devastated by plague, and had buried all his fellow monks with only one dog to keep him company.[6] For Petrarch, all the diligent scholar needed was peace and quiet, a few servants and a dog. He expands on this theme in a letter of 1353 to his friend Ludwig van Kempen, a chaplain to Cardinal Giovanni Colonna; he lists the elements of a simple life: clothes to wear, servants, a horse to ride, a roof and a bed, and a dog for company.[7]

In an entirely different world, the daily life of a pampered court pet is set down in a short descriptive *blason* written for Eleanor of Austria, Queen of France (1498–1558) by the poet Clement Marot (1496–1544). The poem describes how her little pet dog Mignone accompanies her mistress everywhere and sleeps in a specially prepared area.[8]

However, great affection towards pets, especially for a man, could have drawbacks. The excessive devotion for small lapdogs of Henri III of France (r. 1574–89) was seen as extravagant and unmanly, a key character flaw criticized by his Huguenot opponents.[9] Henri would carry his little dogs everywhere and spent much time pampering them. The diarist Pierre de L'Estoile (1546–1611) recorded how the king, on returning from Normandy in 1576, was accompanied by a great quantity of monkeys, parrots, and little dogs, all bought in Dieppe.[10] For Agrippa d'Aubigné (1552–1630), the king's obsession with the *petis chiens de Lyon* (little Lion dogs) had bought about 'a state of great sterility and financial destruction'; when on progress in 1586 to Lyon, the king was seen with a thousand of the little dogs and travelled with 200 of them. They were divided into groups of eight, and each group travelled with a governess, a female servant and a packhorse, and required in total 600 horses, at enormous expense.[11] His obsession with little dogs knew no bounds; he would confiscate little dogs that he liked when travelling around Paris in his coach and even visited nunneries to remove them 'to the great regret and displeasure of the ladies who owned the dogs'.[12] Before leaving for the battle of Mohács in 1526, the final words of King Louis II of Hungary 1526 show where his priorities lay: 'Take good care of the little dogs! And wash them twice a week!'[13]

Feeding of pets

T HE food fed to pets was often of a quality that ordinary people could not afford, and included meat, high-quality bread, milk (a drink reserved usually only for children), and even imported foodstuffs. Naturally the food differed depending on the species of pet.

For pet dogs the staples were bread, often of a fine quality, and milk, occasionally with meat. This is what is said about the Prioress, Madame Eglentyne, in the General Prologue to Chaucer's *Canterbury Tales*:

> Of smale houndes hadde she that she fedde
> With rosted flesh, or milk and wastel–breed[14]

Wastel bread was of the highest quality, made of very fine flour and baked in a hot oven. Roasted meat technically was forbidden in the Benedictine Rule, although it is not clear whether the Prioress was feeding her dogs from her table or having food especially prepared for them.[15] These lines have attracted literary comment, implying criticism. The Prioress seems to care less for the poor than for her spoiled lapdogs, and is a marked contrast with the Second Nun in *The Canterbury Tales*, a pious character who does not own pets.[16]

Household accounts are a useful source, although it is rare to find separate entries for pet food. The accounts of John de Multom of Frampton, Lincolnshire, detail the purchase of bread for 'my lady's dog'.[17] It can be assumed that the diet of pet dogs, besides table scraps, consisted mainly of the food labelled under the general entry *panes pro canibus* (loaves for dogs). The staple was bread, normally made from wheat, though other grains could be used.[18] The dogs were also fed porridge, usually made from oats, bran mash, or barley, often with the addition of peas.[19]

Pet dogs were usually fed apart from other domestic animals and given a superior quality of food. In the household of Richard Mitford, Bishop of Salisbury (d. 1407), his pet dogs, which appear in his accounts from 1406–7, were given at least two loaves of bread per day and often more. These animals were distinct from his hunting dogs, which were kept and fed outside.[20] The accounts of Eleanor de Montfort (1258–82) in 1265 include entries for her chamberlain purchasing milk for her pet dogs that lived in her chamber. The household's hunting dogs that were kennelled outside would not have received milk, although all the dogs ate bread.[21] At the French court during the sixteenth century there was even a *boulengier des petits chiens blancs*, a baker whose speciality was baking bread for little white pet dogs.[22] This diet did not always suffice, as shown in an entry in the journal of Jeanne d'Albret, Queen of Navarre (r. 1555–72), which remarks that her little dog had eaten a letter that she was writing to the King of Spain.[23] There are few specific entries in accounts for special food for pet cats, who probably relied on leftovers and mousing. There is an entry for cheese bought for a cat in the manor of Cuxham in Oxfordshire in 1293–4, but this is a rarity.[24] Pet cats seem to have enjoyed milk, as attested in an Old Irish proverb: *cuirm lemm, lemlacht la cat* (beer with me, fresh milk with a cat).[25]

Pet birds kept in cages, relied completely on their owners for food, and were usually fed a variety of seeds. This could vary; depending on the luxury with which the bird was kept. Chaucer's *The Squire's Tale* presents a pet bird in a cage cushioned with straw and fed fine foodstuffs:

> And strawe hir cage faire and softe as silk
> And yeve hem sugre, hony, breed and milk[26]

In his satirical poem *Speke Parrot* John Skelton describes the exotic bird, 'Daintily dieted with divers delicate spice' being fed imported spices and fruit (almonds, dates, nutmegs, cloves, cinnamon and musk):

> Then Parrot must have an almond or date
> Now a nutmeg, a nutmeg, *cum garyophyllo*,
> For Parrot to pick up, his braine for to stable,
> Sweet cinnamon-stickes and *pleris cum musco*![27]

Food for caged birds rarely appears in accounts, possibly because the quantities purchased were small. The accounts for the household of Pope Urban V (1362–70) mention the purchase of birdseed by a papal apothecary for a specific parrot.²⁸ There are also general entries for birdseed, also purchased by the apothecary, where the identity of the bird is not spelled out. Birdseed purchased in this manner was clearly intended for pets, as birds destined for the table were purchased whole and not fed in the papal court itself.²⁹ This is underlined by the fact that the birdseed was being purchased by the apothecary, and not by a member of the kitchen staff.

The household manual *The Goodman of Paris* informs the young female reader of how to take care of caged birds and those in an aviary. It begins by listing the faults of large aviaries, and suggests the correct method to feed pet birds:

> In the first case [the Hesdin aviary] the fault lieth in that the little birds be fed upon hempseed, which is hot and dry, and they have nought to drink. And in the second case [the royal aviary at Saint-Pol], they be given chickweed or groundsel, sowthistles set in water ever fresh and constantly renewed, changed thrice a day and in clean leaden vessels, and therein with the chickweed and the groundsel all green, all field thistles with their stems well moistened in water, and hempseed sorted and broken up, with the shells removed, and moistened with water. *Item*, let carded wool and feathers be put in the aviary to make their nests. And thus have I see turtle-doves, linnets and goldfinches lay and rear their young. *Item*, you should also give them caterpillars, worms, flies, spiders, grasshoppers, butterflies, fresh hemp in leaf, moistened and soaked. *Item*, spiders, caterpillars and such like things which be soft to the little bird's beak, which is tender.³⁰

Monkeys were fed a variety of foodstuffs, nuts in particular. The late thirteenth-century chronicler Richard of Durham recounted how Robert Coquina, Bishop of Durham (1274–83), kept two spoiled pet monkeys that were fed peeled almonds from a silver spoon. Almonds were an expensive imported foodstuff, but the chronicler merely states that the practice of keeping pet monkeys is customary among high prelates.³¹

> … he kept in his court, after the custom of modern prelates, as some relief from their cares, a couple of monkeys – an old and a young one. One day at the end of dinner, desiring to be refreshed by amusement rather than by good, [the bishop] caused a silver spoon with whitened almonds to be placed in the enclosure of the younger monkey, the bigger one being kept away [from it]. She [the little monkey], seeing the coveted food, and wishing to avoid

being despoiled by the bigger one, made every endevour to stuff all the contents of the spoon into her left cheek, which she managed to do. Then, just as she thought to escape with the spoil, the older monkey was released, and ran to her, seized the right cheek of the loudly screaming little one, drew out all that was stuffed into the left cheek, as if out of a little bag, and refreshed itself, until not a single [almond] was left. Everybody who saw this burst out laughing but I perceived there an image of the covetous of this world, calling to mind that proverb of Solomon in the twenty-second [chapter]: 'He that oppresseth the poor to increase his riches, shall himself give to a richer man and come to want.

The stereotypical fat pet

PETS were prone to being overfed. This might be a result of the emotional attachment to an animal that was a constant companion or it could serve as an ostentatious demonstration of the owner's wealth, indicating a person who could afford to lavish so much fare on an animal whose sole purpose was to amuse and provide companionship.

There was awareness that the rich diet of some pets might have grave consequences for their health. Albertus Magnus covers the entire animal kingdom in his *De animalibus*. During his discussion of the diseases of dogs in general, Albertus comments on the consequences of the unhealthy, excessively rich diet of pet dogs, especially those belonging to ladies, who, it seems, were very prone to spoiling their pets, which were then afflicted with gastric complaints:

> This is seen most often in the ladies' small dogs which almost always die of constipation. Let them be given oatmeal that has been steeped in warm water to the consistency of thick porridge. Or else let them be fed with leavened soft bread and let them be given a little milk whey and they will become loosened and become swift and whole.[32]

In literature, and especially in sermons, the pet was often fat and spoiled. A thirteenth-century sermon by the Dominican preacher Étienne de Bourbon speaks of a spoilt fat dog whose health improved once its owner realized the folly of overfeeding it.[33]

The Dominican preacher John Bromyard takes pet owners to task, and anthropomorphizes the pet into the stereotype of an uncaring and uncharitable aristocrat who takes the best of everything and leaves nothing for the poor:

The wealthy provide for their dogs more readily than for the poor, more abundantly and more delicately too; so that, whereas the poor are so famished that they would greedily devour bran-bread, dogs turn up their noses at the sight of wafer-bread, and spurn what is offered to them, trampling it under their feet. They must be offered the daintiest flesh, the first and choicest portion of every dish. If full, they refuse it. Then there is wailing about them, as though they were ill.[34]

Criticism is often directed at overly emotional owners, who care only about their fat pet's well-being. Of interest here is the warning Geoffroy de La Tour-Landry gave his daughters in the manual of instruction he wrote in the late fourteenth century. He gives the example of a lady who overfeeds her dogs with meat and milk and neglects the poor. Divine punishment comes with the appearance of two small black demonic dogs at her death bed:

There was a lady that had two little dogs and she loved them so much that she took great pleasure in seeing and feeding of them. Every day she made dishes of milk sop for them and then gave the little dogs meat. A friar told her that it was not good that the dogs were fed like that and made so fat while poor people were so lean and hungry. The lady was angry with the friar for these words and would not amend her behaviour. When she was dying, there was an amazing sight, for two little black dogs were seen on her bed and as she was dying they licked her mouth, so that by the time she had died, her mouth was as black as coal.[35]

The author then compares the unchristian behaviour of this lady with Blanche of Castile and other noble ladies who gave extensive charity. It is not the feeding nor the affection towards the pet *per se* that was such an object of criticism, rather the excessive feeding and the neglect of one's duty to care for the poor, who are Christian souls, whereas the pet dogs are just animals. This is an echo of Mark 7:27: 'Let the children first be filled: for it is not meet to take the children's bread, and to cast it unto the dogs.'

The iconography of small dogs depicts them as well-fed specimens without any apparent criticism. However, a miniature in an early fourteenth-century Northern French book of hours possibly alludes to the perils of small dogs overeating: at the bottom of a page in the Hours of the Dead a fat pet dog is shown eating a bone next to a skull and bone (fig. 7).

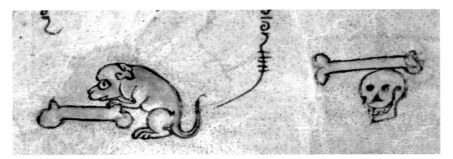

Fig. 7 A fat dog sits next to a bone (Hours of St Omer, *c.* 1320, Northern France)

Perhaps the ultimate dire result of overfeeding a pet is related in the first Life of St Brendan. The Irish saint, on his voyages, encounters an aggressive giant sea-cat. Its origin is explained by the surviving monk on the island on which it lives, who tells how it began as a small animal, but grew large from eating fish.[36] The tale is expanded in the Book of Leinster, which recounts how three students went on a pilgrimage with three loaves of bread and their cat. They arrived at an island where the cat brought them three salmon every day. They decided not to eat the cat's food, and luckily after six days they were rewarded with food from heaven. Unfortunately the cat continued to eat so much fish that it was transformed into the giant sea-cat that attacked St Brendan's party.[37]

Care of pets

THERE are no extant sources that relate specifically to veterinary care for sick pets. However, in the case of dogs, it would be reasonable to assume that if they fell ill, kennel keepers and other professionals would know how to treat them. Albertus Magnus' remedy of feeding constipated overweight pet dogs has already been mentioned; other advice he gives on the general care of dogs includes the topics of breeding, feeding pregnant bitches, and the care of puppies. He suggests starting puppies with whey mixed with buttery milk; at eight months they should be weaned on bread softened with whey. Albertus notes that dogs that had been petted would lose their tracking ability as 'it follows the track of those whom it loves'. He considers that letting dogs sleep a great deal is harmful, especially just after they have eaten and before the food is digested, as 'the intense heat which is around the place of nourishment attracts bad humours to the stomach and the dog is infected and weakened'. He lists the common canine diseases of dogs. Impetigo and scabies require that the dog is bled and the spots anointed with an ointment made from mercury, sulphur, nettle seeds and butter. If worms appear in wounds, then wild tansy juice should be poured on the area. Swellings on the limbs may be cured with a compress of ground marsh mallow and water, sour milk or an ointment of groundsel and lard. Common perils for a dog are spines in the paws or thorns on its coat, which can be drawn out with a mixture of bran and lard. If a dog is growing thin without apparent cause, it should be fed with copious quantities of butter. If the dog still does not get any fatter, Albertus suggests drawing the 'worms under its tongue' with a needle. If all these remedies failed, then the dog is near to death. Sluggishness may be remedied with oat bread, and fleas can be removed by anointing the dog with olive oil.[38] The hunting treatise *The Master of Game* offers similar remedies for the canine ailments, from rabies, scabies, eye and ear troubles to a worm under the tongue. Mange is due to the inherent melancholic nature (excess of black bile) of all dogs, and various ointments are suggested, such as one of honey, verdigris, nut oil, water and valerian leaf.[39]

The most feared canine disease was rabies, as it was known to be transmissible via bites to other animals and humans.[40] The French surgeon Henri de Mondeville (*c.* 1260–*c.* 1320) explains how one can recognize rabies in a dog. The symptoms include drooping ears, grinding teeth, red eyes, drool, an arched back, tail between the legs, infrequent barking and 'tottering as if it was drunk'. The afflicted animal will bark at its own shadow and no longer recognize its master. Mondeville gives a remedy from his native Normandy, which he claims is tried and tested, involving bathing the afflicted animal or person in sea water: nine immersions should cure any rabid dog or person. He insists, 'I have often seen people and animals taken to the seashore who already exhibit the bad signs, at peace and docile as they are led.' There were various elaborate treatments for a patient who had been bitten by a rabid dog, involving special diets, assorted compound medicines (such as theriac), and plasters applied to the wound.

Not all bites from dogs were dangerous. Mondeville placed the bites of pet monkeys and non-rabid dogs together and suggested applying 'crushed salt and onions with honey or with fresh lanolin and oil and warm vinegar.'[41] Apart from medical treatments, owners could also seek other forms of treatment, such as visiting the shrine of St Hubert, a patron saint of rabies in the Ardennes. There the owner could view relics, receive a minuscule fragment of St Hubert's robe to be placed on the wound, or give votive offerings, all in exchange for a return to health of the animal. The saintly cures were not just restricted to humans; Charles, Duke of Orléans (1394–1465) sent all his dogs to St Hubert's shrine to be cured, as he feared that one might be rabid and thus infect the others.[42] Being bitten by a dog, most likely non-rabid, was likely part and parcel of owning them. Maximilian, Archduke of Austria, on the night of his marriage to Mary, Duchess of Burgundy in 1477, was bitten in the bridal chamber by her small lapdog.[43]

Grooming pets is something that would have to have been done regularly, particularly with long-haired pet dogs. Unfortunately, few sources detail the practice, and pets, as ever, are rarely mentioned. An illumination in a fifteenth-century manuscript of *The Master of Game* shows a man with a curry comb grooming two hunting hounds, and similar tools might have been used for long-haired pet dogs, but unfortunately this has to remain conjecture.[44]

Animal accessories

E VEN if it came from a species that had little intrinsic monetary value, an animal could be transformed into a pampered pet of exalted status by adorning it with elaborate accessories. Such is the case of the squirrel, a popular medieval pet, which is almost always described and depicted as being fitted with a collar and chain, usually finely crafted in silver. This practice is depicted in the early fourteenth-century Luttrell Psalter: in one decoration a lady plays with a squirrel that wears a belled collar,[45] while on another folio a lady stands in a coach with a chained and collared squirrel on her shoulder (plate VIII). A fifteenth-century French gold love-ring has a lady with a chained squirrel inscribed inside (fig. 8). A portrait by Hans Holbein the Younger in the National Gallery, London, 'Lady with pet squirrel and starling' shows that the practice of keeping pet squirrels on chains still prevailed in the sixteenth century, as observed in a dialogue in John Lyly's play *Endymion*:

> Tophas: What is that the gentlewoman carrieth in a chain?
> Epiton: Why, it is squirrel.
> Tophas: A squirrel? O gods, what things are made for money![46]

Elaborate pet-themed accessories could be worn by an owner to celebrate affection. A fifteenth-century Italian gold finger-ring has an onyx cameo of a sleeping dog; the following legend is inscribed around it: *kute dormio tute viglio victis parco nullum fugio* (Alert I sleep, safely I watch, I spare the vanquished, I flee from none).[47] A fifteenth-century French gold ring is engraved with a sleeping dog and the inscription *muet* ('silent'; fig. 9).

Fig. 8 Gold engraved love ring, depicting a woman with a chained squirrel
(England, 15th century)

Fig. 9 Gold ring engraved with a sleeping dog and the inscription *muet* ('silent')
(France?, 1400–1500)

Pet collars

While dogs for hunting and guarding were allotted sturdy functional collars, pets tended to wear rather flimsy affairs. These were made of fine leather, adorned with a multitude of bells often manufactured of precious substances such as gold or silver.[48] Collars were designed for dogs and pet squirrels, while cat collars are rarer in the sources. One of the few references appears in a 1498 letter by Tolommeo Spagnolo, a Mantuan courtier visiting Venice, who recounted how he saw 'a most beautiful Syrian cat' sitting in a window wearing a little collar adorned with bells.[49]

These jewelled collars are a symbol of status and appear in public representations of their owners, such as a stained glass window depicting Mary of Burgundy standing with her small short-haired dog tucked under her right arm (plate IV). The dog's neck is adorned with a large ornate collar with hefty silver bells. Another example is the effigy of John Oteswich's wife, with two dogs wearing belled collars (fig. 13). Collars with bells are one of the clear signifiers of pets. Although pets can often appear with just plain collars or even without collars, a collar with bells is a sign of a household animal, as the tinkling bells would be an obvious disadvantage for a hunting dog.

Ladies could keep their pet dogs on leashes, but rather than serving any functional purpose, the leash is a sign that the animal is connected to its owner. In a British Library Psalter a lady holds in one hand leashes attached to three dogs of different colours.[50] Ornate collars were not restricted to dogs. A green parrot in a fifteenth-century English bestiary now in Copenhagen sports a collar with golden bells (plate III).

Even unusual pets could wear collars. When Il Sodoma painted his pet badgers in the cloisters of the Benedictine monastery of Monte Oliveto Maggiore, he depicted one of them wearing a red leather collar with silver studs (plate IX).

Cushions and cages

Pets might be given fine cushions to sit on, and their owners would order the construction of elaborate private living quarters, which could include specially designed baskets, kennels, squirrel hutches and birdcages. An Old Irish legal text mentions how cats, kept indoors by women, sleep in special baskets or on bed pillows.[51] An elaborate dog kennel is described in the romance of Tristan:

> Queen Isolde had made a delightful little kennel of gold and precious stones, such as one might dream of. Inside they spread a rich

brocade for him to lie on. In this way, Petitcreiu was under Isolde's observation, day and night, in public and in private.[52]

This description adheres to the conventions of romance literature, and it is doubtful whether such 'jewelled' kennels were in use in daily life. Nevertheless, the use of brocade cushions for pets is well attested in iconography and literature. A fine example of a carefully constructed squirrel hutch can be seen in an initial D of the Sherborne Missal in the British Library: St Baltildis, in the regalia of a queen, stands by a nut-eating squirrel which is outside its hutch.[53] A similar hutch, accompanied by a chained and collared squirrel, appears in a fourteenth-century Flemish book of hours, now in the Bodleian Library.[54]

Pet birds were kept in cages, which created a market for such items. The accounts for Urban V give expenses for the cages for parrots and other birds kept at his court, and also an iron stick which conventional wisdom recommended for training parrots.[55] Parrots, as expensive exotic birds, could be kept in very fine surroundings: the talking bird in John Skelton's *Speke Parrot* is kept in an ornate cage with a mirror to keep it amused:

> A cage curiosly carven, with a silver pin,
> Properly painted, to be my coverture;
> A mirror of glasse, that I may toot therein.[56]

Birds in cages were normally safe from external threats, but not always from other pets. The parrot narrator in Jean Lemaire's poem *Les Épîtres de l'amant vert* is eaten by a mastiff, presumably when out of its cage. In an illumination for the entry for 'cat' in a mid-thirteenth-century bestiary, a large black cat opens the cage of a caged bird and inserts its paws.[57]

Apart from other birds, a few pets were kept in cages when their owners were travelling. The pet weasel of Alfonso X of Castile accompanied him everywhere in a little cage tied to his saddle. One of Alfonso's *Cantigas de Santa Maria* relates how the Virgin Mary rescues his beloved weasel when it falls accidentally under the feet of his horse, in return for the king's piety.[58]

High status accessories

At the highest level, ornate pet collars displayed status through precious metals and stones. Among the items listed in an inventory drawn up in 1380 on the death of Charles V of France there are several examples of pet accessories. These include a silver collar with bells specifically *pour un petit chien* and a very small *collier à chiene* made with blue cloth adorned with golden *fleur de lys* with three little golden bells and secured by a gold buckle.[59]

Similarly, Isabeau of Bavaria spent extensively on such accessories. In 1387 she commissioned for her pet squirrel a collar embroidered with pearls and fastened by a gold buckle.[60] There were various expenses for her birds, such as green cloth parrot cage covers in 1387 and 1392, and a silver cage made for her birds in 1402.[61] Bright green cloth was used not just for her parrots; her cat had a special cover made from a similar material in 1406.[62]

The same kind of bright green fabric was used for a cage cover of a singing bird owned by another Queen of France, Anne of Brittany, in 1492.[63] This was one of several cages she owned, as far as we can tell by payments for birds in her accounts. They feature alongside entries for the *petits chiens de sa chambre*, which lived constantly with her, although their feeding and general care was entrusted to someone else. The twenty-four dogs all wore black velvet collars, each with four suspended ermine paws, symbolizing the arms of the Duchy of Brittany.[64] Louis XI's greyhound wore a scarlet velvet collar decorated with twenty pearls and eleven rubies.[65] The accounts of his successor, Charles VIII, detail the purchase of parrots, two covers for birdcages (which contained an albino blackbird and two turtledoves that resided in the king's chambers), green cloth purchased for a robe (*habillement*) for a little dog and red cloth for a robe for a pet marmot.[66] The dog collars detailed in the household inventories of Henry VIII include: 'two greyhoundes collars of crimsun velvett and cloth of gold, locking torrettes' (spikes), 'a collar garnished with stole-worke with one shallop shelle of silver and gilte, with torettes and pendauntes of silver and guilte', 'a collar of white velvette, embrawdered with perles, the swivels of silver'. The 'two other collars with the kinges arms, and at the ende portcullis and rose' bore the heraldic Beaufort portcullis and Tudor rose, while 'a collar embrawdered with pomegranates and roses with turrets of silver and gilt' would have been worn by one of Queen Catherine of Aragon's dogs, her symbol being the pomegranate (and the turrets a symbol of Castile).[67]

Although the iconography frequently depicts cloth collars with bells, and occasionally metal ones, the very ornate and jewelled collars mentioned in royal accounts were unlikely to have been used for everyday wear owing to their weight and impracticability. Isabeau of Bavaria's fondness for ordering such accessories could be misleading. In a British Library manuscript containing the works of Christine de Pisan, Isabeau's alert little white dog is shown sitting beside her in her bedroom: and he is collarless.[68] Perhaps the more ornate collars were used only in a public setting when a clear indication of status and wealth was required. In this way a pet could become an ostentatious 'consumer' of wealth through its owner through the magnificence of its upkeep, the delicacy of its feeding, the expense of its accessories and the opulence of its living arrangements.

✦　✦
✦

Fig. 10   Initial, with King David, dog and monkey

4

$\mathcal{L}$iving with $\mathcal{P}$ets

The pet indoors

MEDIEVAL pets had as their true milieu enclosed domestic space. They differed from other animals on which care was lavished, whether fine horses, hunting hounds and hawks, all of which required special attention from trained carers and resided in purpose-built accommodation – stables, kennels and mews. Pets, on the other hand, were free to accompany their owners in all aspects of their life, playing with them or with other pets.

Pets abounded in both public and private interior spaces, from courtyards and halls to private chambers, where their presence was taken for granted. In the early fifteenth-century Bedford Hours an illumination depicting the legend of the Fleur de Lys includes a small brown long-haired dog, wearing a collar, standing at the feet of court ladies, looking up at a king dressed in armour.[1] In another illuminated fifteenth-century manuscript a round, long-haired dog with a curled tail follows the trains of the court ladies in a scene from Jean Wauquelin's *L'Ystoire de Helayne* (1448).[2]

Pets appear in more intimate domestic spaces. In Lorenzo Lotto's early sixteenth-century painting 'Husband and Wife', a fashionably dressed couple sit in a luxurious room, in an opulent setting; an imported carpet is draped over the table. The man points to a tame squirrel on the table, as the lady holds in her left arm a white long-haired dog with a short snout and collar.[3] In the background of a top-left corner roundel in Hieronymus Bosch's oil panel 'The Seven Deadly Sins', a dying man is lying in bed and is attended by priests and other religious figures, as two women sit at a table, with a grey cat at their feet.[4] In a miniature in a book of hours originating from either Bruges or Ghent a man is warming himself by the fire while a woman sets the table, while in front of the table a well-fed grey cat stares at the cosy scene.[5] The pets in these images are not the focus of the compositions, but are accepted as common companions in the domestic spaces they inhabit.

Ostentatious exhibition of a pet in interiors was also common for the many clerics who owned monkeys. A monkey was an expensive and imported pet, as Hugh of Saint-Victor complained in a sermon: 'Even though the ape is a most vile, filthy, and detestable animal, clerics like to keep one in their houses and to display it in their windows, so as to impress the passing rabble with the glory of their possessions.'[6] The spoiled almond-fed monkeys of Robert Coquina, Bishop of Durham we encountered in Chapter 3 would also fit this description. This fashion was evidently prevalent in the upper reaches of the clergy. As an iconographic aside: in 1506 William Warham, Archbishop of Canterbury, presented New College, Oxford, with a splendid silver-gilt salt cellar in the shape of a monkey: plate II.[7]

The Franciscan chronicler Salimbene de Adam, writing in the 1280s, quotes his contemporary Brother Hugh's rebuke to cardinals: 'You spend the whole day idly in your chambers, lazing about. You take delight only in little lapdogs and rings and sleek horses and your kinsmen.'[8]

Pets occupied the very close personal space of their owners, and physical proximity was an indicator of intimacy. Diminutive size, although not an absolute necessity in a pet, facilitated such closeness. Thus most pets were small and portable: small dogs, birds and squirrels. Close contact is an iconographic attribute of pets in their pictorial representations – the pets inhabit very close personal space and are often held in their owners' arms or lie by their feet. Two illuminated initials in a fourteenth-century book of hours from the South Netherlands illustrate this intimacy. On one folio a nun is depicted inside an initial 'D' holding a small white collared dog in her arms (plate VII), and an almost identical pose is adopted by a secular lady inside an initial 'S' in a later folio. In a miniature in the Manesse Codex (c. 1300–40) which links exterior space with the interior, the poet Dietmar von Aist, disguised as a pedlar, sits on a donkey outside as his lady stands at the threshold. She examines the goods on offer, while keeping her small white dog carefully tucked under her arm.[9]

Pets also appear in domestic family interiors, interacting with family members or merely sleeping contentedly. It is not always clear to which family member the animal belongs, though it is often associated with children. In an early sixteenth-century French book of hours a domestic scene of family life is played out as a woman cooks on a fire, while one of her children places more firewood in front of her.[10] In the foreground one child bends over while another rocks a cradle with a swaddled baby sleeping inside. On the right a smooth-haired dog is sleeping; it wears a collar and has its tail curled. On the verso side of the same folio, in a similar domestic setting, a child offers a piece of bread to a little white smooth-haired dog, who sits up, his ears alert. The full-page illumination of a January winter scene in another early sixteenth-century book of hours, the Grimani Breviary, depicts a similarly cosy scene. A family is sitting inside a small house warming itself by the fire, as a grey-haired striped cat sits on the door-ledge of the open door.[11]

Cats were common pets in urban environments because of their skill as mousers and their ability to adapt themselves easily to living in close quarters. Salimbene de Adam recounted how many pet cats, in towns abandoned by Frederick II in northern Italy in 1247, were captured by an enterprising man who wanted to profit from their fur:

> He had caught in his traps twenty-seven fine cats in the burned-out cities, and he sold these pets to furriers. There can be little doubt of this, because in peace time they had been pet cats [*domestici*] in those cities.[12]

Salimbene was told this tale by the trapper himself, while residing in Imola. The trapper took all the pet cats he could find, both large and small. Salimbene had an eye for detail regarding the perils awaiting urban cats. He recorded a great plague in 1284 that affected only cats.[13]

Children would grow up with pets in their houses and doubtless played with them. Fifteenth-century schoolbooks illustrate this. One speaks of a family dog called Whitefoot, and a fifteenth-century poem written in a grammar school boy's text mentions that there was a little dog in a house, kept in special quarters, and cared for by the lady of the house:

> Clim, clam, the cat leapt over the dam
> My dame hath in a hutch at home
> A little dog with a clog;
> Hey dogs, hey![14]

A similar poem written in a schoolboy's text, either as an exercise set by the master or an original creation of the student recounts: 'At my house I have a jay'. The schoolboy is using the poem to describe the different sounds of the bird compared to other animals. Clearly having a jay at home was an ordinary matter.[15]

Pets in the dining hall

Dogs and cats frequently appear in the iconography of feasts and less formal dining: a reflection of their place in such spaces in real life. The animals are usually quite small, in itself a sign that they were probably pets, quite apart from other contextual evidence. A common motif is a fight between a dog and a cat, or an exchange of hostile glances between two pets that are oblivious to anyone else. This motif is frequently found in images of the Annunciation or the Last Supper, in which the animals play no textual role but instead underline the domesticity of the scene.

In a miniature of the Annunciation in the British Library's London Hours, a tabby cat fights a small smooth-haired dog, who wears a collar covered in bells. The pair give battle in the middle of a tiled floor, between the Virgin Mary and the Archangel Gabriel, but they are not themselves relevant to the Gospel story.[16]

Animals can also appear individually in scenes of this sort. In an early sixteenth-century Annunciation by Lorenzo Lotto, an alarmed tabby cat runs away from the Archangel Gabriel and towards Mary, as if perceiving the presence of the angel in the room.[17] In Cosimo Rosselli's fresco of the Last Supper (1484), in the Sistine Chapel in Rome, a small dog and slightly larger cat snarl at each other in the central foreground in front of the table, while on the far left a very small white dog, wearing a collar, stands on two legs in front of two men.[18] By contrast, in Pietro Lorenzetti's Last Supper in the Basilica of St Francis in Assisi, the two animals studiously ignore each other. The cat sits by the fire while the small dog licks a plate of leftovers on the ground.[19] The distinction between a pet and other domestic animals is underlined in a fourteenth-century fresco of the Wedding Feast at Cana in the baptistery of Padua Cathedral. Here two hounds gnaw bones next to the servants, while a small long-haired grey dog sits on the high dais next to Jesus, a reflection of its elevated status.[20] This situation was not without tensions: a *bas-de-page* miniature in an early fourteenth-century book of hours from Artois, now in the British Library, illustrates a large lean hunting hound biting the back of the small fat little dog who in turn nips the hound on the nose.[21]

Pets are visible in more private dining scenes as well. In an illumination in an early sixteenth-century breviary a well-fed grey cat pounces on a mouse in front of a small table at which a couple are dining.[22]

By the fifteenth century, despite the widespread practice of having animals in close contact with diners, many courtesy manuals claimed it was not genteel for animals to roam around the dining hall, sit on the table, or be fed by hand or patted by owners. Courtesy books discourage the custom:

> Yf thy nown dogge thou scrape or clawe
> That is holden a vyse emong men knawe.
> Where-sere thou sitt at mete in borde,
> Avoide the cat at on bare worde,
> For yf thou stroke cat other dogge,
> Thou art lyke an ape teyge with a clogge.[23]

Albertus Magnus comments on how feeding dogs from one's own plate could make a dog neglect his duties: 'The most ignoble genus of dogs before one's table are those that are thought to be on guard but which frequently so place themselves that they keep one eye on the door and one on the generous hand of the master.'[24] Dogs could even be allowed on the table: in the illumination for January in *Les très riches heures de Jean Duc de Berry*[25] there are two little dogs on the dining table in front of the Duke of Berry, and one is even leaning over and starting to eat from a plate.

Pets in chambers

PETS had free access to sleeping quarters, the most intimate physical space. This was something that concerned the authors of fifteenth-century courtesy books. Huge Rhode's *Book of Nurture* suggests that on preparing a chamber one must 'auoyde the dogs, and shutte the doors' and similarly John Russell's *Boke of Nurture* requests that one 'dryve out dogge and catte, or els geue them a clout'.[26]

In a misericord in Seville Cathedral (1464–74), a kneeling woman pats a small dog in a decorated room.[27] In an early sixteenth-century drawing by Lorenzo Lotto a young cleric is seated at his desk, in front of which is a very small dog, sitting on a plump cushion placed on a small bench. The dog wears a collar and has his head turned towards his master (fig. 11). The presence of the dog is taken for granted.

Pets resided in private chambers at their ease, either at the foot of the bed, the main item of furniture, or on the bed itself. In Vittore Carpaccio's 'Dream of Saint Ursula' (1495), a small short-haired dog, wearing a collar, lies at the foot of St Ursula's bed, looking towards the viewer. The same dog (along with another which does not appear in the final version) is in a preparatory sketch as well, underlining the importance of a contented small dog as an accessory in depictions of bedrooms.[28] In the church of San Fermo Maggiore, Verona, Pisanello's fresco of the Annunciation (1426) shows the Archangel Gabriel standing on the left, while on the other side the Virgin sits on a long bench in an elegant and well-furnished bedroom. In the foreground, near the Virgin's feet and looking towards the angel, stands a small white dog with a belled collar.[29] An early sixteenth-century stained glass panel shows Tobias and Sarah sleeping together in a bed on their wedding night, accompanied by a small, white, long-haired dog (plate V).

Pets might sleep on, or even in, the bed with their owner, as attested by the poet John Gower (1330–1408) in his *Confessio amantis*, where he describes the little dog and birds in his mistress's bedroom:

Fig. 11 An ecclesiastic in his study with a pet dog
(drawing by Lorenzo Lotto, Italy, early 16th century)

> I pleie with hire litel hound
> Now on the bed, now on the ground,
> Now with hir brides in the cage.[30]

The dire consequences of letting pets sleep in or on beds is a topic of various short narratives, though the practice itself is not condemned. Usually the tales involve mistaken identity. For instance one such *exemplum* from the thirteenth century recounts how a knight, on returning home, stabs his wife when he sees a shape under the sheets besides her. On drawing back the sheet he discovers that she has merely been sleeping with her dog.[31] In another, a knight kills his mistress in the dark of her bedroom, mistaking her for her dog, which had previously bitten him.[32] Another tale concerns a knight who is rejected by a lady. He returns in disguise and lets her cat scratch him. For his discretion after this incident, she becomes his mistress. The knight then refuses to marry her, claiming that he is afraid of her cat.[33] A prioress at Newington was alleged to have been smothered by her cat while she slept.[34]

Heinrich Cornelius Agrippa (1486–1535), author of various magical and astrological treatises, kept two dogs, a black male called Monsieur and a bitch called Mamselle. Agrippa was very affectionate towards Monsieur, who was allowed to eat beside him and sleep on his bed. Agrippa's work on magic led some contemporaries to think Monsieur was a familiar demon.[35]

When Richard II was deposed by Henry of Lancaster, Richard's greyhound Math deserted the king. The dog, which previously had always fawned on his royal master, ignored him and raced to Henry with great cheer. Henry saw this is an auspicious sign, especially as the greyhound was already one of Henry's badges. He let Math sleep on his bed, as the royal dog had given a clear sign of approval of the change of kingship.[36]

Pets were allowed into spaces where access was granted to few apart from chosen servants and retainers. They are present in numerous representations of women in childbirth, a scene that was out of bounds for men, but not for pets. We see this in depictions of the birth of the Virgin or John the Baptist. In a miniature of the birth of the Virgin in the mid-fifteenth-century Hours of Catherine of Cleves, a striped cat sits on the tiles by the fire licking its paws, as St Anne is handed the swaddled Virgin Mary.[37] Pets abound in the scene of the Birth of John the Baptist in the early fifteenth-century Hours of Milan. In the foreground a small long-haired white dog eats a bone at the foot of the bed, an alert grey cat stands protectively over a bowl of milk, complete with spoon, while St Elizabeth lies in bed with the infant John.[38] Similarly, in a miniature of the birth of John the Baptist in the early sixteenth-century Grimani Breviary, a well-fed (possibly pregnant) grey cat looks up as St Elizabeth is handed the baby.[39] This motif is not confined to religious scenes. A miniature in a fifteenth-century Alexander Romance in the British Library has one woman in a bed, another swaddling the baby, while a dog chews a bone.[40]

An Old Irish poem written by an unknown monk in Carinthia on the margin of his copy of St Paul's Epistles in the eighth or ninth century extols the role his pet cat, Pangur Bán, plays as a faithful companion for a monk at his desk:

> I and Pangur Bán, my cat
> 'Tis a like task we are at;
> Hunting mice is his delight
> Hunting words I sit all night.

Better far than praise of men
'Tis to sit with book and pen;
Pangur bears me no ill will,
He too plies his simple skill.

'Tis a merry thing to see
At our tasks how glad are we,
When at home we sit and find
Entertainment to our mind.

Oftentimes a mouse will stray
In the hero Pangur's way:
Oftentimes my keen thought set
Takes a meaning in its net.

'Gainst the wall he sets his eye
Full and fierce and sharp and sly;
'Gainst the wall of knowledge I
All my little wisdom try.

When a mouse darts from its den,
O how glad is Pangur then!
O what gladness do I prove
When I solve the doubts I love!

So in peace our tasks we ply,
Pangur Bán, my cat, and I;
In our arts we find our bliss,
I have mine and he has his.

Practice every day has made
Pangur perfect in his trade;
I get wisdom day and night
Turning darkness into light.[41]

Pets outdoors

I F a pet was taken outside into the fresh air it was usually confined
to an enclosed garden and kept close to its owner, either sitting near
the owner's feet, held tightly in the owner's arms or on a leash. In the
iconography of garden scenes, pets are paraded in the constant company
of their owners. A fourteenth-century French ivory mirror in the British
Museum shows a woman holding a little dog in her left arm as she stands
in a garden with her lover. A fourteenth-century French ivory comb in

the Victoria and Albert Museum depicts three pairs of lovers:[42] on one side a lady sits in a garden patting a small dog, while the reverse shows a lady standing with a dog in her arms. In a fifteenth-century miniature in a manuscript at the Bibliothèque de l'Arsenal a couple sit on the grass while a smooth-haired dog wearing a red collar sits next to them.[43] A very common motif in depictions of couples is a small dog next to the lady. In the fourteenth-century Queen Mary's Psalter a marginal image shows two couples on a bench, in which a lady on the far right has a small dog on her lap.[44] Similarly, an early fourteenth-century manuscript of the Romance of the Grail has an illumination of Lancelot talking to a lady on a bench: the lady pats the head of a small black and white dog, wearing a collar, which sits on her lap and looks at Lancelot.[45] A mid-fifteenth-century misericord in Gloucester Cathedral represents a lady standing in a garden with a small dog at her feet looking up at her.[46] In Sir David Lindsay's satirical *Papyngo* in 1529, the parrot narrator, allegedly James V's pet, describes how he is aired in the garden by his caretaker, perching on the trainer's wrist.[47]

In a miniature in an early sixteenth-century Flemish book of hours, ladies oversee the construction of a garden while holding small dogs in their arms. On the next folio a pair of lovers wander in a garden as a small brown curly-tailed dog stands nearby.[48] In the Grimani Breviary the miniature for the month of April has a lady sitting on the ground cradling a small brown and white spaniel-like dog on her lap. Another little dog, which appears to belong to a group of ladies and gentleman who are walking along, sits on the lady's skirt, barking at the dog in her lap.[49] The little dog in the *Romance of the Chatelaine of Vergi* is let out alone into a garden for exercise as a sign that his owner's lover may visit her, but this appears to be the limit of the animal's freedom.[50] Gardens, the outside province of the pet, share many of the same characteristics as pets: both are products of a tamed and artificial nature, destined only for amusement and distraction.

Perhaps the most detailed literary treatment of the whereabouts of pet dogs appears in the fourteenth-century French poet Eustache Deschamps' *Un chien doit presque tout scavoir*. Here the ubiquity of dogs is underlined, from palaces to fields, from churches to dining halls. Their unruly behaviour (misbehaving in church, fighting under tables) is taken for granted:

> I marvel more and more each day
> at a phrase so common it's become cliché
> when people want a put-down now they say,

'He's got the brain of a dog; he's about
as ignorant as can be.' But I'd point out
a dog is well informed since he
wanders where he wants habitually;
to palace, council – isn't it the truth? – they go
to taverns, and to fields, and to, and fro:
most of what we know a dog must know.

Dogs go to churches every single day
and piss on the vestments of the priests,
and go to funerals and wedding feasts,
to butchers, and orations, bedrooms; they
go to the cloister and the dorm, and go
to convents and kitchens, every household. Where
there are feats of arms, bold deeds or fair,
many dogs are often gathered there.
The heralds will confirm that this is so:
most of what we know a dog must know.

Dogs go to eat in dining rooms, and they
can hide and quarrel while they are below
the table, bickering over offal; they can go
into the houses of the great and find a way
to sleep in those grand beds, and tear
the carpets up, and go to markets where
there's cheese, and to the mill, the baker's go
to gardens, cellars, where they're beaten, and dogs lie
on all the river barges passing by:
most of what we know a dog must know.[51]

Travelling with pets

WHEN venturing further afield, as would frequently happen with noble households that changed lodgings regularly, the pet travelled with its owners in a closed wagon, inhabiting a movable domestic space. This practice is visible in an image from the early fourteenth-century Luttrell Psalter. One of the ladies in this scene has a chained squirrel perched on her shoulder as she looks out of the back of the carriage, while a servant is handing a small but podgy dog, wearing a collar, to another lady (plate VII). A large guard dog walks underneath the carriage, in marked contrast to the pampered animals inside, illustrating the difference between the lives of the pet, a non-functional animal, and the working dog. This situation had not changed two and half centuries later when John Caius wrote in *De canibus Britannicis* (1570):

> These puppies the smaller they be, the more pleasure they prouoke, as more meete play fellowes for minsing mistrisses to beare in their bosoms, to keepe company withal in their chambers, to succour with sleepe in bed, and nourishe with meate at bourde, to lay in their lappes, and licke their lippes as they ryde in their waggons.

This passage indicates the intimacy associated with small pet dogs, who are kept in private chambers, allowed on beds, overfed with meat and taken everywhere on their owner's laps, including in 'waggons' and even allowed to lick their mistresses' lips.[52]

The owner might travel without a pet, but still send for the animal if needed. This was often the case with birds, which were relatively easy to transport in cages. The accounts of Isabeau of Bavaria reveal that her own birds were sent for when she was on the move. In March 1416 she asked for her turtle-doves and little birds to be sent from Paris. Later that year, in July, she had her little birds taken from Vincennes to Saint-Germain-en-Laye. While in Troyes in 1420, during treaty negotiations with the English, she sent for her little singing birds of various species, for her *plaisance et esbatement*.[53] Marie d'Anjou, wife of Charles VII of France, kept many animals, particularly during her long stay in Chinon; in November 1454 she made a payment to her valets who had brought her pet starling and parrot.[54]

When outside the acceptable limits of either a garden or a carriage, the pet was kept under close surveillance, or held firmly by its owner. This is the situation in a miniature in an early fourteenth-century book of hours from the South Netherlands, where a lady rides pillion behind a man, clutching her little white dog in her lap.[55] In a painting by Bounamico Buffalmacco, 'The Triumph of Death', *c.* 1350, in the Campo Santo Monumentale in Pisa, a hunting party includes a lady riding with one hand cradling a small white dog. Buffalmacco had problems with pets while painting this fresco. Apparently a pet baboon, owned by Bishop Guido of Arezzo, started playing with his paints and smeared them over the frescos he had previously painted.[56]

In a *bas-de-page* illumination in the early fourteenth-century Macclesfield Psalter a lady stands between a man on horseback on the left and a wildman on the right. In her right arm she cradles a small grey dog that looks up at her. Its small size and physical proximity emphasizes intimacy, and like the lady, provides a civilized domestic contrast to the unkempt wildman.[57] The presence of the pet and lady as a symbol of the tamed as distinct from the untamed is also apparent in a full-page illumination from a fifteenth-century French manuscript of *Le Livre de échecs armoureux moralisées*.[58] Here a lady entitled 'Nature' stands guard with a key at the entrance of an enclosed garden, which is carefully cultivated and occupied by three other ladies bearing the labels 'Venus', 'Juno' and 'Pallas', allegorical figures from the *Romance of the Rose*. Lady Nature has a tiny white dog at her feet. The pet, like the garden itself a product of an artificial and tamed nature, looks outwards with the lady towards the untamed rocky and forested wilderness that lies beyond the garden, and at the two men standing in the wilderness looking in. One of the men holds a large hunting hound by a chain. This animal is perfectly at ease in its surroundings, in stark contrast to the tame and gentle little dog that, like its owner, belongs in the enclosed garden. Like the garden where it is kept, it is tended, watched and enclosed.

Pets in the city

SMALL animals which can be identified as pets appear in various representations of urban life. They do not usually play a major role in the iconographic scheme, but instead add interest to the pictorial narrative. In urban scenes the animal, usually in a playful mood, appears in the foreground, adding lightness and domesticity.

Pet animals are common in depictions of urban crowd scenes. In Santa Maria Novella, Florence, there is a fresco by Filippino Lippi (1457–1504) showing St John restoring Drusiana to life. A crowd of women and children stand in the background to the side of the miracle, observing the event; in the foreground a small spaniel tugs at the sash of one of the children, lending a playful air to the serious religious scene. Similarly in Carpaccio's oil painting 'Miracle of the True Cross on the Rialto' (*c.* 1494), crowds are depicted near the Rialto Bridge in Venice, with the streets overflowing with spectators and the Grand Canal full of gondolas. In the foreground on the right a small dog sits in a gondola. It has its tail hanging over the side of the boat, and is made eye-catching through the use of bright white paint. It sits quite apart from the rest of the occupants of the gondola and, like the crowd, bears witness to the miracle.[59] Among many other examples, the painting of 'St Peter Healing a Cripple and the Raising of Tabitha' by Masolino da Panicale (*c.* 1383–*c.* 1447) shows a monkey sitting on a window ledge in the buildings in the background, oblivious to the crowd below watching the miracle.[60]

Animals also appear in less crowded urban scenes. In a full-page miniature in a book of hours in the British Library, St Barbara is shown in conversation with her father in a city street with tall buildings on either side. In the foreground two small dogs are fighting. Whether they belong to either of the human pair is unclear, and their symbolism is also uncertain. Are they intended to add animation and lightness to the scene or is their small-scale fight representative of St Barbara's discussion?[61]

Pets appear in urban professional interiors, such as the jeweller's shop depicted in a Paris manuscript. In this scene the husband attends to a couple and the woman to a male buyer. In the foreground a monkey and a medium-sized white hound wearing a collar sit on the tiles. On the counter itself, among the displays of costly jewels sits a small short-haired collared dog, which appears to be quite at home. The little dog represents the domesticity of this urban shop, and its presence as a quality animal emphasizes the luxury of the goods on sale there.[62] Similarly, in a depiction of a medical dispensary in a Cambridge medical manuscript, a little dog sits in the lap of a doctor.[63]

Pets in monasteries and convents

M OST of the evidence for the prevalence of pet keeping by members of religious orders comes from criticism of the practice. The main argument put forward by religious authorities against keeping pets in enclosed institutional spaces was that they had no place in such a sacred environment. They had no functional role, and had a negative effect on both the owner and the community by distracting them from religious duties and disrupting contemplative life. The pet-keeping secular clergy could more easily ignore such prohibitions as they were not bound by institutional rules.

Pet keeping was not encouraged in the mendicant orders either, even though they had a more external ministry than monks. In 1260 the General Chapter of Narbonne ruled that members of the Franciscan order could keep only cats and certain birds. The Franciscan chronicler Salimbene de Adam differentiated between the love of wild animals, part of the image of the order's founder, and pet keeping by the order's members. He saw the former as a commendable trait of the saint and the latter as a frivolous pursuit which caused the pet-owner to lose the respect of his fellow friars. Here the criticism is directed at delighting in animals for one's own pleasure, rather than communicating with wild animals to celebrate Divine Creation:

> I have seen in my own Order, which is the Order of the blessed Francis and the Friars Minor, some lectors who despite being highly

learned and of great sanctity, nevertheless had a blemish on account of which they are judged by others to be frivolous men. For they liked to play with cats, little dogs and little birds, but not as the blessed Francis played with a pheasant and a cicada while delighting in the Lord.[64]

The general discouragement of the practice may explain why there is very little iconography showing pet keeping in religious communities. This is in marked contrast to imagery of secular women, for whom the keeping of pets is presented as a normal and acceptable. However, in an early fourteenth-century book of hours from the Netherlands there are two unusual images of nuns with pets. On one folio a nun in black habit works with a distaff while on her right a white cat catches and plays with the spool.[65] On another folio, inside an initial 'D', a nun in brown habit clutches a little white dog (plate VI).[66] This manuscript is full of images of animals and people in topsy-turvy situations. The religious pictured are often engaged in subversive activities, so this is possibly an expression of gentle criticism of members of the clergy, and may indicate that pet keeping was a common practice.[67]

Animals appear throughout monastic grounds in the fresco cycle of the life of St Benedict in the monastery of Monte Oliveto Maggiore (Tuscany) begun by Luca Signorelli (1497–8) and completed by Il Sodoma (1502 or 1505). Two of these frescos are particularly interesting. One depicts Benedict presiding over the monks as they eat their frugal dinner. In the foreground in front of the table cloth, a dog and cat snarl at each other, apparently fighting over table scraps. Their presence is not indicated as anything out of the ordinary in the fresco. In another fresco a group of prostitutes try to enter the monastery and seduce the monks. They are preceded by their dog, which like them is an ornate specimen, a small curly-haired breed with a coat whose luxuriousness matches the women's fine clothing. Here the dog performs another function, representing the frivolous secular world intruding, unwanted, into the monastic world.

There was no universal canonical prohibition against pet keeping, as there was of hunting. Many individual houses or some entire orders enacted regulations against keeping animals. Some forbade all animals and others only certain species. The Order of Grandmont forbade all animals 'except bees, which do no harm to neighbours'.[68] The Cistercian Order in their first *Instituta Generalis Capituli* banned the keeping of animals for pleasure.[69] Despite numerous efforts by individual ordinances, injunctions and sternly worded letters after visitations, pet keeping was widespread among men and women in religious orders. The visitation letters were concerned mostly with distraction from duties and the presence of pets in the sacred space of the church itself.

Sometimes specific houses tried to issue strict ordinances on the matter. In 1295 the ordinance of Walter of Wenlock, Abbot of Westminster, firmly stated that 'We wish that no one of our household should have a dog or bird, and if anyone does bring in a dog or bird and keeps it for three days, it is our ruling that he gives it to whomever we please.'[70] William Alnwick, Bishop of Lincoln, wrote to Daventry Priory after his visit in July 1442, informing them of a practice he believed should be stopped: 'Also every monk keeps dogs on his own account, by which the alms of the house, as in the broken meat of the table, are wasted.'[71] William should have been relieved that he just had to deal with dogs. The canons of Notre-Dame in 1245 had a veritable menagerie in the cloister, and Eudes, Legate of Saint-Siège, banned them from keeping such 'useless' animals as monkeys, crows, deer and bears.[72]

A pet raven plays a part in a Cistercian narrative of an abbot and a stolen ring. The abbot of Corvey is described a worldly man, fond of courtly ritual and a far cry from St Bernard of Clairvaux, the founder of the order. When washing his hands the abbot leaves his gold ring on a table. A raven, which is kept as a pet by members of the abbot's household, snatches the ring and hides it in a nest. The abbot, on discovering the loss, launches a public sentence of excommunication on the unknown thief. The raven, unaware of its guilt, began to 'sicken little by little, to loathe his food, to cease more and more from his droll croakings and other irrational follies whereby he was wont to delight the minds of fools who neglect the fear of God'. By the time the bird's feathers have fallen out, the abbot's servants are puzzled and ask their master for help. He promptly realizes what has happened, and orders the nest to be examined. On discovering the ring, the sentence of excommunication is lifted and the raven is restored to health.[73]

Injunctions against pet keeping were often directed against nunneries. Thus Hugo Seton, Archdeacon of Ely, after visiting Chatteris in 1345, issued injunctions against dogs and birds being kept by the abbess or any nun, especially when the animals were put under the choir bench during divine services.[74] He had to issue an almost identical injunction against Ickleton Priory in the same year, repeating the prohibition of keeping a *canem seu caniculum* (dog or puppy), in the choir of the church.[75] Similarly, two Yorkshire Cistercian houses, Keldhome and Rosedale, were visited by Archbishop Greenfield in 1314–15, and the nuns were subsequently forbidden to take their small dogs into sacred space. In Keldhome (1314) the prioress was strictly instructed to exclude little dogs (*caniculos*) from the choir, cloister and other places. Nuns who disobeyed this injunction were to be punished. In Rosedale (1315) the prioress and sub-prioress were ordered to forbid little dogs from the choir or church, as the animals would 'impede the service and hinder the devotion of the nuns'.[76]

William of Wykeham, Bishop of Winchester, issued a stern injunction in 1387 to the nunneries of Romsey, Wherwell and St Mary's, Winchester, against taking a variety of animals into church; the nuns were paying more attention to their pets than the Holy Offices. The species listed included birds, rabbits and dogs, which were regarded as frivolous and distracting creatures. Although the nuns were forbidden from bringing their pets into the sacred space of the church itself, under pain of a one-day bread and water fast per animal, the bishop was not concerned with the keeping of pets in the nunnery itself.[77] A set of reformed rules enacted in the nunnery of Langendorf in Saxony, in the early fifteenth century, insisted that 'cats, dogs and other animals are not to be kept by nuns as they distract from seriousness'.[78]

Eudes Rigaud, Archbishop of Rouen (1248–75), listed pet keeping among other scandalous conditions, such as the wearing of secular dress and costly food, in monastic houses in his register. He visited Saint-Sauveur, Evreux, in 1250 and ordered the nuns to get rid of their small dogs, birds and squirrels. But he had to issue a prohibition of the very same practice again in 1258, and then yet again in 1269. Similarly the sisters of Holy Trinity in Caen were forbidden from keeping larks and small birds in cages in 1250, but the birds were still there when Eudes returned in 1256. On visiting Saint-Léger des Préaux in 1257, he merely noted the presence of two small dogs and three squirrels. When in 1268 the archbishop ordered Eustacia, an ex-prioress at Villarceux, to remove a bird whose squawking disturbed some of the older nuns, she replied, to quote the archbishop, in a manner 'which greatly displeased us'. Evidently the ex-prioress had tolerated no complaints about her noisy bird during her tenure of office.[79] The abbess Marie de Bretagne of Fontevrault, like the prioress at Villarceux, was not content with a mere pet dog or cat, but had a parrot listed among an inventory of goods made at her death in 1477.[80]

Despite occasional injunctions against them, pets appear to have been part of monastic life, especially in nunneries. Many regulations, instead of banning them entirely, tolerated pets as long as there were not too many of them and they kept quiet. The wording of the complaints against pet keeping often stressed the excessive number of pets kept and the taking of animals into inappropriate areas, especially sacred spaces. Presumably if pets were kept at all, they should have been confined to the cloisters. As

Fig. 12 A woman holds a dog (Book of Hours, Utrecht, *c.* 1460)

long as the owners had only one quiet animal, kept it under control and still managed to perform all their devotions, a blind eye would be turned to the practice.[81] In the margins of Beaulieu Abbey's thirteenth-century account book there is a small rough drawing of a pet cat with the name of 'Mite' inscribed above.[82] At Westminster Abbey, where Walter of Wenlock had passed statutes against pet keeping less than a century before, a collar was bought in 1369 for a dog called Sturdy, owned by the abbot himself.[83]

In the fifteenth century the prioress of St Helen's, Bishopsgate was ordered by the local dean of Kentwood to remove most of the dogs, but allowed to keep one or two.[84] Similarly a letter was sent by the chancellor of Bishop Nykke of Norwich in August 1520 to the prioress of Flixton, Elizabeth Wright, ordering her to remove all dogs within a month except the one that she would prefer to keep.[85]

Deep affection for pets on the part of those in nunneries was also tolerated. A late fourteenth-century *exemplum* tells of a little girl who is brought up as nun and taught that she must love. She begins by loving the dog and bird of her abbess, but later decides to love the Christ child with all her heart after viewing his image. Although the abbess's pets are not the focus of the story, their presence is not condemned. Instead the young girl's devotion to them is seen as a lower form of the love she will later feel for the Christ child.[86]

In some monastic cases, for certain species or if permission had been given, the pet could stay. In the *Ancrene Riwle*, a guide for anchoresses, a ruling stated:

> Unless need compels you, my dear sisters, and your director advises it, you must not keep any animal except a cat ... Now if someone needs to keep one, let her see to it that it does not annoy anyone or do any harm to anybody, and that her thoughts are not taken up with it. An anchoress ought not to have anything which draws her heart outward.[87]

Cats could be justified on practical grounds, and might be kept under the official guise of destroyers of vermin.[88] This would explain why cats, which were often relegated to a lowly status of mousers outside monastic walls, became a very familiar pet among those in religious orders. There were even 'official' cats for Exeter Cathedral, where there are entries in the accounts (from 1305 to 1467) for the *custodibus et cato* (to the keepers and the cat) and *pro cato* (for the cat), amounting to a penny a week (to supplement the animal's diet, apart from the pests it was supposed to control). There is still a cat-hole in the door of the north transept wall.

When secular women lodged in nunneries their pets might cause disturbance and annoy the nuns. The flaunting of pets, like dress, was a sign of secular lifestyle. In 1440 the prioress of Langley complained about a lady who occupied a set of rooms within the priory: 'Lady Audley, who is boarding here, has a great many dogs, so many that when she comes to church, her twelve dogs follow, who make great noise in church, stopping the nuns in their psalms, and by this, the nuns are terrified.' The visiting Bishop of Lincoln, William Alnwick, knew that a formal injunction could not be issued against Lady Audley, as she was not a nun, and merely declared that she be asked to remove her dogs from the church and choir.[89] In a similar vein, at Legbourne in 1440, Dame Joan Pavy complained to Bishop Alnwick that a Margaret Ingoldesby, a secular woman who slept at night in the nuns' dormitory, 'brings along her birds, whose chirping breaks the silence and the nuns' sleep is disturbed'.[90]

Perhaps the most negative consequence of pet keeping by nuns appears in an early fifteenth-century vision of purgatory. It condemns the practice as unworthy of one who has taken vows, a sinful symbol of an earthly life that should be discarded when taking the veil. In the vision the author sees the soul of a fellow nun in purgatory, pursued by 'a lytel hound and a lytel catte ... al of fyr brennyng'. It turns out that these animals act so because 'thay wer hir mawmettes the whil sho was on lyve, and sho sett hyr hert to mych on such foul worms'.[91]

Pets in universities

M OST of the evidence for clerics keeping pets at universities comes from statutes attempting to keep the practice in check. Like regulations against pet keeping in nunneries, the fact that they were issued in the first place demonstrates that it was a common problem in need of control. The frequency with which prohibitions were reissued suggests that they were either ignored or were futile attempts to curb an established custom. Although pets would have been more suitable for a life dedicated to study in urban interior quarters, some students still had ties to practices associated with the lay world, and kept hunting animals. Consequently many university regulations banned the keeping of hawks along with caged birds. University students might also get themselves into trouble with animals by engaging in riotous behaviour and games. An *exemplum* by Jacques de Vitry (*c.* 1160/70–1240) tells of a group of Parisian students playing with a cat by making it throw a die they had placed on its paw. Depending on how the die fell, the cat would either be taken and fed or sold for its skin.[92]

The statutes of various Oxford and Cambridge colleges suggest that the authorities there were fighting against the importation of hunting animals – symbols of the students' previous secular lives – and the keeping of small animals as pets. Having animals was clearly considered a distraction to scholars, who were forbidden from keeping them either in the public areas or their private chambers.

The fourteenth-century statutes of Peterhouse, Cambridge, forbade the keeping of any type of dog, a ban which presumably included pets as well as hunting dogs.[93] At Oxford, New College and All Souls had the same prohibition, but in their fifteenth-century statutes they added the keeping of ferrets, animals that could have been pets or used to catch small game.[94] The statutes of New College railed against giving bread to dogs instead of the poor. King's College, Cambridge, not only followed New College's line regarding the distribution of bread to dogs, but also attempted to cover almost any possible animal that could be brought into college premises. Besides barring all types of birds and dogs, King's, clearly fearing their students' imagination, added badgers, foxes, deer, monkeys, wolves and bears to the list of prohibited animals.[95] At Oxford, both Magdalen and Corpus Christi proscribed singing birds in cages, along with other animals.[96] Corpus Christi, perhaps like King's College, Cambridge, anticipating that students would try to break the rules, tried to encompass most species of singing birds in their list, and specified thrushes, blackbirds, starlings and nightingales.[97] In the fourteenth century, along with criticizing animals as a distraction for students and that bread was given to animals instead of poor people, the regulations of The Queen's College, Oxford, also claimed that the animals might infect the air around the students.[98]

Similar rules were enacted at Continental universities. Birds and beasts were banned in Paris, and a statute of 1453 at Heidelberg forbade the keeping of animals and birds; 'little birds' were specified among the prohibited animals.[99]

Leaving now the actual medieval pet sleeping on beds, running around enclosed gardens and being held on laps, we shall now turn to pets in medieval iconography.

✦ ✦
✦

5
ℙets in 𝕴conography

REFERENCES to depictions of pets in iconographic sources have abounded throughout this book, but in this chapter I shall focus on certain common motifs in a few genres.[1] A large proportion of these portray pets with women; although there are many depictions of secular men with animals which *could* be pets, it is harder to interpret them, as the animals might have a dual function – dogs could be hunting hounds, for example. The pet, rather than just being a symbol of faithfulness, is an identity marker of noble women in general. The virtue of fidelity, especially involving death or self-harm, is often ascribed to dogs, specifically those owned by lay men; the pets of women and clerics are associated more with affection and close companionship. There is a close connection between pets, status, and identity, both in public images such as seals and funerary monuments, and in private images of identity, such as donor portraits in manuscripts.

Pets on funeral effigies

FUNERAL effigies remind the living of the deceased, as well as being public representations of personal identity. Although funeral effigies are formal representations of the dead, they are often individualized by details in the carving, through inscriptions, styles of robes or armour. The animals depicted in funeral effigies, normally at the feet of the figure, play a part in establishing the identity of the deceased.

The presence of pets has usually been explained in symbolic terms, with many art historians declaring them to be symbols of fidelity in the case of secular women and men, and faith in the case of clerics.[2] The gender distinction on the use of the animals is quite marked. Men often have at their feet lions, which are symbols of bravery and fortitude, or hounds, symbols of loyalty. This is not to discount the fact that both these animals can be used as heraldic symbols on tombs of certain individuals. A small companion dog at the feet of a female effigy might symbolize loyalty, but it is the loyalty of a pet, rather than the faithful-until-death hound on masculine tombs. The status of the dog on female effigies as a pampered non-functional pet is usually underlined by the addition of a multi-belled collar.

Furthermore, women's dogs often appear in pairs, which is very rarely seen on male tombs. The artistic convention for such dogs is to depict small round well-fed specimens, with little belled collars. These collars are one of the defining iconographic accessories of a pet that distinguish them from the uncollared or plain-collared hounds of lay men. Small dogs wearing collars covered in bells also appear in the effigies of clerics. As with legal seals, the mere presence of pet dogs is not an indicator that the individual really did keep pets, but does point to the social reality of widespread pet keeping by women. I do not deny that the presence of small dogs could have had a symbolic meaning in effigies of women, but for any such metaphor to work, it requires that little round collared dogs are associated with a lady's identity as a person.

These little dogs abound on memorial brasses, whether it is an individual brass of a lady, such as that of Margaret de Camoys (Trotton, Sussex, *c.* 1310) which has a small dog at her feet, or joint memorial brasses of couples, such that of Richard Torryngton and his wife Margaret (Great Berkhampsted, Hertfordshire, *c.* 1356).[3] Their brass depicts an alert lion at Richard's feet while Margaret has two self-absorbed belled collared dogs at hers, one of whom is curled up asleep.[4] In the brass of Robert de Freville and his wife Clarice (Little Shelford, Cambridgeshire, *c.* 1400) Robert, dressed in armour, has both his feet on top of a large hound; Clarice's two little belled dogs are not under her feet, but instead lie down among the folds of her gown; one gazes upwards towards the lady while the other looks down at something in the distance. Unlike Robert's attentive hound, his wife's little dogs appear easily distracted.[5] A common artistic convention has the men standing on animals, while in female effigies the animals are usually sitting down on the hem of the robe.

We find the same on monumental tombs. The tomb of Louis II, Count of Flanders (Louis de Male, d. 1384), has a lion at the count's feet, while little dogs rest by the feet of his wife and daughter, who lie on either side of him. The fourteenth-century marble effigies of Charles V and his wife, Joanne of Bourbon, in the Abbey of Saint-Denis, show Joanne with two alert round-nosed little dogs at her feet.[6] The marble effigy of Anne of Burgundy (d. 1432), wife of John, Duke of Bedford and Regent of France, formerly in the Celestine Church in Paris, also has two little dogs by her feet.[7] The fifteenth-century double tomb in the church at Norbury, Derbyshire, of Ralph Fitzherbert (d. 1483) and his wife Margaret, has a lion sitting at Robert's feet, while his wife is accompanied by an very small dog on the side of her tomb, adorned with the *sine qua non* belled collar. A pair of portly collared dogs sit at the feet of the wife of one John Oteswich in their early fifteenth-century double effigy in St Helen's Bishopsgate (originally in St Martin Outwich) (fig. 13).

The gilt effigy of Mary of Burgundy (d. 1482) in the church of Notre Dame in Bruges has two little dogs at her feet. Interestingly, the dog on the right of Mary's effigy closely resembles the small white dog on her lap in the patroness image in her book of hours, and the one she holds in a stained glass panel formerly in the Chapel of the Holy Blood in Bruges (plate IV). In this panel Mary holds in her right arm a small white smooth-haired dog with folded ears; the dog, whose neck is adorned with a wide collar carrying gold bells, looks out towards the spectator, in contrast to Mary's demure gaze. In all three depictions the smooth-haired dog has very particular triangular folded ears, and possibly they represent the same animal.[8]

The tombs of clerics use dogs in the same way as the tombs of women. The tomb of William Courtenay, Archbishop of Canterbury, 1386–91, in Canterbury Cathedral depicts a small dog with short round ears wearing a multi-belled collar at his feet.

Fig. 13 Effigy of John Oteswich's wife on tomb in St Helen Bishopsgate, London
(formerly in St Martin Outwich; early 15th century)

As these animals are symbols of identity for the deceased, they are for the main part anonymous, despite resembling their living counterparts, festooned with bells and well fed. A few have names etched on their collars but this is not a common occurrence. The name 'Terri' is etched on the collar of a dog at the foot of Alice, Sir John Cassy's wife, in a brass of *c.* 1400 in Deerhurst church, Gloucestershire, while 'Jakke' is on a dog collar on the effigy of Sir Brian de Stapleton, in Ingham, Norfolk, 1448.[9] The dogs on the effigy of French knight Jehan de Seure (d. 1391) at Ozouer-le-Repos, Seine-et-Marne, are identified by names on their collars, 'Parceval' for the hound at Jehan de Seure's feet and 'Dyamant' on the collar of his lady's dog.[10]

The conventions used in traditional funerary monuments are also to be observed in other commemorative objects whose aim is to perpetuate memory of individuals. In the St William window in the north choir transept of York Minster there is a small white dog with a multi-belled collar at the feet of Lady Roos (d. 1438).[11] A fourteenth-century misericord in Norwich Cathedral depicts a standing couple, identified by the heraldry in the supporters as Sir William Wingfield of Letheringham (d. 1378) and his wife Margaret Boville. Sir William has a lion at his feet, while at Margaret's a little dog stands.[12]

Pets on seals

PERSONAL seals used to certify documents as legal attestations of authority were public symbols of their owners' identity, and thus are linked to funeral effigies, which similarly fulfilled a function of personal identity. Unlike the many decorative images in manuscripts of generic ladies with their pets, both seals and funeral effigies are supposed to represent a certain individual, so the inclusion of a pet becomes a significant motif. Representing a pet on the seal or effigy emphasizes a certain status through the possession of an animal which was destined only for leisure.

The presence of pets along with their owners can be seen in many English and French seals belonging to noble women issuing documents.[13] The pet is a symbol of the aristocratic identity of the female owner, just as noblemen will often be portrayed on horseback and both sexes often carry falcons, hunting being a preserve of the nobility. Pets are not found as an iconographic motif in male personal seals, which is understandable given the non-masculine undertones of a small spoilt animal kept for pleasure and companionship.

In iconographic terms, the most common pose is for the pet, usually a dog, to sit at its owner's feet or to be ensconced in their arms, stressing the intimacy between the pair. The pet represents more than just a luxury item that is an essential part of the owner's high status; it is a facet of the owner's public depiction, to be viewed by all who would deal with the document to which the seal would be attached. I have examined English and French seals in the British Library from the twelfth to the fourteenth centuries which represent the owner with an animal. I shall not discuss seals depicting animals by themselves, since they usually have heraldic implications or allude to the owner's name. (For example, the twelfth-century seal of one Alicia Capra depicts the lady with a small goat.)[14]

The seal of Isabella, Countess of Gloucester and Mortain, of the late twelfth century, depicts the lady holding a small bird in her hand.[15] Such a portrayal of the owner with a small singing bird is uncommon; most female personal seals with birds depict the woman holding a hawking bird (easily identified by the jesses attached to the falcon), emphasizing the connection between hunting, nobility and authority. Occasionally both pets and hunting birds, a mixture of the domestic and exterior worlds, can appear in the same seal, as is the case of Matilde, Countess of Boulogne, dated to 1236. This shows the countess holding a falcon in her left hand while a small dog rests at her feet.[16]

As small dogs were the most popular medieval pet, they understandably appear on the majority of seals depicting pets. The seal of Eleanor de Montfort, Countess of Leicester, mid-thirteenth century, depicts her standing with a small dog at her feet.[17] A similar motif appears in the seal of Johanna Aumbesas, *c.* 1307, of Carshalton, Surrey.[18] Apart from pets sitting at the feet of their owners, they also appear in seals in their owner's arms. Margareta de Nevyle of London, *c.* 1315, holds an extremely small dog in the crook of her left arm on her seal[19] while Juliana, widow of Richard de Norton (*c.* 1344, of Long Itchington, Warwickshire) clutches her little dog in both arms.[20]

Fig. 14 Seal of Marie d'Issouldon, Countess of Eu (*c.* 1256)

The motifs can be combined, as on the late thirteenth-century seal of Matilda of Hardredshilla, who holds a little dog tightly in her arms while a small dog resting at her feet looks up at her.[21] Even if the pet is not physically touching the owner in the seal image, there can still be a connection between the two, which stresses the emotional attachment, affection and intimacy between them. An example of this is the seal of Marie d'Issouldon, Countess of Eu, *c.* 1256, which depicts the standing Marie holding a *fleur de lys* as she bends her head to look at her small dog that leaps up enthusiastically towards her (fig. 14).[22]

An example of a seal with a non-canine pet is that of Denise de Montcherney, late thirteenth century, who stands with a small squirrel by her feet.[23]

Although pets are never seen in the personal seals of men, in rare cases a man might use a woman's seal to certify a document. The grantor of a charter in the British Library, Thomas Cursoun (of Eyntre, Norfolk), sealed the document with three seals, one of which is an anonymous lady's seal depicting a woman with a small dog at her side.[24] But the general rule is not broken here; it is still a lady's seal, merely being used here by a man for whatever purpose it served at the time.

Pets in patron portraits

IMAGES of individual women and their pets are not necessarily close reproductions of the owner in question or the pet. Rather, their very existence is an interesting indicator of how pets were transformed into a recognizable and necessary accessory of a noble woman. This can be seen in donor portraits in manuscripts and in other portraits of an owner and their pet. The pampered and privileged condition of pets is emphasized in images when they are represented in areas that were forbidden to many, such as private chambers or sitting next to their owners, sharing the same seat and thus status. In an early fifteenth-century French manuscript miniature, Isabeau of Bavaria, Queen of France, sits apart from her ladies on a separate cushioned bench, while the author Christine de Pisan presents her book. An attentive long-haired white lapdog with a pointed nose shares the bench with the queen, transforming the pet into the queen's equal, above the other ladies who sit below (or even kneel, as in the case of Christine de Pisan).[25] In a manuscript of works presented to Anne of Brittany there is a full-page miniature of the seated queen receiving the book, while a small white dog sleeps on the hem of her dress.[26] The animal is seen as a perfectly acceptable companion to its royal owner in this image. Only the queen and her pet dog are sitting down; all the other participants in the scene are either standing, as are her ladies-in-waiting, or kneeling, like the author.

Pets are symbols of their female owners, and their presence in images of women demonstrates how pet ownership is connected to perceptions of female identity. Yet we should not take the presence of the pet as a mere artistic convention of such identity, for there is overwhelming evidence that a large proportion of noble women owned such pets and kept them as close, both emotionally and physically, as visualized in images.

Apart from the specific genre of donor portraits, pets abound in personal portraits from the late fifteenth century, and 'it is evident that the inclusion of a beloved pet or other animals was a deliberate gesture on the part of both sitter and artist'.[27] This is exemplified by Jean Clouet's painting of Marguerite d'Angoulême, sister of François I and Queen of Navarre (1492–1549), c. 1530, where she has a green parrot perched on her finger. The parrot could be seen merely as an allegorical symbol of purity and devotion (partly thanks to the popularity of *Les Épîtres de l'amant vert* among the circle of French royal women) but it could also have been a pet, just like the dog the same sitter holds in a later pastel portrait by François Clouet (son of Jean Clouet).[28]

Pets and prayer in books of hours[29]

THE pet's presence in the personal life of the owner extended into prayer space. Pets are frequently close to women in prayer, incongruous though this may seem. They may be involved in the scene in a variety of ways. This is particularly evident in the iconography of 'patroness portraits' in personal books of hours, in which the pet can mimic the pose of the owner in prayer in an attitude of reverence or can merely act as a companion at the scene. Although pets do not appear in all patroness images, they are a common motif, forming part of the patroness's identity, who might have had pets in real life.

In the thirteenth-century Hours of Yolande de Soissons, her little black dog looks up the statue of the Virgin and Child in worship, as does Yolande herself.[30] More conventionally, the pet may accompany its owner without any reverence or participation in the religious scene. The pet, unlike its owner, may be distracted by the cares of the secular world, possibly a warning to all. A prime example of this appears in an early fourteenth-century northern French book of hours in the British Library.[31] This book, owned by an unknown lady, is notable for the presence of many pets illuminated throughout the manuscript along with other animals and hybrids (dog-headed grotesques are particularly prevalent). The artist, knowing that his patron was a lady, decided to illuminate the manuscripts with many images of pets, or he may have been instructed by the patron to include them.

Parrots and other caged birds also abound in this manuscript. On fol. 6v a parrot with bright green and blue wings flies out from a small cage with a wooden perch. (An empty bird wooden cage appears on fol. 9r.) More parrots, notable for their orange beaks and green wings, are depicted on fols. 42r and 121v. A small well-fed little dog is present throughout the manuscript, sometimes in the scene as the patroness-owner prays and sometimes by itself, overeating or annoying other animals. There are scenes in which this dog appears without its owner. In fol. 6v it is wearing a belled collar and standing on his hind legs. (This is the only depiction in which the animal is coloured brown; elsewhere it is grey.) On the *bas-de-page* of fol. 34r a small grey male dog stands on hind legs grasping and chewing a bone that is almost as high as he is, a possible allusion to spoiled pets; this fat bell-collared animal is very different from the hunting hound on fol. 24r which is long, leaner and has a plain collar. As noted in Chapter 3, a belled collar is one of the iconographic markers of a pet dog and, judging from entries in accounts, was a common accessory. On the *bas-de-page* of fol. 64v the fat little grey dog appears by himself, with his head curved towards his body. On fol. 79v (*bas-de-page*) a large lean hunting hound bites the back of the small fat little dog which is biting the bigger dog on the nose. On *bas-de-page* of fol. 88v, in the section of the Hours of the Dead, on the left the fat little grey dog crouches greedily over a big bone, while on the right of the page sits a skull and the same bone, a possible reflection on mortality, which is common in illuminations for the Hours of the Dead (fig. 7). On fol. 106v (centre of the *bas-de-page*) is the small grey fat dog with belled collar, looking right. On fol. 121v the little grey dog, wearing a red collar, sniffs at a bush.

The most interesting illuminations are those in which the patroness and the pet dog appear together as the lady prays.[32] In all these depictions the dog, unlike his devout owner, is very distracted. On fol. 39r, to the side of the main illuminated initial depicting a religious scene, a wimpled woman in a grey *vier*-lined gown with a red collar, prays in the direction of the initial, with her hands in a position of reverence, her eyes firmly directed towards the religious scene. Next to her, her fat grey dog sits curled up, looking downwards towards the actions of the hybrids on the *bas-de-page*.

On fol. 49r the lady (now in a blue gown with white collar and red sleeves) prays towards the Gospel scene in the initial. On the right her small fat dog sits on the grass and leans against a tree, his bored face turned towards the main scene (plate VI). Further on, in fol. 56r, the lady (in a white gown with red sleeves) prays towards the religious scene in the initial. A dog, which appears to be the portly grey specimen who normally accompanies her, is directly below her on the *bas-de-page*, completely out of the prayer space, leaping in the direction of a green bird drinking from a fountain. At the centre right of fol. 60r, to the side of the main square illuminated initial, the lady (in a yellow gown with blue sleeves), has her book of hours placed in front of her, while her leaping little grey dog is behind her, jumping on the hem of her gown. Like all the other illuminations of this pair, the animal is playful and not remotely in touch with the solemnity of the occasion. The frivolous pet forms a marked contrast with the devotion of its owner. Similarly, in an early sixteenth-century painting by Lorenzo Lotto depicting 'Christ taking leave of his mother', the religious scene takes place in the centre of the canvas but on the lower left hand side a lady prays with her book of hours, while a small curly-haired dog toys with the folds of her dress, without reverence or awareness of Christ.[33]

The pet can even interact with the potential reader of the book, as in the Hours of Catherine of Cleves, in which the dog looks out at the viewer (i.e. the reader of the book, presumably the owner herself) while the patroness observes the scene of the Crucifixion.[34] Similarly, in a folio in the Hours of Mary of Burgundy, as the patroness is reading her own book of hours, the dog on her lap looks out towards the audience.[35] The pet, an emblem of the secular world, can be separated from its owner as she prays, or from the religious scene by a physical barrier, visible in a Flemish manuscript titled *Traites de Morale*, in which Margaret of York, Duchess of Burgundy, prays at an altar. Her little pet dog can be seen in the next room, separated clearly by a wall.[36] In the same way, the Hours of Margaret Tudor has a miniature in which the small smooth-haired dog is below on the earthly plane, sitting in front of the altar, while above it the Virgin and the Child in halo look down on the praying Margaret Tudor, Queen of Scots.[37]

Pets and scholars

S MALL domestic animals are a common motif in iconographic representations of scholars. Dogs are often interpreted as symbols of intellectual keenness and fidelity. Besides faithfulness, the dog represented intellectual enquiry, taking the role of a hunter for further wisdom. (Spaniels are particularly associated with this trait.) On the other hand, dogs were also linked to the planet Saturn and melancholy, an ailment often associated with scholars.[38] The small dog as a humanist motif is explored by Patrik Reuterswärd in his article 'The Dog in the Humanist's Study', where he argues that symbolism of the dog in regard to intellectual keenness and fidelity derives mainly from Basil of Caesarea (regarding the reasoning of dogs) and Horapollo's *Hieroglyphica*.[39]

Nevertheless, it seems clear that despite such symbolic connotations, the presence of a pet in depictions of scholars also reflects the social reality of widespread pet keeping by this group of men, as evidenced by the numerous mentions of pets in their letters and literary compositions. The pet appears to have become a normal accessory of a scholar in his study along with a desk, writing implements and books; this is not merely an iconographic device. Moreover, the animal did not always have to be a dog. Cats also appear in the imagery of scholars, and despite their traditional negative symbolic connotations, I see their function in much of the imagery as akin to that of small dogs, a sign of contented domesticity and an acknowledgment of their presence as pets. Although cats do not share the intellectual keenness so often ascribed to dogs, any negative symbolism would be out of place in a scholar's quiet study.[40] It is clear from the feline elegies discussed in Chapter 6 that having a pet cat is not seen as extraordinary. In fact, because of their small size and agility, cats often occupied a closer physical proximity than dogs (by sitting on desks, for example). The diminutive size of the pets reflects their presence as interior animals, and their role as companions.

The domestic space of the scholar and the small animal in iconographic representations usually belongs to the private sphere. The scholar normally sits at his desk alone, in an interior setting, either reading or writing. The animal is usually asleep, curled up in a tight position, on the other side of the desk. When the animal is awake it is to acknowledge the presence of others who are entering the room, or to pay attention to an extraordinary event. The animal's sleeping pose may reflect the desired tranquillity of the scholar. The following images may serve as examples; Petrarch, as the archetypal humanist, appears in the majority.

All posthumous iconography of Petrarch shows him with small dogs or cats. This is despite the absence of any contemporary evidence that he owned either a cat or small dogs. In reality, most of his pet dogs were large, but it appears that later readers had a fixed notion of his owning a small dog, which would be more in keeping with a scholar's lifestyle. A depiction of Petrarch in a manuscript of his work in the State Library of Darmstadt shows him sitting at his desk in a closed study; in the foreground, on the right side of the desk, a small dog is curled up, his head away from the poet.[41] In a manuscript now in Milan, the illuminator Francesco di Antonio dei Chierico depicts Petrarch at his desk deep in thought, as a striped cat sits in profile by his feet, its head turned towards him.[42]

A fresco of Petrarch in his study by Altichiero da Zevio, in the Sala dei Giganti (Padua, 1379) shows him sitting at his desk on an outside balcony.[43] Although the background depicts the countryside, Petrarch appears to have merely transplanted his study outdoors, as he is shaded by an overhanging ledge, sitting at his desk, with a small brown dog curled up nearby. This small dog appears in exactly the same position in another fresco by Altichiero, in the Oratory of St George, Padua, where it is depicted at the bottom of a flight of small stairs.[44] Above the dog stands Petrarch, at the top of the stairs, at the extreme left. The scholar is firmly closed off by the balcony. The domain of the scholar and his pet is the interior; the exterior is seldom depicted. When it is, the scholar is shown confined in a closed balcony, thus turning the exterior into an artificial interior space.

However, not every image of Petrarch with a dog is of this sort. In a miniature in a manuscript of Petrarch's *Rime e Trionfi*, made in Mantua *c.* 1465, Petrarch sits in a garden with his beloved Laura. A white long-haired portly dog of the Melitaean type sits obediently at her side, but is clearly *her* dog, not his, and the image conforms to the motif of lovers in gardens with pets.[45]

The motif of the sleeping dog appears in an illumination of the Flemish scholar Jean Miélot in his study.[46] On the side of his desk is a sleeping dog of medium size, resting its head on its paws, head in Miélot's direction. In the frontispiece to Conrad Celtis' *Amores*, 1502, a small long-haired dog is curled up by his feet; the name-tag 'Lachne' is printed below its face.[47] Both these images emphasize the pet as a quiet and unobtrusive companion of the scholar.

Wakeful pets occur when a third party interferes with the scholar's repose. In a manuscript in the Huntingdon Library, the humanist poet Boccaccio, lying on his bed, views an apparition of Petrarch coming through the door, as the cat at the foot of his bed looks towards the viewer.[48] Similarly, in a miniature of *Histoire de Charles Martel* the calligrapher, translator and compiler David Aubert is surprised by Charles the Bold, Duke of Burgundy (1433–77), his two dogs adopt differing poses (fig. 15). The smaller dog, a white-collared specimen, continues to sleep by the feet of the scholar, while the other, slightly larger dog greets the visitors. Thus, the lone scholar's pet is usually asleep, whereas a scholar with company has an alert animal. The image of the scholar and pet can

Fig. 15 Charles the Bold surprising David Aubert in his study with dogs
(*Histoire de Charles Martel*, Bruges, before 1472;
the illumination is attributed to Loyset Liedet)

also appear in a public interior, in which the protagonist is in the company of other scholars. The animal in this case is normally alert. It performs the role of the audience and appears to be actively listening to the debate going around it.

Pets and scholarly saints

S AINTS and their pets have already been discussed in Chapter 1. A fruitful source of pet iconography is associated with scholarly saints, who are often depicted with small dogs, reinforcing the idea of the small dog as an attribute of the scholar. In these cases, the dog's presence is not related to saintly behaviour, as would be the case of St Cuthbert with otters or St Francis with wolves.

Vittore Carpaccio's depiction of the vision of St Augustine (1502–8) in the Scuola di San Giorgio degli Schiavoni, Venice, shows the saint caught at the moment when a bright light shines through the windows of his study and he miraculously hears the voice of the dying St Jerome. The unearthly visitation is witnessed by his small white curly-haired dog, who sits in profile looking alertly towards the divine light and participating in the scene.[49] In his *Confessions* Augustine mentions that he kept hunting dogs, but the small dog portrayed here is unmistakably of the kind destined solely for interior companionship. In this case St Augustine is alone. However, there is iconography of Augustine as a scholar with company in which he also has an alert dog. In Benozzo Gozzoli's (d. 1497) fresco 'St Augustine Reading Rhetoric and Philosophy at the School of Rome' (*c.* 1463–5), in San Agostino, San Gimignano, the saint appears in a classroom of scholars. In the centre foreground sits a small brown dog, with ears pricked. Similarly, as St Augustine preaches in a Flemish panel showing scenes from his life life, a small brown dog sits looking out towards the viewer under his lectern.[50] A dog appears between Augustine and Cicero as they dispute in a fifteenth-century French manuscript of *The City of God* (fig. 16).

Several scholarly saints are commonly depicted with small animals that are clearly represented as pets, even though their hagiographies associate none of them with the keeping of small animals. Often, as the saint in question needs his identifying animal (as in the case of St Jerome and his lion, and those animals that symbolically represent the Evangelists), the two animals must be portrayed together, and the symbolic animal of the saint adopts the resting attitude of the pet. In Dürer's engraving of St Jerome in his study (1514) both the lion and a small dog are asleep in the foreground of the image (fig. 17). Similarly, a cat appears in the study of St Jerome (along with the lion), in the painting of the saint (*c.* 1475) by Antonello da Messina.[51] A manuscript image of St Luke in a copy of the Acts of the Apostles and the Apocalypse at Hatfield House shows him with his traditional ox along with a short-haired collared dog, which looks up at the writing saint.[52] A similar image appears in a full-plate illumination of the evangelist St Mark writing the gospel. Apart from his symbolic lion at his side, a grey striped cat sits on the floor in the same room.[53]

✦ ✦
✦

Fig. 16 Augustine disputing with Cicero (Paris, *c*. 1475)

Fig. 17 St Jerome with lion and dog (engraving by Albrecht Dürer, Nuremberg, 1514)

6

Pets in Literature

LITERARY sources have been used throughout this book to illustrate everything from pet names to descriptions of their sleeping quarters. This chapter will examined some particular genres of literature in which pets appear with great frequency.

The pet as a symbol of love in courtly literature

IN romance literature the presence of the pet is closely connected to love and emotional attachment. Pets, nearly always small dogs, can play various roles, usually one of aiding and abetting the lovers.

A common role in this tradition is the pet as representative of the absent lover; in his absence, the pet takes his part as a companion and comfort to the lady. The pets are usually love-tokens given by the lover to his lady. The most famous pet exchanged between lovers is the small lapdog from Avalon, Petitcreiu, which features in various versions in the romance of Tristan. In Gottfried von Strassburg's early thirteenth-century *Tristan*, Petitcreiu is no ordinary lapdog, it is a *Feehündchen*, a little fairy dog that Tristan takes from his owner Gilan. Petitcreiu has long fur of every known colour that dazzles all on sight; on its collar is a magical bell that banishes all sadness when it heard.[1] Being a magical creature, Petitcreiu does not bark nor eat nor drink, though like any good lapdog it is eager to please and relishes play. Petitcreiu is given to Isolde by Tristan for comfort in his absence, and the dog's role as a replacement for Tristan is clearly stated by Gottfried von Strassburg:

> He [Petitcreiu] never came out of her sight, he was always led and carried where she could see him. Nor did she have this done for any relief it might give her. She had it done (so we are told) to renew her tender love-pangs out of affection for Tristan, who had been moved by love to send her Petitcreiu.[2]

Petitcreiu becomes Isolde's constant companion, to be carried around everywhere by her, and is the focus of her emotional attachment to Tristan. She removes the bell from the dog's collar, for with her lover absent, she would prefer to dwell in unhappiness. The dog's magic ability to assuage sadness is thus lost; instead its presence serves only to remind Isolde of her loss.[3] Although Petitcreiu is not to be found in all versions of the Tristan romance, the dog is ubiquitous in the iconography of the pair. A late fourteenth-century misericord in Lincoln Cathedral depicts the lovers meeting while Isolde's waiting woman carries the small dog.[4] Another fourteenth-century misericord from Chester Cathedral shows the lovers accompanied by Petitcreiu who stands at Isolde's feet peering into a small pond that separates the pair.[5] The traditional pairing of the lovers with Petitcreiu is repeated in other iconographic mediums. An early fourteenth-century French ivory casket portrays the lovers sitting under a tree with the small dog on Isolde's lap (fig. 18).[6] Petitcreiu's head is pressed against her chest, thus symbolizing the intimacy of the relationship between the lovers. In a mid-thirteenth-century manuscript of the romance, Tristan displays the small dog on a leash (with the written label 'Pitcrei' above the animal), just before presenting it to Isolde.[7] Although Isolde may not always have Tristan, she does have Petitcreiu, who represents whether he is absent or present. However, by destroying the bell, the dog's magical palliative function is lost, and it becomes just another lapdog, albeit wondrous hued, rather than a 'bearer of happiness'.[8]

Fig. 18 Ivory casket plaque depicting Tristan, Isolde and Petitcreiu (Paris, 1325–50)

Huidan, Tristan's hunting dog also figures in the story, as Tristan trains him silently in the grotto. In the Middle English *Sir Tristem* Huidan even accidentally swallows some of the love potion drunk by the couple, and, under its influence, loves them in his canine way:

> Thai loved with al her might
> And Hodain dede also.[9]

Although pets often accompany the lady in the absence of the lover, they need not always be a symbolic replacement of the lover and may simply perform their natural role of offering companionship to their sorrowful owner. Such is the dog, described as a *chiennet*, in Guillaume Machaut's fourteenth-century *Le Jugement dou Roy de Behaigne*, who stays with its lady in mourning for her dead lover, as one who can share her sorrows. The narrator describes the situation:

> I saw a lady approaching along a narrow pathway, thick with grass; she was pensive and all alone except for a small dog and a young girl. Yet in her restrained way she seemed overwhelmed with grief.[10]

The literary motif of the comforting small dog reappears in Chaucer's *Book of the Duchess*, in which wandering the narrator meets such an animal.[11]

> I was go walked fro my tree,
> And as I wente, ther cam by me
> A whelp, that fauned me as I stood,
> That hadde y-folowed, and coude no good.
> Hit com and creep to me as lowe,
> Right as hit hadde me y-knowe,
> Hild doun his heed and Ioyned his eres,
> And leyde al smothe doun his heres.

The pet can be a go-between, and aid to the lovers. Animals frequently play this role (for example, the message-delivering swan in Marie de France's *lais* of *Milun*) but pets, since they are always in the company of their owners, are perhaps ideally suited to take this part.[12] A parrot acts as an inventive go-between for the lovers in Arnaut de Carcasses's thirteenth-century *Las novas del papagay*, setting fire to the husband's castle so the lovers can finally meet.[13] Another psitticine intermediary is the parrot in *Le Chevalier du Papegau*, who lends assistance in King Arthur's love affairs.[14] A pet dog acts as a go-between in the thirteenth-century *Romance of the Chatelaine of Vergi*, where the lady signals to her lover that he may visit her whenever she puts her little dog into the garden.[15] For Michael Camille the aim of the dog in this romance is to: 'disguise or euphemize the sexual act – to keep it a secret'.[16] Depictions of this particular romance always show the dog as a key component, witnessing the lovers' pledge, sitting with his mistress, being put out into the garden, present at the lovers' embrace and at their final discovery. A fourteenth-century ivory casket now in the British Museum is covered with scenes from this romance, and the small dog is visible in practically all of them, from their first meeting to the lovers' tragic end (fig. 19).[17] It is so much a part of the action that, even after being put out in the garden to signal the lover's entry, it is immediately present in the next panel when the lovers meet and then embrace, as if the trio are inseparable. The same romance was also a popular subject for metal badges. Two lead-tin examples dating from the late fourteenth to the early fifteenth centuries, both found in the Netherlands, show the lovers in an adulterous embrace while observed by the lady's kinsman behind a tree. On both badges, the little dog stands in the middle, looking towards the lovers.[18] As in depictions of *Tristan*, the pet is so essential for the dénouement of *The Chataleine of Vergi* that its presence is an essential part of any iconographic depiction of the tale.

However, a pet may act as a less illicit go-between in courtly literature, and its role is not always as an accessory to adultery. A lady's pet, since it is part of her identity and persona, could be used to gain a polite introduction. This as demonstrated by the narrator in Machaut's *Le Jugement dou Roy de Behaigne* who uses the pet, ignoring its slight hostility,

Fig. 19 Ivory casket plaque depicting scenes from *The Chatelaine of Vergi* (France, 1325–50)

to introduce himself in a non-threatening or incriminating way towards its female owner:

> When I had come so near them that I could see them quite clearly and openly, the little dog, which didn't know me at all, began to yelp. I noticed that the lady, who well understood proper behaviour, was startled and called to it. But the dog paid very little heed to her call; he approached me barking and sunk his teeth into my robe. I grabbed him and, in his fright, he stopped barking. In my heart I was delighted to bring him back to his mistress, for it gave me the opportunity and occasion to go where I wished; therefore I kept stroking his coat.[19]

Here the dog plays a role in defending and representing his owner: his presence is the polite method by which a man and a woman in the romance can meet. Although some of the pets' roles in romances are not indicative of their use in real life, here many of the details appear to be courteous methods of dealing with a stranger's unruly pet. There is the lady who knows it is rude for one's pet to bark at strangers, and the accepted intimacy one can have with a small pet, which is accustomed to being picked up and stroked.

It is also possible for the pet to attempt to hinder the lady's love affair. In Thomas de Saluces's late fourteenth-century *Le Conte des trois perroquets*, a lady is watched by her three pet parrots while her husband is away. She meets her lover and the next day interrogates the parrots. The first two speak of the affair so she kills them with the help of her maid: they plan to blame their deaths on her cat. The third parrot, deciding that discretion is the better part of valour, keeps quiet and the husband on his return learns nothing.[20]

Pets become a common iconographic motif in tales of love. A *bas-de-page* illustration in an early fourteenth-century book of hours from the South Netherlands shows lovers embracing while a small dog at the lady's feet looks up at them (fig. 20). Certain pets, such as squirrels and rabbits, are often transformed into a sexual metaphor, representing the lover. In much secular iconography a small pet is closely associated with the lady's body, sitting on her lap, clutched close to her chest or slavishly sitting at her feet in adoration. The small dogs portrayed in the late fifteenth-century 'La Dame à la licorne' tapestry series are vivid examples of the type. In the tapestry 'A mon seul désir', a long-haired white dog sits facing the audience on a brocade cushion positioned on a bench next to the lady, and in the tapestry 'Le Goût', a long-haired white dog stands on the train of the lady's dress, looking up at her.[21]

Despite the prevalence of pets as love tokens in romance, there is little evidence for the practice in real life, where pets, if presented as gifts to ladies, came from acceptable males such as husbands, fathers, other relatives, vassals and retainers.

Fig. 20 Lovers embracing, with pet dog looking up at them
(Book of Hours, Netherlands, early 14th century)

Personal elegies

V ERSES written by lay scholars eulogizing their pets and those of their friends often received acclaim, and were widely imitated. The strong emotional attachment of scholars to their pets was not seen as an eccentricity but rather as a typical response to owning a companion animal. Although there may be an element of self-deprecating humour in some of these elegies, the emotional sentiment portrayed should not be taken as mere literary exaggeration or stylized convention. Elegies to personal household pets are a different category from the mock-eulogies of an animal species for which there is no emotional attachment. For example, there is a wealth of difference between the *Muscae encomium* (Praise of the Fly) of the humanist Leon Battista Alberti (1404–72) and his *Canis*, which praises a dog he actually owned.[22] *Canis*, written in 1441–2, has been described by a modern scholar as a 'tongue-in-cheek eulogy for his dog'.[23] But it need not be considered a mere mock funeral oration.[24] Although Alberti may have written the work from a satirical viewpoint, it is clear that he considered his great affection for this dog would not provoke surprise among his contemporaries. He presupposes that an elegy for a beloved dog would not be out of the ordinary and describes the deceased creature as the 'very best and the most loved'. Despite the elegy's elevated style, exaggerated emphasis on canine heritage and frequent use of classical allusions, it expresses emotional attachment to a dog who delighted his owner with his games and joy.[25]

The evidence for scholars keeping pets mainly comes from their letters and literary compositions, and above all, elegies and epitaphs written when a pet died.[26] But as well as marking the owner's emotional attachment to his animal, these works function as exhibitions of the writer's skill through the use of the Classical model of elegy. Latin was their primary literary language, although the vernacular was used at times.[27] The most influential classical authors for this genre were the recently discovered Catullus, along with Ovid, Statius, Martial and the *Planudean Anthology*, a group of Greek epitaphs collected in the fourteenth century by the Byzantine scholar Maximus Planudes.[28]

A very popular Latin two-line epitaph to a dog appears in many Petrarch manuscripts and is often attributed to him:

> Care Zabot, tibi parva domus, breve corpus habebas
> Et tumulus brevis est, et breve carmen habe.

> Dear Zabot, your house was small, your body small
> Your tomb is small, so take this short song.[29]

Despite there being no mention of a dog named Zabot (or any variation of the name) in any of Petrarch's correspondence, Zabot has passed into legend as his dog. This epitaph probably contributed to the association of Petrarch with small dogs in all subsequent iconography and many imitative elegies, some of which even mention Zabot by name. Later scholars living in confined urban quarters, and thus restricted to keeping only small dogs, may have liked to imagine their prototype keeping one too.

One such imitative elegy to Petrarch's pet was written by the poet Rapello in the early sixteenth century. It was one of the many epitaphs composed on the death of Borgettus, the beloved little dog of the humanist poet Antonio Tebaldeo (1463–1537):

> Here lies Borgettus, queen of dogs,
> Who on earth was Tebaldeo's living idol,
> Just as Cabat was to the divine Petrarch.[30]

Many scholars wrote elegies for birds, but unless there is evidence of genuine bird-keeping by the author, one must assume that the majority, especially those on sparrows, were literary exercises imitating Catullus' highly regarded sparrow poems (*Carmina* II and III).[31] Nevertheless, despite the profusion of poems dedicated to nightingales, parrots, starlings and sparrows, it is difficult to determine if such works were composed in memory of particular birds. For this reason it is better to concentrate on elegies for dogs and cats. Individuality is more common in these compositions and it easier to get a sense of whether they were written for an actual pet.

In Antonio Tebaldeo's epitaph to his dog Borgettus, it is possible to discern behind the somewhat inflated language genuine emotion and an attachment to the 'most charming little dog'. The little white dog is elevated to almost human status, described as faithful, pure and beloved. There is an appropriation of human funeral rites for the animal, which is buried by its owner and placed in a stone urn. There is a further attempt to anthropomorphize Borgettus, who is describes as worthy of heaven although the author concedes that dogs might not be allowed into paradise, and requests therefore a shining star *in memoriam* of his dog.[32]

Tebaldeo's epitaph for Borgettus was incised on a tombstone in his garden.[33] The practice of placing the animal in a tomb or urn does not appear to have been unusual, judging from an earlier epitaph by the scholar Flavio Biondo (1392?–1463). The animal in question was a young puppy; the poet feels the loss sorely and laments the cruel fate that took away his pet, ending by stating that the animal's ashes were placed in an urn.[34]

Not only did owners write epitaphs for a lost pet; it was common for scholarly acquaintances to share the owner's mourning. This can be seen in the contributions of Tebaldeo's friends and fellow-scholars who also mourned his dog. I have already mentioned Rapello's little Italian epitaph for Borgettus, which compares the dog to Petrarch's Zabot. Ercole Strozzi (1473–1508) wrote a longer, 213-line elegy to Borgettus; the verse asks rhetorically who could not weep at the funeral of such a faithful and beloved dog, before embarking on a long digression on funeral monuments and faithful animals of Classical antiquity, from Corinna's parrot (Ovid), Lesbia's sparrow (Catullus), Odysseus's Argos, King Garamantes's dogs (Pliny the Elder) to Cerberus in Hades.[35] More indicative of the emotions attached to the keeping of pets appears in the elegy for Borgettus (*In obitum Borgetti catuli*) by Andrea Navegero (1483–1529).[36] It begins by describing Borgettus as a 'charming little dog with winning ways', who played games for his master, and was dearly loved and would be missed. In return the dog loved his master as a two-year-old girl would love her mother. This maternal metaphor is taken from Catullus' *Carmen* III, in which the poet declares that the dead sparrow knew its mistress Lesbia in the same way that Lesbia knows her own mother. There is an emphasis on close physical contact between the owner and the animal, with descriptions of the small dog sitting in his master's lap and jumping around near him. These lines again recall Catullus' description of the sparrow jumping around on Lesbia's lap. The dog's habit of begging for food at the table, while standing on his hind legs, is described as normal and uncensored behaviour. The last line underlines the owner's affection for the little dog, whose unexpected and quick departure to the Underworld is greatly lamented – another echo of Catullus. Navegero repeats almost verbatim the phrase 'Oh, wretched sparrow', merely changing the species – 'Oh wretched little dog.'[37]

Begging at the table is a topos of domesticity; it is used again in an epitaph by Pietro Gherardo in his *Epitaphium catellae*. The little multi-coloured smooth-haired dog is unnamed here, but many of the affectionate emotions described are similar to those of Borgettus. The dog is not reprimanded for his habit of barking at guests; instead his behaviour considered as done 'in a winning manner with a charming face'. Like Borgettus, as described by Navegero, this dog also begs at the table by standing on two legs. Even his barking in the house was considered a delightful characteristic, and his dominance at the table and sleeping on the bed is remembered.[38]

Navegero and Gherardo's poems both make it clear that these pets were allowed to inhabit their owners' close physical space, whether sitting on laps, sleeping on beds or being fed at the table. A very intimate domestic arrangement between the scholar and his pet is described in the late sixteenth century by Cesare Orsini's (1570?–1640?) epitaph to his dead cat, *Alla gatta uccisa*, written in Latinized Italian. The cat is described as his light and dearest companion, who is always around day and night. Even when the owner is called to supper, the cat wanted to give 'a thousand caresses' and coaxed tidbits from the dishes. The cat is described as constantly following him whenever he steps into the hall and is ready to lie down in front of the owner whenever it detects that he is melancholy. The ability to recognize an emotional state is a rather intriguing attribute for a cat, as melancholy is more commonly associated with dogs. The cat follows him into his study, prowling and pawing around his books and letters. It thus becomes the perfect scholar's companion, rousing him from unhappy thoughts, and sitting on his desk and leaping over his books to provide amusement. A long digression on the physical closeness between the owner and his cat follows. The cat jumps into his lap with gentle paws, climbs up his shoulders, licks his face, purrs to the delight of his owner's ears and playfully bites his hand. Orsini ends his elegy by mentioning the cat's constant happy disposition which always cheered him up.[39]

Another feline elegy is *Canzone nella perdita d'una gatta* by 'Il Coppetta', Francesco Beccuti (1509–1553). This long elegy is unusual for being written entirely in Italian: most other Italian poets and scholars of the period wrote their pet elegies in Latin.[40] After lamenting the cat's death, Coppetta quickly speaks of intimacy, remembering how it slept on his feet at night, and how he has lost his beloved treasure ('l'amato tesoro'). There was a very close relationship between the cat and its owner: the cat would playfully bite his foot and then go to sleep on his shoulder, presumably while the poet was writing at his desk. The cat even attempted to pull off its master's gloves. It also kept mice in check, and these now wander freely around, annoying the poet, to his great despair. Coppetta concludes with a request for a monument in the stars for his lost pet, but whereas Antonio Tebaldeo wished for one star to memorialize his dog, Coppetta asks for two new and shining stars, that will for ever represent the eyes of his beloved cat.[41]

Joachim du Bellay (1522–1560), a French poet, critic and member of the Pléiade, wrote in the 1540s the celebrated poem *Épitaphe d'un chat* lamenting the loss of Belaud, his cat. A. H. Tomarken has pointed out several similarities between this and Coppetta's elegy, arguing that Du Bellay imitated Coppetta's elegy when composing his own work.[42] *Épitaphe d'un chat* begins with an elaborate physical description of the animal in question: 'This is Belaud, my little grey cat', although he proceeds to specify that the cat was not entirely grey, but had fine satin-like silvery grey fur, with a small white patch. Further individual details are given: Belaud had a little muzzle and small teeth, short ears, a black nose 'of ebony', a silvered chin and delicate paws. The close relationship between the two is emphasized by the cat being allowed to sleep on the bed and even steal food from his master's plate (and mouth). Belaud normally sat on a chair by the table and had a fondness for cheese. In a rare note on animal hygiene, Belaud is commended for being clean. The cat is not without his uses, as he eliminates mice, especially those that nibble at Du Bellay's ears and verses. Two lines clearly sum up Belaud as the beloved companion of his study, bed and table ('Belaud estoit mon cher mignon, / Belaud estoit mon compagnon / À la chambre, au lict, à la table') and as an animal that participates in all of Du Bellay's life. He even insists that a cat is more suitable pet than a spoiled little dog, perhaps because Belaud assists him in his work but does not need constant care and attention. Several lines lament the incomparable loss of his cat, and later on regrets that Belaud had no offspring.[43]

The trend for scholars to write elegies continued throughout the sixteenth and early seventeenth centuries. The Italian scholar and physician Julius Caesar Scaliger (1484–1558) wrote a personal elegy for a little dog called Balbina. He laments the death of the little barking dog, whose loss affects him greatly.[44] Similarly, the French Calvinist scholar Theodore Beza (1519–1605), who spent most of his life in Switzerland, wrote 'On the domestic delights of a little dog', a highly personal portrait of his dog, without resorting to any direct classical references. The dog is described as having a snub nose and a squint, little eyes that showed love, and short curly ears. Its wagging tail would soften his master's sorrows and the dog was, all in all, a beloved companion.[45]

Tomarken suggests that 'such expressions of acute grief became so conventionalized that it is difficult to judge their sincerity'.[46] I would dispute this suggestion. Parody is definitely evident in animal elegies where there is no personal or emotional attachment to the animal. Members of the Pléiade wrote various *blasons* (short descriptive poems) on animals such as flies and donkeys, but these are different in character from the personal pet elegies, where the animal is personalized and individualized; there is genuine emotional attachment in the composition, no matter how conventionalized. Nevertheless, just because the animal in question is a common species of pet, the elegy need not be a personal statement of grief. Pierre de Ronsard (1524–1585), the leader of the Pléiade, wrote a lengthy poem on cats, *Le Chat, à Remi Belaux*, which is a historical description of cats and a rather impersonal piece. (Ronsard disliked cats intensely and once proclaimed that 'A cat will never enter my bedroom'.)[47] In this case, it is definitely not an elegy to a personal and beloved pet. However, a work such as du Bellay's *Épitaphe d'un chat*, like many of the contributions of the Italian humanists, is not a mere exercise in literary sophistry that happens to take a pet as its subject. Instead it demonstrates the affection of a scholar-owner towards his pet. In fact, despite being over 200 lines long, Du Bellay seldom rambles into an exhibition of classical allusions but remains focused on his description of delight in his deceased pet. He proudly proclaims his affection and grief at the loss of his pet, a personal loss now publicized. There are no attempts to mask affection or to defend the ownership of the pet. Owning a pet for a scholar is seen as a common occurrence, nothing to be commented on, apart from possibly being eulogized in verse. Du Bellay's *Épitaphe d'un chat* influenced other feline epitaphs in French, such as François Maynard's (1582–1646) *Plainte sur la mort d'une chate*, which laments the passing of his cat, a fluffy black and white animal admired by all.[48]

My final example of the pet-keeping and elegy-composing scholar is the Flemish humanist Justus Lipsius (1547–1606), who claimed that his love of dogs and gardens was exceeded only by his love of books. He lectured with dogs by his side at the University of Louvain. He had them painted, and they are included in the engraved portrait that frequently appears in his published work.[49] Four dogs are named in his correspondence – Melissa, Saphyrus, Mopsus and Mopsulus, although he may have owned more. When Melissa died, he requested that his friends write poems in her memory. He defended such behaviour, claiming that since the Italian scholar Celio Calcagnini (1479–1541) had erected monuments to his dead cat, he wished to do the same for his little dog.[50] Lipsius shortly received a contribution from Victor Giselinus which described the little dog as very playful, even with the household cat, possibly another of Lipsius' pets.[51]

More details on Lipsius's dogs Saphyrus, Mopsus and Mopsulus (all living at the time) appear in a long letter written to his students in January 1600, in which he praised dogs as the ideal companion for a scholar.[52] Although this epistle can be construed as a rhetorical exercise for his students, it fits into the genre of encomia on dogs. Lipsius's aim was to persuade his students that dogs are both the ideal companions of scholars and have qualities those scholars should aspire to: resolve, cleverness, vigilance, and faithfulness to their work.[53] He even adds personal anecdotes, including one about his grandmother's loyal little terrier, who would not leave her deathbed and after her death, in its grief, dug a hole and tried to bury itself in the garden.[54]

Near the end of the letter he writes six little personalized and affectionate poems – two for each of his three dogs. The first, Saphyrus, is described as a little Dutch dog with white fur and a purple-brown head and ears (with a little white wedge on his head). At thirteen years old he is quite ancient, although when young he was very beautiful and charming.[55] A little poetical elegy follows, narrated by Saphyrus, claiming to be the jewel of all dogs in Belgium due to his beauty and charm. To these qualities Saphyrus adds cleverness (according to Lipsius, one of the attributes that dogs share with scholars) and ends on a humorous note, claiming to be a little bit human-like, owing to a fondness for wine which has caused gout.[56] Next is Mopsulus, two years old, a gift from Lipsius's friend Arnoldo Borcourt, a lawyer from Antwerp. He has a white body with one yellow eye, a short and blunt red muzzle speckled with white, a snub-nose and a cunning and snappish temperament.[57] Like Saphyrus, Mopsulus narrates a little poem, in which he is described as the master's companion who shares his bed. In fact, he claims to be the master's master (*Domini dominus*) and is greatly loved, despite not being the best-looking of dogs.[58] Here Lipsius, without any self-censure, shows the status his dogs enjoyed in his home, spoiled and treated almost as equals. Finally comes Mopsus, a three-year-old dog of Scottish origin.[59] His fur is a solid chestnut colour, although speckled with golden hairs around the edges of the eyes, mouth, inner paws and thighs, and under the tail, along with two little golden spots over one eye. Mopsus has a wide and upright chest, scattered with white spots, and is very handsome.[60] The poem related by Mopsus speaks of his beauty and large body (unlike the previous two little dogs, where the term *catellus* is used, Mopsus is called a *canis*), and how he endears himself to the lord, lady or maid-servant, being full of honesty and simplicity and quite deserving of Heaven.[61] These six compositions personalize each dog, both by detailed physical description and by remarks on their personality; they are a clear testament of Lipsius's affection for all three.

In the following year, 1601, the elderly Saphyrus accidentally fell into a cauldron of boiling water. In a letter to his friend Philip Ruben, Lipsius wrote both an epigram and an epitaph, the latter being for the dog's tomb in his garden. The epigram describes Saphyrus as 'a true small jewel, not a little dog', a play on the dog's name, dead at the old age of fifteen. Lipsius speaks of the affectionate relationship between the two, how the dog would wag his tail, waiting for him at the threshold, bouncing about and barking, demanding attention and entertaining his master with his games. The elegy ends with a supplication to the spirits of the underworld to be kind to the dog; as a fellow canine, Cerberus should show him particular sympathy.[62] The epitaph for the tomb proclaims the name of the dog, Saphyrus of Holland, and how he was Lipsius' delight, known for its intelligence, charm and physical appearance. The sad circumstances of the death appear along with the age of the dog.[63]

Although elegies and tombstones for scholars' pets were commonplace, not all agreed on their propriety. The early seventeenth-century Jesuit writer François Garasse found such things blasphemous and placed in this category both du Bellay's *Épitaphe d'un chat* and Lipsius's epitaphs and monuments to his little dogs.[64] Nevertheless such censure was not the norm. Lipsius' situation was in no way unique or eccentric; we have seen that well before his time the keeping of a small dog had become part of the scholar's lifestyle. Strong emotional attachment to the animal was viewed as an unremarkable result of sharing a confined domestic space. Many of the elegies and epitaphs stress how well the pet fits into the scholar's lifestyle, as it cheers its master when he is sad, amuses him at all times, shares his desk (and table and bed) and provides a welcome distraction from study.[65]

Court elegies

ALL the elegies discussed above were written for the writer's own pet or for that of a friend. However, there is a rich vein of pet elegies written for patrons at royal and aristocratic courts. One of the most notable early sixteenth-century courtly pet elegies is *Les Épîtres de l'amant vert* ('The Letters of the Green Lover') composed by Jean Lemaire de Belges in 1505, and published in 1511. In these two French epistles in verse, the author adopts the voice of the recently deceased parrot of his patroness, the newly widowed Marguerite of Austria.[66] Apart from keeping parrots, Marguerite was known for her fondness for the popular *le jeu de Papegay*, which consisted of shooting with a bow and arrow an image of a parrot stuck on a pole.[67] Like all parrot elegies, it draws heavily on Ovid's *Amores* (Book II.6, on Corinna's dead parrot) and Statius's *Silvae* (Book II.4, on his friend Atedius Melior's dead parrot).[68]

Following the model of a Petrarchan love poem, Lemaire attempts to comfort the grief-stricken Marguerite by presenting the theme of the loss of a loved one and their joyous state in heaven. Marguerite had lost both a husband, Philibert II of Savoy, in 1504, and a parrot, eaten by a dog, in 1505.

In the first epistle the parrot Amant Vert is left alone by Marguerite as she leaves the château of Pont d'Ain to meet her father in Strasbourg. The narrator/parrot then explains how, overcome by despair at being abandoned by his owner, he is going to throw himself into the jaws of a dog. He finds a mastiff, who thoughtfully waits for the bird to finish his poem before administering the *coup de grace*.[69] Marguerite was pleased by the poem and suggested that the poet write another.

In the second epistle the parrot/narrator, guided by Mercury, travels to paradise. There the parrot is greeted by L'Esprit Vermeil (the Rosy Spirit), a parrot who had been the pet of Marguerite's mother, Mary of Burgundy (1457–82). L'Esprit Vermeil acts as the parrot's Beatrice (with Mercury in the guise of Dante's Virgil). The parrot proceeds to describe his life in the Elysian Fields, which is populated with animals from history, literature, hagiography and myth. These include Catullus' sparrow, the geese that raised the alarm when the Gauls attacked Rome, the she-wolf that suckled Romulus and Remus, the cockerel that crowed after St Peter had denied Jesus Christ, St Anthony's pig, St Roch's dog and St Jerome's lion, among others.[70] The epistle ends by assuring Marguerite that her pet, like all the departed, is happy in heaven. Both epistles present serious themes of devotion, loss, and eventual contentment after death, in a light-hearted manner.

Apart from Marguerite of Austria, other readers were similarly delighted. Anne of Brittany, Queen of France, who would later become Lemaire's patron after he left Marguerite of Austria's service, adored the parrot epistle and made the effort to memorize it. It influenced the Scottish poet and courtier Sir David Lindsay to write *The Testament and Complaynt of our Soverane Lordis Papyngo* in 1529, which takes the same model. Here, the parrot, supposedly James V's pet, writes two satirical poems, one to his master and one addressed to the Scottish court.[71]

However, most animal poems written for a court patron did not have the length or scope of Lemaire's. Pierre de Ronsard wrote a poem for Charles IX (r. 1560–74) on the king's lapdog Courte (*Courte, chienne du Roy Charles IX*) with a line that exemplifies the spoilt pet dog at court, coming to the table to take biscuits and marzipan from the king's hand. In a similar vein to Jean Leamaire's otherworld travelling parrot, in Ronsard's *Heureux sejours des espritz precieux* there is a meeting between the shades of two of Charles IX's dogs, Beumont the greyhound and Courte the lapdog.[72] Joachim du Bellay wrote his *Épitaphe d'un petit chien* as his contribution to a small poetical competition with Olivier de Magney for elegies praising Peloton, a dog belonging to Jean d'Avanson, French ambassador in Rome (1511–64). Peloton is described in detail, up to its habit of tinkling the bell on its collar when happy.[73]

Similar elegies for the pet of a noble patron were composed by the poet Torquato Tasso (1544–95), for Barbara of Austria, the Duchess of Ferrara

(1539–72, the second wife of Alfonso II d'Este, Duke of Ferrara). Both are written in Italian and titled 'Weeping on the death of Violina, the little dog of the most serene Duchess of Ferrara'. The first one speaks of the tomb of the little dog, where it rests 'in holy peace among the sweet violets'. The second speaks from the point of view of the duchess, who laments and weeps at the loss of her dog.[74]

The poet Seraphino de Aquila (1466–1500) wrote two canine poems in Italian for a clerical patron, the influential Cardinal Ascanio Sforza (1455–1505). Unlike the other elegies in this chapter, both these poems are for a living dog and written in a light and jocular manner, for example, the first line of one imitates a dog barking 'Hau, hau, hau, I cannot speak'. One of the elegies is titled 'Attached to the collar of Ascanio's dog' which may refer to a light-hearted presentation of the poem to the cardinal. Both elegies emphasize the kindness of the owner and the animal's devotion.[75]

Other notable examples of Italian animal elegies were composed in praise of Pope Leo X's white elephant, Hanno. This animal arrived in 1514, as part of a delegation from Manuel I, King of Portugal, and belongs to a tradition of giving exotic animals as gifts. Hanno was not strictly a pet, since it was kept in a special enclosure on the Borgo Sant'Angelo and used in spectacles. However, Leo X was extremely fond of the elephant. When it fell ill in 1516 physicians were summoned; when it died in June it was buried in the Cortile del Belvedere. The artist Raphael, assisted by Giulio Romano, was commissioned to paint a large fresco of the creature. Leo X wrote an epitaph for Hanno, which was put in Latin hexameters by Filippo Beroaldo, the Roman poet who also composed elegies for Isabella d'Este's dog, Aura.[76]

As we saw in Chapter 2, the death of Isabella d'Este's dog produced a flurry of elegies. Presumably these were sent with letters of condolence to Isabella, although they do not survive in the Gonzaga Archive. However, a large collection of elegies to Aura by dozens of authors survives in a small handwritten booklet.[77] As the compositions come from authors based in a variety of locations (including Ferrara, Rome and Mantua), the poems must have been copied from the original versions which were presumably on loose sheets.[78] Although the style of the elegies vary among the authors, all share common ground in commemorating Isabella's pet in lavish praise, often emphasizing her current grief or her deep affection for the dog. Common themes include descriptions of the dog (such as its size and character), laments for the dead animal, reports of the owner's grief, classical allusions and models, references to graves and tombs, the trope of how the dog will be remembered in the stars, and its life in the Underworld.

Typical examples include 'Hendecasyllable of the death of the little dog Aura, the beloved of Isabella d'Este' by the Mantuan scholar Carlo Agnelli.[79] The little dog is praised for being faithful and resides now in her new home in the Elysian Fields. The pet will be remembered for years, and was so well behaved that she never needed to be punished with either a stick or Isabella's hand. Everyone loved the little dog, who was so charming, was stroked with caresses and had her lovely little face kissed. At the end of Agnelli's poem, he laments that evil day in which the delightful Aura died. His next poem is titled 'When the lady cried for the death of the little dog'. He begins again by lamenting the animal who was so beloved and over whom tears are being shed. He talks of the circumstances of the dog's death, of a 'shameless, impudent, and daring dog' whose passion for the 'chaste Aura' resulted in her fall from the cliff and subsequent painful demise. This refers to the dog that Aura and Mamia (Isabella's other pet dog) were fighting over when she fell. Agnelli's next poem is 'To the owner of the little dog so that she might hold back tears', in which he implores Isabella to restrain her great grief. It laments the death of the sweet Aura, who was always so beautiful and charming and was kissed a thousand times, until fate caused her death, which was followed by tears.

Scattered through the collection of epitaphs in the manuscript are several that would be suitable for a tomb; one of these proclaims: 'Aura the little puppy / the darling / of Isabella of Mantua / by her mistress in an urn / she has been buried'. However, there is no indication which one was finally used. Agnelli's suggestion imitates the model of classical epitaph and declares that the tomb is for 'Aura Parthenie the charming and playful puppy, whose bones now rest here'. The Parthenie reference is one of the many allusions in the elegies to the little animal's chastity. It appears to be a reference to the death of the little dog while fighting with another for an unfulfilled 'love'. The epitaph ends with the traditional classical salutation 'Ave viator' and details of Isabella, the owner. Calandra, Isabella's secretary, contributed an elegy on the playful Aura's ascent to heaven, and how she will join the star Procyon.[80] Since Aura is a little dog, connecting her to Procyon (Alpha Canis Minoris) the luminary of Canis Minor, this is very fitting.

The courtier Mario Equicola sets a unique tone by writing of the heavens howling with grief, along with the stars and the Egyptian dog-headed deity Anubis. His other verses personalize the dog, who would wag her tail and nibble Isabella's fingers. He even added a mention of Isabella's other little pet dog and Aura's companion Mamia.[81] Battista Scalona, the Marchese's secretary, had in 1510 composed elegies for another of Isabella's pets, Martino the cat. In one of his contributions he remarks how Aura's pleasing little tricks would now be entertaining the Muses.[82]

Conclusion

THIS book has shown the complexities which lay behind pet keeping in the medieval period (and to an extent, the early modern period), and has brought to life the experiences of owners and their pets. Here I shall summarize the main themes from the previous chapters.

Pet keeping is a component in the wider scheme of human–animal relationships. In a culture of anthropocentrism, mankind had dominion over all the beasts. Pets, though, were treated kindly, and led a spoiled, privileged life, completely dependent on the whim of their owner, who had elevated the animal to the category of companion. The pet's status was wholly dependent on the human owner's perception of the animal's affection as genuine.

Being a pet exempted the animal of any traditional utilitarian function, but instead placed the emphasis solely on a social and psychological role: as animal companions, which received and were perceived by their owners as giving affection. This role relied on an invisible emotional bond between the human and animal.

Does the privileged position of pets, allowed indoors (and into more private spaces, such as bedrooms), place them above other domesticated animals? Do they become 'honorary humans', leaving behind their inferior animal condition? Many of the rituals of pet keeping appear to point at least to an ambiguous animal–human status. Pets were given names, allowed to roam indoors with as much as freedom as humans, and rather intriguingly, at their deaths, were greatly mourned over. It should be apparent from the discussion owners' grief in Chapter 2 that this transcended mere ritual on the death of an animal, and instead was treated as a tragedy and a loss which the owner had to bear.

Pets were seen as individual repositories of affection and companionship. An owner felt affection for his or her very own pet, not just for any pet that might happen to be present. Pets were seen both as capable of giving and receiving affection. Their owners perceived their animals as adept in mitigating their concerns and cares. This raises the question of animal intelligence. Were pets seen as different from other animals merely because they had been accorded their role by a decision of their owner?[1]

But as well as being kept for affection and companionship, pets formed a part of their owners' identity and were almost always connected to status. Having a pet often demonstrated their owners' desire to emphasize their elevated position in society and show off their material assets. The stereotypical overweight medieval pet was a sign of status, demonstrating that the owner affectionately gave excessive food to a beast that fulfilled no useful function, and only served to amuse.

Pets benefited from many freedoms in interiors, as they were allowed to roam in all spaces, including sleeping quarters. They also occupied the close personal space of their owners, sitting on laps or by their feet. In exterior space, pets' freedoms were curtailed; they might be kept on a leash, restricted to an enclosed garden or held tightly in its owner's arms.

When they showered their pets with care and affection did medieval owners truly consider their animals' needs, or were they just playthings? It is true that pets were lavished with fine food, including imported nuts, white bread and an abundance of milk, unnecessary for weaned animals. Similarly they were displayed with specialist and often costly accessories (including collars, leashes, chains, and cages). They were allowed into intimate quarters, and were always present, whether frolicking in gardens or demanding table-scraps at dinner. But were these things done for the benefit of the pet or for the benefit of the owner? Thomas Aquinas writes that pity towards animals can provoke pity towards human beings, which is the ultimate justification of the sentiment.[2] In the many sources covered in this book, pet owners rarely appear to act without consideration for the animal itself. Whether exercising the animal or playing with it, these activities were seen as beneficial for both parties, not just for the owner.

Some practices, such as the feeding of fine fare, were, at least in the eyes of the owner, perceived to be beneficial solely to the pet. But even this is not the complete picture. Given that both overfeeding and the feeding of inappropriate food (for an animal) was such a motif of criticism of medieval pet owners, it could be argued that these were done not just out of affection for the animal (on the assumption that this was what the pet would want), but as a show of conspicuous consumption, flaunting a cosseted animal to all. Affection and the desire for display could go hand in hand.

There are further ambiguities. Pets could be both costly to purchase (particularly if exotica) and to maintain if luxurious expenditure was demanded (silver-belled collars, brocade cage-covers). However, a pet could be bought cheaply, or even received as a gift, and elaborate accessories were not essential. Pets might be status symbols, but they could be very reasonably priced symbols. This point might have been appealing. Merely owning a pet gave the impression that one could indulgently afford to spoil an animal kept solely for amusement and companionship.

Tolerance for pet keeping was nuanced, as pets were often forbidden to those living in institutional space, such as monasteries and universities, where they were perceived as a distraction. But some religious houses reached a compromise, and allowed pets as long as they were few in number and did not enter into sacred spaces. In general, pet keeping was accepted as long as owners did not heap excessive care upon their pets or neglect their duties.

Although pets were commonly kept by women and clerics, they were acceptable companions for scholars. Indeed, they became part of the identity of the lay scholar, as a fitting quiet and small companion for one's study. Literary compositions eulogizing a personal pet were a popular genre, and emphasized the ubiquity of the pet in a scholar's lifestyle.

✦ ✦
✦

Notes

1 The Medieval Pet

1 L. Spitzer, 'On the Etymology of Pet', *Language* 26:4 (1950), pp. 533–8. The noun is likely to be derived from the Scottish Gaelic *peata* (tame animal). Reference from *Oxford English Dictionary*: J. B. Paul, *Accounts of the Treasurer of Scotland*, VII (1900), p. 274.

2 K. Thomas, *Man and the Natural World: Changing Attitudes in England, 1500–1800* (Oxford, 1996), pp. 112–15; L. Bodson, *L'Animal de compagnie: ses rôles et leurs motivations au regard de l'histoire* (Liège, 1997); A. Manning and J. Serpell, eds., *Animals in Human Society: Changing Perceptions* (London, 1994); E. A. Moore and L. M. Snyder, *Dogs and People in Social, Working, Economic or Symbolic Interaction* (Oxford, 2006); J. E. Salisbury, *The Beast Within: Animals in the Middle Ages* (London, 1994).

3 P. Edwards, *Horse and Man in Early Modern England* (London, 2007).

4 L. Moessner, 'Dog – Man's Best Friend: A Study in Historical Lexicology', *English Historical Linguistics 1992 = Current Issues in Linguistic Theory* 113 (1992), pp. 208–18. L. Davidson, 'The Use of Blanchete in Juan Ruiz's Fable of the Ass and the Lap-Dog', *Romance Philology* 33 (1979), pp. 154–60 discusses the Castilian term *blanchete* and its relation to similar terms in other European vernaculars.

5 William Lambard, *Eirenarcha or The Offices of the Justices of the Peace* (London, 1588), p. 278. Cf. E. Fudge, *Perceiving Animals: Humans and Beasts in early modern English Culture* (Urbana, IL, 2000), pp. 132–4. Fudge points out the legal problem of pets, where the law does not recognize the pet 'not because the recreational animal does not exist, but because it does not fit the legal notion of what an animal is for.'

6 Marie de France, *Fables*, ed. and trans. H. Spiegel (Toronto, 1987), pp. 68–71. The fable is titled 'De l'asne ki volt jüer a sun seignur'.

7 Adelard of Bath, *Conversations with his Nephew: On the Same and the Different, Questions on Natural Science, and on Birds*, ed. and trans. C. Burnett (Cambridge, 1998), pp. 110–17.

8 Thomas Aquinas, *Summa contra gentiles* (Madrid, 1967), pp. 665–71: book II, ch. 82 'Quod animae brutorum animalium non sunt immortales'. See R. Sorabji, *Animal Minds and Human Morals: The Origins of the Western Debate* (Ithaca, NY, 1993) and P. G. Sobol, 'The Shadow of Reason: Explanations of Intelligent Animal Behaviour in the Thirteenth Century', *The Medieval World of Nature*, ed. J. Salisbury (New York, 1993), pp. 109–22.

9 J. A. Serpell, *In the Company of Animals* (Oxford, 1986), part II, ch. 4 ('Pets in Tribal Societies'), esp. p. 53, discusses several cases of pet keeping by societies living at a subsistence level, and concludes that 'the existence of pet-keeping among so-called "primitive" peoples poses a problem for those who choose to believe that such behaviour is ... a by-product of Western decadence and bourgeois sentimentality'.

10 Canon 15 of the Fourth Lateran Council (1215) forbade clerics from hunting and keeping of hounds and hawks. N. P. Tanner, ed., *Decrees of the Ecumenical Councils* (London, 1990) vol. 1, p. 243.

11 S. Salih, *Versions of Virginity in Late Medieval England* (Cambridge, 2001), esp. pp. 2 and 17; M. Rubin, 'The Person in the Form: Medieval Challenges to Bodily "Order"', in *Framing Medieval Bodies*, ed. S. Kay and M. Rubin (Manchester, 1994), pp. 100–22.

12 See F. Kelly, *Early Irish Farming: A Study Based Mainly on the Law-Texts of the 7th and 8th Centuries AD* (Dublin, 1997), esp. pp. 120–2, and F. McCormick, 'The Domesticated Cat in Early Christian and Medieval Ireland', *Keimelia: Studies in Medieval Archaeology and History in Memory of Tom Delaney*, ed. P. F. Wallace (Galway, 1988), pp. 218–28.

13 Alfonso X, *Cantigas de Santa Maria*, ed W. Mettmann (Coimbra, 1959–72), vol. 3, pp. 257–8 (no. 354). The king's affection is expressed thus: 'Este pesar foi por hua bestiola que muit' amava el Rei'.

14 London, British Library, Ms. Cotton Cleopatra D.VIII, fol. 115r. The manuscript dates from the end of the fourteenth century. For contents see H. L. Ward, *Catalogue of Romances in the Department of Manuscripts in the British Museum* (London, 1883), pp. 200 and 249. The manuscript described by Ward as 'A collection of exempla, moral precepts, etc., mainly extracted from the *Vitae Patrum*. Latin.' The exemplum in question is quoted by Ward in vol. 3, p. 641, no. 25.

15 Cambridge, Trinity College, Ms. 0.1.20 [I, 53], fol. 265r, 'Chirugia' (possibly by Robert of Parma) the manuscript is from the first half of the thirteenth century. Cf. T. Hunt, *The Medieval Surgery* (Woodbridge, 1992), pp. 76–7. The folio in question (265r) gives instructions for an ointment receipt and has an illustration of a medical dispensary, lined with storage jars, herbs, pestles and a cauldron. In the manuscript the dog is coloured yellow. The exemplum of the doctors and the monkey is in London, British Library, Add. Ms. 11872, fol. 89 [*c.* 1400, Italian]. Cf. Ward, *Catalogue of Romances*, vol. 3, p. 694, n. 30.

16 Thomas, *Man and the Natural World*, pp. 109–10; B. Boehrer, 'Shylock and the Rise of the Household Pet: Thinking Social Exclusion in the Merchant of Venice', *Shakespeare Quarterly* 50:2 (1999), pp. 152–70; and C. Gómez-Centurión, 'Chamber Animals at the Spanish Court during the Eighteenth Century', *The Court Historian* 16:1 (2011), pp. 43–65.

17 For a general overview on these species, see J. Clutton-Brock, *Domesticated Animals from Early Times* (London, 1981), pp. 34–45 (dogs), 106–12 (cats) and 145–9 (ferrets and rabbits). Also see R. Delort, *Les Animaux ont une histoire* (Paris, 1993).

18 Two excellent articles that provide a general overview are S. Menache, 'Dogs: God's Worst Enemies?', *Society and Animals*, 5:1 (1997), pp. 23–44, and S. Menache, 'Dogs and Human Beings: A Story of Friendship', *Society and Animals* 6:1 (1998), pp. 67–86.

19 Clement of Alexandria, *Paidogogos*, book 3, ch. 4. The poet Martial wrote a hendecasyllabic poem on the death of one named 'Issa' (*Epigrams*, I.109). On pet dogs in the Ancient World, see J. M. C. Toynbee, *Animals in Roman Life and Art* (Baltimore, 1996), pp. 108–22; F. D. Lazenby, 'Greek and Roman Household Pets', *The Classical Journal* 44:5 (1949), pp. 299–307; and T. P. O'Connor, 'Pets and pests in medieval and Roman Britain', *Mammal Review* 22 (1992), pp. 107–13.

20 Desiree Scott, a historian of Crufts, has defined a landrace as a 'A group of dogs with some similarities of appearance and behaviour that form the basis of one or more pedigree dog breeds.' This covers a wider group than a modern breed, which Dr Scott defines as 'A population of animals of one species that may be distinguishable from other populations of this species with regard to some conspicuous characteristics that are genetically determined, but are defined as a breed by an official registration body because of their common descent from the same group of founders. Official division of the population may lead to the creation of further breeds. Decision by the registration body may allow unrelated individuals to be added to a breed's register.' Compare this to the definition of breed in Clutton-Brock, *Domesticated Animals from Early Times*, p. 41: 'A breed is a group of animals that has been selected by man to possess a uniform appearance that is inheritable and distinguishes it from other groups of animals within the same species.' Medieval landraces and breeds of dogs are very diverse phenotypically, often sharing just some physical characterics. Many thanks to Dr Scott for all her assistance.

21 See A. Erlande-Brandenburg, *La Dame à la licorne* (Paris, 1978).

22 See J. Cummins, *The Hound and the Hawk: The Art of Medieval Hunting* (London, 2001), p. 47.

23 London, British Library, Add. Ms. 12531, fols. 4r and 5r. dated to *c.*1530. There are other pets in this manuscript, on fol. 5r Doña Ines holds a small bird while an unnamed lady in the upper right side of the folio holds a caged bird. Fol. 10r has Doña Constança with a different dog, this time a long grey haired little dog, just like the one that appeared with Doña Ermesenda in fol. 5r. Numerous monkeys, birds and other small animals are depicted near ladies through the manuscript. Fol. 4 is reproduced in T. Kren and S. McKendrick, *Illuminating the Renaissance: The Triumph of Flemish Manuscript Painting in Europe* (London, 2003), p. 461, and all the cited folios are available online via the British Library website.

24 John Caius, *Of Englishe Dogges: The Diversities, the Names, the Natures, and the Properties,* trans. A. Fleming (1578). All quotations come from Fleming's translation.

25 Shakespeare, *Two Gentlemen of Verona,* Act 4, scenes 2 and 4. Also see B. Boehrer, *Shakespeare among the Animals* (Basingstoke, 2002).

26 *The Master of Game: The Oldest English Book on Hunting,* ed. W. A. and F. Baillie-Grohman (London, 1904), pp. 105–22 [text is modernized].

27 Medieval animal symbolism is a hugely rich field. To examine at length the literary and theological symbolism of animals commonly kept as pets (dogs, cats, monkeys, parrots and so on) is beyond the scope of this book. An introduction to the field is provided in J. M. Ziolkowski, 'Literary Genre and Animal Symbolism', in *Animals and the Symbolic in Mediaeval Art and Literature,* ed. L. A. J. R. Houwen (Groningen, 1997), pp. 1–23, and a good starting point for individual species is B. Rowland, *Animals with Human Faces: A Guide to Animal Symbolism* (London, 1974). Also see Menache, 'Dogs and Human Beings', esp. p. 77.

28 Tobias 6:2 and 11:4. For a discussion on the mainly negative attitudes towards dogs in the Jewish, Christian and Muslim traditions, see Menache, 'Dogs: God's Worst Enemies?'.

29 *Hildegard von Bingen's Physica: The Complete English Translation of her Classic Work on Health and Healing,* trans. P. Throop (Rochester, VT, 1998), pp. 217–18.

30 A modern translated edition of one manuscript, Oxford, Bodleian Library, Ms. Bodley 264, appears in R. Barber, trans., *Bestiary* (Woodbridge, 1999), p. 2. The bestiary stories of canine fidelity come originally from Pliny the Elder. See Pliny the Elder, *Natural History,* ed. J. Henderson and trans. W. H. S. Jones (Cambridge, MA, 1997), book VIII, ch. lxi, pp. 101–3.

31 *The Goodman of Paris,* ed. and trans. E. Paris (Woodbridge, 2006), pp. 72–3. See also *Le Menagier de Paris,* ed. G. E. Brereton and J. M. Ferrier (Oxford, 1981), ch. 7, pp. 181–2. On the loyal greyhound see A. Classen, 'The Dog in German Courtly Literature: The Mystical, the Magical, and the Loyal Animal', in *Fauna and Flora in the Middle Ages: Studies of the Medieval Environment and its Impact on the Human Mind,* ed. S. Hartmann (Frankfurt, 2007), pp. 69–72.

32 Alexander Neckam, *De naturis rerum librum duo* (London, 1863). Cf. A. Smets, 'L'Image ambiguë du chien à travers la littérature didactique latine et française (XIIe–XIVe siècles)', *Reinardus* 14 (2001), pp. 243–53.

33 For a general overview and a copious amount of feline iconography, see K. Walker-Meikle, *Medieval Cats* (London, 2011).

34 D. Gray, 'Notes of Some Medieval Mystical, Magical and Moral Cats', in *Langland, the Mystics and the Medieval English Religious Tradition,* ed. H. Phillips (Cambridge, 1990), p. 193. Cf. P. D. A. Harvey, *A Medieval*

Oxfordshire Village, Cuxhom, 1240 to 1400 (Oxford 1965). Gray's article is an excellent source on medieval cat lore.

35 Bartholomeus Anglicus, *On the Properties of Things*, trans. John Trevisa, ed. M. C. Seymour *et al.* (Oxford, 1975), pp. 1228–9.

36 Albertus Magnus, *On Animals*, trans. K. F. Kitchell & I. M. Resnick (Baltimore, 1999), p. 1523.

37 Thomas de Cantimpré, *De natura rerum*, ed. W. de Gruyter (Berlin and New York, 1973), vol. I, p. 151. Cf. *Ibid*, p. 1523 for translation.

38 *Hildegard von Bingen's Physica*, p. 200.

39 https://blogs.bl.uk/digitisedmanuscripts/2018/12/cats-get-off-the-page. html and https://medievalfragments.wordpress.com/2013/02/22/paws-pee-and-mice-cats-among-medieval-manuscripts/ (accessed 12/05/2020).

40 Geoffrey Chaucer, *The Canterbury Tales*, Manciple's Tale, lines 175–82 (*The Riverside Chaucer*, ed. L. D. Benson (Boston, MA, 1987), p. 284).

41 Chaucer, *The Canterbury Tales*, Wife of Bath's Tale, lines 348–54 (*The Riverside Chaucer*, p. 109).

42 Bartholomeus Anglicus, *On the Properties of Things*, pp. 1228–9.

43 *The Exempla or Illustrative Stories from the Sermones Vulgares of Jacques de Vitry*, ed. T. F. Crane (London, 1890), n. 209.

44 M. H. Jones, 'Cats and Cat-skinning in Late Medieval Art and Life', in *Fauna and Flora in the Middle Ages*, ed. Hartmann, pp. 97–8. Cf. Caxton's *Royal Book*. Jones's article discusses many medieval feline proverbs.

45 Gray, 'Notes of Some Medieval Mystical, Magical and Moral Cats', and S. Lipton, 'Jews, Heretics, and the Sign of the Cat in the *Bible moralisée*', *Word and Image* 8 (1992), pp. 362–77. An image of St Dominic pointing to the devil disguised as a large black cat climbing a rope appears in The Hague, Koninklijke Bibliothek, Ms. 72 A 24, fol. 313v (available on the library's website). See the entry 'Cats and other animals in sermons' (compiled by Fabrizio Conti, Central European University) in the Medieval Animal Data-Network website, which lists a variety of references to devilish cats.

46 C. L'Estrange Ewen, ed., *Witch Hunting and Witch Trials* (London, 1971), pp. 317–21. Cf. G. R. Quaife, *Godly Zeal and Furious Rage: The Witch in Early Modern Europe* (Beckenham, 1987) and A. C. Kors and E. Peters, ed., *Witchcraft in Europe, 400–1700: A Documentary History* (Philadelphia, 2001). For associations of dogs with the Devil, see B. A. Woods, 'The Devil in Dog Form', *Western Folklore* 13:4 (1954), pp. 229–35. And for details of possible pets accused as familiars, see J. A. Serpell. 'Guardian Spirits or Demonic Pets: The Concept of the Witch's Familiar in Early Modern England, 1530–1712', in *The Animal/Human Boundary* (Rochester, NY, 2002), pp. 157–90.

47 W. George and B. Yapp, *Naming of the Beasts: Natural History in the Medieval Bestiary* (London, 1991), pp. 91–2. The authors contend that most medieval monkeys would have been African tailed monkeys of genus *Cercopithecus*.

48 L. Bourgain, *La Chaire française au XIIe siècle d'après les manuscrits* (Paris, 1879), p. 12, n. 4, from an unpublished sermon (Paris, Bibliothèque nationale de France, Ms. Lat. 14934, fol. 82r). Cf. H. W. Janson, *Apes and Ape Lore in the Middle Ages and Renaissance* (London, 1952), p. 30.

49 For an extensive study of monkey symbolism, see Janson, *Apes and Ape Lore*.

50 E. Dawes, 'Pulling the Chestnuts out of the Fire', in *Animals and the Symbolic in Mediaeval Art and Literature*, ed. L. A. J. R. Houwen (Groningen, 1997), p. 156, on these simian characteristics quotes Philippe de Thaon, Jean Le Fèvre de Ressons (after 1376) and *Les Caquets de l'accouché* (1622).

51 Dawes, 'Pulling the Chestnuts out of the Fire, pp. 155–69. The first written versions of the fable appear in the sixteenth century, where the animal is usually a pet dog; later the monkey's dupe becomes a gullible cat, as in the version in Fontaine.

52 Kuntsmuseum Basel, Kupferstichkabinett (Inv. 1823.139).

53 Thomas de Cantimpré, *De naturis rerum*, book IV, ch. 96, p. 161 . Cf. Janson, *Apes and Ape Lore*, p. 80. Thomas moralizes this story: any creature that cannot accept bitterness is not worthy to taste higher sweetness.

54 Albertus Magnus, *On Animals*, pp. 1534–6. Albertus also describes (p. 1522) the *mamonetus*, a small monkey from the East which is seen in Europe as a pet.

55 Bartholomeus Anglicus, *On the Properties of Things*, p. 1247. Cf. Janson, *Apes and Ape Lore*, p. 82.

56 For a general overview of the history of rabbits see Delort, *Les Animaux ont une Histoire*, pp. 299–319, and on rabbit symbolism see Rowland, *Animals with Human Faces*, pp. 133–5.

57 A. Franklin, *La Vie privée d'autrefois: arts et métiers, modes, mœurs, usages des Parisiens du XII au XVIII siècle d'après des documents originaux ou inédits*, vols. 24 (Paris, 1899), ch. 1, pp. 30, 31–3.

58 Giorgio Vasari, *Le vite de' più eccellenti pittori scultori e archittettori nelle redazioni del 1550 e 1568*, ed. R. Bettarini (Florence, 1966–87), vol. 5, pp. 381–2.

59 For details on caged birds, including selected literary and iconographical evidence, see W. B. Yapp, 'Birds in Captivity in the Middle Ages', *Archives of Natural History* 10:3 (1982), pp. 479–500, and W. B. Yapp, *Birds in Medieval Manuscripts* (London, 1981). Also see W. M. Lindsay, 'Bird-Names in Latin Glossaries', *Classical Philology* 13:1 (1918), pp. 1–22.

60 G. R. Owst, *Literature and Pulpit in Medieval England: A Neglected Chapter in the History of English Letters & of the English People* (Cambridge, 1933), p. 27 (*Summa Predicatorum*, s.v. *consilium*).

61 *The Complete Poems of John Skelton*, ed. P. Henderson (London, 1948), p. 231, lines 16–17. On medieval parrots, see George and Yapp, *Naming of the Beasts*, pp. 162–4.

62 London, British Library, Ms. Egerton 945, fol. 214r (miscellaneous offices and prayers, dated to the last quarter of the thirteenth century, France); British Library, Ms. Egerton 1151, fol. 50 (English book of hours, dated third quarter of the thirteenth century). The parrots in the following manuscripts from the British Library (Ashmole 1525, fol. 17r; Burney 139, fol. 1; Harley 3244, fol. 51v; Oriental 2626, fol. 8; Yates Thompson 39, fol. 1) and the Koninklijke Bibliotheek, The Hague (76 E 4, fol. 6r; KA 16, fol. 99v). All illuminations available on the libraries' websites. There are several depictions of parrots in Yapp, *Birds in Medieval Manuscripts*, pl. 11 (British Library Add. Ms. 47682, fol. 10r), 15 (British Library, Ms. Royal 19 B.xv, fol. 37v) and pl 47 (British Library, Ms. Egerton 1070, fol. 34v).

63 C. Grössinger, *The World Upside Down: English Misericords* (London, 1997), p. 42. M. Prestwich, *Plantagenet England, 1225–1360* (Oxford, 2005), p. 122. The most detailed accounts for parrot upkeep appear in the papal accounts from Avignon.

64 Arnaut de Carcasses, *Las novas del papagay*, in *Les Troubadours: le trésor poétique de l'Occitanie*, ed. R. Lavaud and R. Nelli, vol. 2 (Bruges, 1966), pp. 214–35; *Le Chevalier du Papegau*, ed. F. Heuckenkamp (Halle, 1896) is dated to the fifteenth century or earlier. The other two works date from the early sixteenth century; Jean Lemaire de Belges, *Les Épîtres de l'amant vert*, ed. J. Frappier (Lille and Geneva, 1948); *Works of Sir David Lindsay*, ed. D. Hammer (Edinburgh, 1931–6), vol. 1, pp. 55–90. For 'Speke Parrot' see *The Complete Poems of John Skelton*, ed. Henderson, pp. 259–81. Cf. M. T. McMunn, 'Parrots and Poets in Late Medieval Literature', *Anthrozoös* 12:2 (1999), pp. 68–75; S. Thiolier-Méjean, 'Le Motif du perroquet dans deux nouvelles d'oc', in *Miscellanea Mediaevalia*, ed. J. C. Faucon, A. Labbé and D. Quéruel (Paris, 1998), pp. 1355–75. For parrots in early modern literature, see B. Boehrer, '"Men, Monkeys, Lap-dogs, Parrots, Perish All!" Psittacine Articulacy in Early Modern Writing', *The Modern Language Quarterly* 59:2 (1998), pp. 171–93.

65 Oxford, Bodleian Library, Ms. Buchanan e. 3, fol. 74r (available on the Bodleian Library website).

66 B. Boehrer, *Parrot Culture: Our 2500-Year-Long Fascination with the World's Most Talkative Bird* (Philadelphia, 2004). Pliny the Elder, *Natural History*, book 10, ch. 58.

67 P. D. A. Harvey, 'After Adam: Naming the Animals in the Middle Ages and Later' and M. Jones 'Animal Names', both unpublished papers presented at the London Society of Antiquaries, December 2003. I am very grateful

to both authors for sending me copies of their papers, which were of great help in writing this section.

68 *The Complete Poems of John Skelton*, ed. J. Scattergood (New Haven, CT, 1983), pp. 71–106.

69 *Dictionnaire étymologique de la langue françoise*, ed. G. Ménage (1750), vol. 2, p. 309. Cf. Franklin, *Vie privée* p. 269. Other generic French animal names include Martin for an ass, Robin for a sheep and Guionne or Jeanne for a goat.

70 National Archives, P756. Cf. *Proceedings of the Society of Antiquaries* (March, 1886). Cf. Jones, 'Cats and Cat-skinning in Late Medieval Art and Life', p. 98.

71 *The Complete Poems of John Skelton*, ed. Scattergood, pp. 71–106.

72 *Gammer Gurton's Needle*, ed. C. Whitworth (London, 1997).

73 Jones, 'Cats and Cat-skinning in Late Medieval Art and Life', p. 98.

74 R. Henryson, *Fables* (Edinburgh, 1802).

75 The names of Reynard's animal companions are popular generic names for animals as well. The include Gorpil the the fox, Isengrin the wolf, Noble the lion; Brun, the bear; Bruiant the Bull; Chantecler the cockerel, Pinte the hen. Courte the mole, Belin the ram; Beaucent, the wild boar; Tardif the snail; Tybert the cat; Conin the rabbit; Coard the hare; Frobert the cricket, and Bernard the ass. In Shakespeare's *Romeo and Juliet*, Act 3, scene 1, Mercutio calls Juliet's cousin Tybalt 'King of Cats' for this very reason.

76 London, British Library, Add. Ms. 48978, fol. 47. The Account Book of Beaulieu Abbey is dated *c.* 1270. A pen drawing of the cat with its name tag appears in the top left margin.

77 Kelly, *Early Irish Farming*, p. 123.

78 Kelly, *Early Irish Farming*, p. 121.

79 J. Armitage Robinson, *The Abbot's House at Westminster* (Cambridge, 1911), p. 10.

80 N. Orme, *Education and Society in Medieval and Renaissance England* (London, 1989), pp. 80, 83, 85; D. Thompson, *A Descriptive Catalogue of Middle English Grammatical Texts* (New York and London, 1979), p. 150.

81 Harvey, 'After Adam'.

82 M. St Clare Byrne and B. Boland, ed. *The Lisle Letters: An Abridgement* (Chicago, 1983), p. 150.

83 'On Certain Rare Monumental Effigies', *Transactions of the Bristol and Gloucestershire Archaeological Association* 35 (1902), p. 99.

84 Chaucer, *The Canterbury Tales*, The Nun's Priest's Tale, line 617 (*The Riverside Chaucer*, p. 260).

I St Roch with an angel (pointing to a plague bubo on his leg) and the dog
with a loaf of bread in its mouth (Book of Hours, Flanders, *c.* 1525)

II The Ape Salt, presented to New College, Oxford, by Archbishop
Warham in 1516 (silver-gilt, ruby & crystal, *c.* 1450–1500)

III A parrot with a gold belled collar (Bestiary, England, 15th century)

IV Stained glass panel of Mary of Burgundy holding
a dog with a belled collar (Bruges, c. 1500)

V Stained glass panel of Tobias and Sarah on their wedding night,
with sleeping dog on bed (Germany, *c.* 1520)

VI Woman at prayer with a pet dog
(Hours of St Omer, Northern France, *c.* 1320)

VII Nun with a small dog in her arms
(Book of Hours, Netherlands, early 14th century)

VIII Ladies in a carriage, one is handed a small dog, another stands with a chained squirrel on her shoulder
(Luttrell Psalter, Lincolnshire, c. 1320–40)

IX Giovanni Antonio Bazzi ('Il Sodoma'), self-portrait with pet badgers
(detail from the Life of St Benedict fresco sequence, Abbazia di Monte Oliveto Maggiore)

85 'On Certain Rare Monumental Effigies', p. 99.

86 Details of this effigy were supplied by Dr Malcolm Jones of the University of Sheffield.

87 Harvey, 'After Adam'. The manuscript of *The Master of Game*, formerly from the estate of HRH the late Duke of Gloucester, was sold at Christies, 2006. M. Thiébaux, 'The Medieval Chase', p. 269, n. 46

88 Jones, 'Animal Names'.

89 *Journal de Louise de Savoye* in S. Guichenon, *Histoire généalogique de la royale maison de Savoye* (Turin, 1778–80), vol. 4 (part II), p. 462.

90 Leon Battista Alberti, *Apologhi ed elogi*, ed. R. Contarino (Genoa, 1984), p. 146.

91 R. Hutchinson, *The Last Days of Henry VIII* (London, 2005), p. 166. Cf. P. Edwards, 'Domesticated Animals in Renaissance Europe', in *A Cultural History of Animals in the Renaissance*, ed. B. Boehrer (Oxford and New York 2007), p. 93.

92 *De mulieribus claris* and *Cité des dames* respectively.

93 London, British Library, Ms. Harley 4431, fol. 4v. This illumination is available online via the British Library's website.

94 Munich, Bayerische Staatsbibliothek, Ms. Gall. 11, l. 2; reproduced in M. Meiss, *French Painting in the Time of Jean de Berry: The Limbourgs and their Contemporaries* (London, 1974), pl. 13.

95 San Marino, Huntingdon Library, Ms. HM 268, fol. 153, and Glasgow, University of Glasgow Library, Ms. Hunter 372, fols. 65r and 104v respectively. The first two illuminations are reproduced in K. Scott, *Later Gothic Manuscripts* (London, 1996), and both illuminations from Hunter 372 are available via the University of Glasgow's website.

96 *Le Menagier de Paris*, ed. G. E. Brereton and J. M. Ferrier (Oxford, 1981), p. 130.

97 Entry for 'Eleemosyna' in John Bromyard, *Summa prsedicantium* (Venice, 1586), fol. 229r. Cf. Owst, *Literature and Pulpit in Medieval England*, p. 11.

98 Owst, *Literature and Pulpit in Medieval England*, p. 327.

99 Entris for 'Custodia' and 'Furtum' in *Summa Praedicantium*; cf. Owst, *Literature and Pulpit in Medieval England*, p. 264.

100 Franco Sacchetti, *Il Trecentonovelle*, ed. E. Faccioli (Turin, 1970), novella 109, p. 288. Cited in C. Frugoni, *A Day in a Medieval City*, trans. W. McCuaig, (Chicago/London, 2005) p. 109. Many thanks to Irina Metzler for this reference.

101 On the classical origins of this belief, see Pliny the Elder, *Natural History*, book VIII, pp. 304–5.

102 A facsimile of the 1486 edition appears in R. Hands, ed., *English Hawking and Hunting in The Boke of St Albans* (Oxford 1975), p. 80.

103 Richard of Durham, *The Lanercost Chronicle*, trans. Sir H. Maxwell (Llanerch, 2001), pp. 36–7.

104 National Archives, Exchequer Accounts, 406/30, printed in A. R. Meyers, ed., *The Captivity of a Royal Witch: The Household Accounts of Queen Joan of Navarre, 1419–21* (Manchester, 1940).

105 Olaus Magnus, *Description of the Northern Peoples*, ed. P. G. Foote (London, 1996–8), p. 848. The quotation from John Chrysostom appears to be spurious as it is not found in any of the saint's writing; it may be a creation by the author.

106 Anon, ed., *A Collection of Ordinances and Regulations for the Government of the Royal Household made in Divers Reigns, from King Edward III to King William and Queen Mary. Also Receipts in Ancient Cookery* (London, 1790), p. 150, on the 'Ordinances made at Eltham in the XVIIth year of King Henry VIII (1526)', transcribed from London, British Library, Ms. Harley 642.

107 See H. Waddell, *Beasts and Saints* (London, 1953) for translations of many pre-Franciscan saintly animal encounters, including all those cited here. For St Jerome in particular, see D. Salter, *Holy and Noble Beasts: Encounters with Animals in Medieval Literature* (Woodbridge, 2001), pp. 11–24, and for Insular saints and animals, see D. Alexander, *Saints and Animals in the Middle Ages* (Woodbridge, 2008). On early Christian martyrs and animals, see M. A. Tilley, 'Martyrs, Monks, Insects and Animals', *The Medieval World of Nature*, ed. Salisbury, pp. 93–107. The animals often refuse to kill the martyr. Cosmos and Damian cured animals as well as people, and a dog in the Acts of Peter speaks so that its can bear witness against Simon Magus.

108 Clemente Sanchez de Vercial, *The Book of Tales by A.B.C.*, ed. and trans. J. E. Keller, L. Clark Keating, Eric M. Furr (New York, 1992), no. 329 (264), pp. 220–1.

109 Salter, *Holy and Noble Beasts*, pp. 25–52.

110 For details of St Hugh's pet swan see D. H. Farmer, *St Hugh of Lincoln* (Oxford, 1985). The altarpiece mentioned is now in the Art Institute of Chicago.

111 Rowland, *Animals with Human Faces*, pp. 63–4. An manuscript illumination of St Dominic with all his attributes, including the dog, can be seen in The Hague, Koninklijke Bibliotheek, Ms. 74 G 36, fol. 104v, available on the library's website.

112 Rowland, *Animals with Human Faces*, p. 63.

113 Jacobus de Voragine, *The Golden Legend*, ed. F. S. Ellis (London, 1931).

114 Further examples can be seen in London, British Library, Ms Egerton 2125, fol. 09v, and Bodleian Library, Ms. Douce 264, fol. 21r. Both are available online.

115 The entire account appears in an engrossing book, J.-C. Schmitt, *The Holy Greyhound: Guinefort, Healer of Children since the Thirteenth Century* (Cambridge and Paris, 1983), which details the popular religious rituals associated with the shrine, the long-standing narrative of the faithful pet killed by the master (first attested in the Sanskrit Panchatrantra in the sixth century BC, where the pet is a mongoose), and the survival of the cult up to the early nineteenth century.

2 Getting (and Losing) a Pet

1 M. K Dall, *Court Roll of Chalgrave Manor, 1278–1313* (Streatley, 1950), p. 32. Cf. B. A. Hanawalt, *The Ties that Bound: Peasant Families in Medieval England* (Oxford, 1986), p. 256.

2 British Library, Add. Ms. 18351, fol. 3r, col. 2. Cf. F. C. Tubach, *Index Exemplorum: A Handbook of Medieval Religious Tales* (Helsinki, 1969) and J. A. Herbert, *Catalogue of Romances in the Department of Manuscripts in the British Library*, vol. 3 (London, 1910), p. 416, no. 11. This manuscript dates from the fourteenth century although the story exists in thirteenth-century compilations of *exempla*.

3 Kew, National Archives, E 101/352/13 m. Cited in J. C. Parsons, ed., *The Court and Household of Eleanor of Castile in 1290: An Edition of British Library Additional Manuscript 35294* (Toronto, 1977), p. 112, no. 172.

4 Thomas Rymer, *Foedera* (The Hague, 1739–45), vol. 4, p. 53. Cf. Meyers, *The Captivity of a Royal Witch*.

5 G. L. E. Du Fresne de Beaucourt, *Histoire de Charles VII* (Paris, 1881), vol. 1, p. 13. Cf. Franklin, *La Vie privée d'autrefois*, vol. 20, p. 324, n. 1.

6 A. Vallet de Viriville, *Histoire de Charles VII* (Paris, 1862–5), vol. 3, p. 277. Cf. Franklin, *La Vie privée d'autrefois*, vol. 20, pp. 324–5.

7 M. A. R. de Maulde-La-Clavière, *Jeanne de France, Duchesse d'Orléans et de Berry* (Paris, 1883), p. 7. Cf. Franklin, *La Vie privée d'autrefois*, vol. 24, ch. 1, p. 37.

8 'Item the same day to a servaunt of William ap Howell for bringing of a popyngay to the Quene to Windesore xiij s. iij d' [9 July 1502]: N. H. Nicholas, *Privy Purse Expenses of Elizabeth of York* (London, 1830).

9 Regarding the gift of seventeen dogs for stag hunting by the queen to the King of France, her accounts mention the expenses of the dogs' caretakers. Parsons, *The Court and Household of Eleanor of Castile*, p. 114, line 25.

10 This gift of a falcon ('ostoir'), along with his keeper, appears in a letter between the two rulers, Kew, National Archives, SC 1/18, no. 118, in M. Vale, *The Princely Court: Medieval Courts and Culture in North-West Europe, 1270–1380* (Oxford, 2001), appendix IX, p. 371. There are numerous sources on the exchange of hunting dogs, falcons, and horses between

rulers and aristocrats in the period, but this topic is beyond the scope of this book.

11 The elephant is chronicled and illustrated by Matthew Paris in his *Chronica Majora*, Cambridge, Corpus Christi College, Ms 16, fol. 4r. On medieval menageries throughout Europe, see G. Loisel, *Histoire des menageries: de l'antiquité à nos jours* (Paris, 1912).

12 Walter Map, *De nugis curialium*, ed. and trans. M. R. James (Oxford, 1983), pp. 26–31, esp. p. 28.

13 M. St Clare Byrne, *Lisle Letters*, vol. 2 (London), pp. 21, 30–1. Cf. K. MacDonach, *Reigning Cats and Dogs: A History of Pets at Court since the Renaissance* (London, 1999), p. 249.

14 See the entry 'Custodia' in Bromyard's *Summa praedicantium*, fol. 170r. Cf. in Owst, *Literature and Pulpit in Medieval England*, p. 264.

15 See the Middle High German original (with a modern German translation) in Gottfried von Strassburg, *Tristan*, vols. 1–3, ed. K. von Rüdiger and F. von Ranke (Stuttgart, 1998), ch. 25, lines 15765–16402. An English prose version can be found in *Tristan with the Surviving Fragments of the Tristan of Thomas*, ed. and trans. A. T. Hatto (Harmondsworth, 1960), pp. 249–56. A study of the dogs in the Tristan romance can be found in L. Gnaedinger, *Hiudan und Petitcreiu: Gestalt und Figur des Hundes in der mittelalterlichen Tristandichtung* (Zurich, 1971).

16 London, British Library, Add. Ms. 8877. The Roll of the Countess of Leicester is edited in T. H. Turner, ed., *Manners and Household Expenses of England in the Thirteenth and Fifteenth Centuries* (London, 1841), pp. 8 and 57.

17 Turner, *Manners and Household Expenses of England*, pp. 8 and 57. On the low value of cat skins, see Jones, 'Cats and Cat-skinning in Late Medieval Art and Life'.

18 Kelly, *Early Irish Farming*, p. 122. Also see McCormick, 'The Domesticated Cat in Early Christian and Medieval Ireland'.

19 Kelly, *Early Irish Farming*, pp. 120–1.

20 D. Jenkins, *The Law of Hywel Dda: Law Texts from Medieval Wales* (Llandysul, 1986), pp. 180–3.

21 M. A. Scheler, ed., *Lexicographie latine du XIIe et du XIIIe siècle* (Leipzig, 1867), p. 35, no. 70. Since Jean de Garlande's work is lexicographical in nature, he mentions practically every Latin term for a species of bird, not just those sold in Paris. A poem written in 1325 speaks of Parisian bird sellers, H. Bordier, ed., *Les Églises et monastères de Paris* (Paris 1856). Cf. Franklin, *La Vie privée d'autrefois*, vol. 20, p. 223–4.

22 Tax records for cage makers and bird sellers appear in the *Livre de la Taille pour l'an 1292* (Paris, 1837), p. 526; cf. Franklin, *La Vie privée d'autrefois*, vol. 20, p. 225–6. V. Gay, *Glossaire archaéologique du Moyen Âge et de la*

Renaissance, vol. 1 (Paris, 1882), p. 247 gives various Old French names for bird cages.

23 Philippe de Commynes, *Memoirs*, trans. M. Jones (London, 1972), pp. 392–3. Cf. MacDonach, *Reigning Cats and Dogs*, pp. 40–1.

24 See Walker-Meikle, *Medieval Cats*, and E. Pascua, 'From Forest to Farm and Town', in *A Cultural History of Animals*, vol. 2: *In the Middle Ages*, ed. B. Resl (Oxford, 2007), p. 102. Hence the term for tabby-cats in Italian: *soriani*, from Syria. The word 'tabby' is derived from the French *tabis*, a striped silk, from the Arabic *'attabiya*, from the Attabiy quarter of Baghdad, where the cloth was first made.

25 *Aubrey's Brief Lives: Edited from the Original Manuscripts*, ed. O. Lawson Dick (London, 1949), p. xxxvi.

26 Although there no complete catalogue of material in the Gonzaga archive, A. Luzio and P. Torelli, *L'Archivo Gonzaga a Mantova*, 2 vols. (Ostiglia and Verona, 1920–1) is very helpful. Archivio di Stato, Mantova, Archivio Gonzaga [henceforth ASMN AG], b. 2993, libro 5, no. 42. Cf. C. M. Brown, *Isabella d'Este and Lorenzo da Pavia* (Genève, 1982), pp. 245–6. There is no trace in the archives whether Salimbeni was successful in this mission. For a study of pets at a later court, see Gómez-Centurión, 'Chamber Animals at the Spanish Court during the Eighteenth Century'.

27 ASMN AG, b. 1438, no. 350: 'Essendo stato per nostro cugnto messer Federico da Casalmazor auisato imo constreto ex uostra IlLustrissima signoria haueria apiacer dedui gatti suriani et Io hauendo Insteso questo come seruidore de uostra IlLustrissima Signoria subito andai dalquanti amici nostri zentilhomini constringendoli mene Facessino auere ecosi Incerti monasteri datuti fome risposo non hauerne dequelli che uostra IlLustrissima signoria forsi haueria apiacer cioe che fossero zoneneti, ma tuti mano promeso che altempo cioe quando sarano nati me seruirano e Io desideroso di Far cosa che sia In piacer de uostra IlLustrissima signoria Faremo haueti el uostro Intentu epiu presto sara possibile: alquale sempre mericomando e saro seruidor che uostra IlLustrissima signoria …'. Cf. A. Bertolotti, "Curiosità storiche mantovane: I gatti e la gatta della Marchesa di Mantova Isabella d'Este', *Il Mendico* 9:8 (1889), pp. 6–7.

28 ASMN AG, b. 1438, no. 351–2 [13 October 1498]. Cf. Brown, *Isabella d'Este and Lorenzo da Pavia*, p. 246.

29 ASMN AG, 2992, libro 9 no. 82v: 'Ptolemeo … Se ne portarai el gatino suriano ne farai cosa grata …'

30 ASMN AG, b. 1439, no. 409 [25 June 1501]. Cf. Brown, *Isabella d'Este and Lorenzo da Pavia*, p. 245].

31 The letter to Alvise Marcello is ASMN AG, b. 2993, libro 12, fols. 61v–63 [27 June 1501]. Cf. Brown, *Isabella d'Este and Lorenzo da Pavia*, p. 246. The letter to Francisco Trevisano [30 June 1501] is ASMN AG, b. 2993, libro 12, fol. 63r: 'Se non hauemo resposto perma cella littera vostra circa la perdita

de la gatta et proceduto che non hauerimo hauuto le precendente quale dicati hauerene scripto …'

32 ASMN AG, b. 1438, no. 359 [27 November 1498]: 'Del gatesino soriano quale mandai, non pote' maie trovare de melo. Farò la diligencia averene uno pù belo se 'la sarà posibile.' Cf. Brown, *Isabella d'Este and Lorenzo da Pavia*, pp. 47–8, no. 21.

33 ASMN AG, b. 2992, no. 90 [30 November 1498]. Cf. Brown, *Isabella d'Este and Lorenzo da Pavia*, p. 48, no. 22.

34 ASMN AG, b. 1438, no. 257. 'Non lasso trasto afare per ritrovar uno bello gatto – ma f[?] que non li ho ventura.' The date of this letter is unclear, possibly from October 1498, at the time when Lorenzo da Pavia was looking for a cat.

35 ASMN AG, b. 1438, no. 614 [19 March 1499]. Cf. Brown, *Isabella d'Este and Lorenzo da Pavia*, p. 48, no. 23.

36 ASMN AG, b. 1439, nos. 310–11 [3 August 1501]. Cf. Brown, *Isabella d'Este and Lorenzo da Pavia*. There is no letter from Isabella confirming that she decided to keep this cat

37 ASMN AG, b. 1140, no. 293 [17 June 1503]. Cf. Brown, *Isabella d'Este and Lorenzo da Pavia*, p. 74, no. 75.

38 ASMN AG, b. 2915, libro 201, no. 21v [13 August 1508]: 'Da vostro fratello non volemo altro se non che 'l ni facci havere dui gatti soriani belli et da soreci buoni, ma uno maschio et una femina, et vadesi alla bonhora …' Cf. Brown, *Isabella d'Este and Lorenzo da Pavia*, p. 115, no. 143.

39 ASMN AG, b. 2498, no. 236 [9 February 1519]: 'Illustrissima et Excellentissma Madamma & Signora mia colendissima, hora quattro giorni per el magnifico Domino Antonio de bologna mi fu richiesto el gatto mio per unirlo cum la gatta di Vostra Excellencia …' Sent by Iacobo Antonio Stella from the village of Castelgoffredo.

40 All these references were compiled by Krisztina Arany, Central European University. They are available at the Medieval Animal Data-Network under the entry 'Cats and other animals in domestic correspondence', with all the document references in the Archivio Segreto Prato, Archivio Datini, along with digitized documentary links. There are also assorted references to peacocks in the letters. Many thanks to Alice Choyke for alerting me to these documents.

41 ASMN AG, b. 2482, no. 111 [21 April 1511]: 'Signore La Fanina gli di passati partori tre figlioli una cagnolina uiua dui maschi morti la cagnolina hebbe la signora donna Hippolita et gli post nome Fratilla. poi la damma nha fatti quattro. la IlLustrissima signora uostra madre racordandose de vostra signoria me ne ha dato uno per lei il pui bello et piaceuolino dil mondo rossetto sfazato de peza biancha in mezo la fronte in mezo el collo unaltra ha il collo quasi tutto intorniato de circulo bianco gli piede tutti balzani la punta de la coda bianca tutto allegro con bel musino Io con consentimento

de la *p*arta Madama gli ho posto nome Zephyro alludendo ad Aura de madama. Credo che la signoria vostra hauera un bel cagnolo. io non gli manca de diligencia per alleuarlo ben accostumato et piaceuolo. Zorzino ha hauuto una sorella, messer Benedetto Lacioso laltra messer Francesco Cantelmo el terzo ma quel de vostra excellencia e il piu bello di tutti come era debito.'

42 ASMN AG, b. 2485 [28 March 1512]: 'Questi di la Mamie cagnolina di madama uostra madre partori prima doi cagnoli morti poi uno cagnolino et una cagnolina dopplicati cioe gionti insieme tutti gemini ex cetto che hauano una sola testa morti. Questo credo non habbia scritto messer Amico che in tutti lo altre cose me remetto a lui: La ditte Mami era grauida chel uostro Zephyro.'

43 R. Thomas, 'Perceptions Versus Reality: Changing Attitudes towards Pets in Medieval and Post-Medieval England', in *Just Skin and Bones? New Perspectives on Human–Animal Relations in the Historical Past*, ed. A. Pluskowski (Oxford, 2005), pp. 95–104. The author also concluded that the number of cats and dogs found on archaeological sites in England in the medieval and post-medieval period is low. On p. 101 he gives the case of red squirrel bones found on deposits in Dudley Castle; these must have been brought in by a human agent, but it is uncertain whether they were kept as pets or used for skinning.

44 A. Riedel, *The Animal Remains of Medieval Verona: An Archaeozoological and Paleoeconomical Study* (Verona, 1994), pp. 24–7 (for further details on the age of the animals and their size see p. 25). The author also asserts that the excavated Veronese cats were generally small and slender. Dog remains, although less common than those of cats, show dogs of different sizes abounded in the city. Excavations in Vác, Hungary, paint a similar picture. Canine remains of different sizes have been excavated, but it is impossible to determine their exact function, the same case appears with feline remains. See L. Bartosiewicz, *Animals in the Urban Landscape in the Wake of the Middle Ages: A Case Study from Vác, Hungary* (Oxford, 1995), pp. 59–61).

45 C. Smith, 'Dogs, Cats and Horses in the Scottish Medieval Town', *Proceedings of the Society of Antiquaries of Scotland* 128 (1998), pp. 869–870, 881.

46 Thomas, 'Perceptions Versus Reality', pp. 97 and 101, and C. Platt, *Medieval Southampton: The Port and Trading Community, AD 1000–1600* (London, 1973), pp. 103–4.

47 St Clare Byrne and Boland, *The Lisle Letters: An Abridgement*, p. 150.

48 'Journal de Louise de Savoye', in Guichenon, *Histoire généalogique de la royale maison de Savoye*, vol. 4 (part II), p. 462. Cf. Franklin, *La Vie privée d'autrefois*, vol. 24, p. 46–7. For a debate concerning the journal's authorship, see M. Dickman Orth, 'Francis de Moulin and the Journal of Louise of Savoy', *Sixteenth Century Journal* 13:1 (1982), pp. 55–66.

49 W. P. Baildon, ed., *Court Rolls of the Manor of Wakefield* (Leeds, 1901), vol. i, pp. 235–6. Cf. Hanawalt, *The Ties that Bound*, p. 256.

50 The entire elegy, *Flete, Canes* (Weep, dogs) is edited in J. Préaux, 'De Culex de Virgile a son pastiche par Thierry de Saint-Thrond', *Présence de Virgile: Actes du colloque* (Paris, 1978), pp. 195–208. Translation from J. M. Ziolkowski, *Talking Animals: Medieval Latin Beast Poetry, 750–1150* (Philadelphia, 1993), pp. 272–3. See M. Jean Préaux, 'De Culex de Virgile a son pastiche par Thierry de Saint-Thrond', in *Présence de Virgile: Actes du colloque* (Paris, 1978), pp. 195–208, on the influence on Thierry's elegy of Virgil's *Culex* (attributed to the poet from the first century AD). Préaux's article supplies the Latin text of the eulogy. The elegy contains various classical references such as Ovid's parrot and Virgil's gnat.

51 Lines 7–14 and 23–27 (of a total of 1382). The entire poem is edited in *The Complete Poems of John Skelton*, ed. Scattergood, pp. 71–106, under the title 'Phylyp Sparrow'. For an interpretation of the poem, see S. Schibanoff, 'Taking Jane's Cue: Phyllyp Sparowe as a Primer for Women Readers', *PMLA* 101:5 (1986), pp. 832–47.

52 Ziolkowski, *Talking Animals*, pp. 244–5; K. Breul, *The Cambridge Songs: A Goliard's Song Book of the XIth century* (Cambridge, 1915), p. 62, cf. E. Power, *Medieval English Nunneries* (Cambridge, 1922), p. 589.

53 *Testamenta Eboracensia*, ed. J. Raine, III (London, 1865, for 1864), p. 255n. Greyhounds are also the supporters of the Neville arms.

54 The death of Isabella's dog Aura in 1511 is mentioned in J. Cartwright, *Isabella d'Este, Marchioness of Mantua, 1474–1539: A Study of the Renaissance* (London, 1903), vol. 2, pp. 56–6, and discussed in A. Luzio and R. Renier, 'La coltura e le relazione letterarie di Isabella d'Este Gonzaga', *Giornale storico della letteratura italiana* 35 (1899), pp. 44–7. A very good general article on pets at the Mantuan court is C. Cottafavi, 'Cani e gatti alla corte di Gonzaga', in *El Ceppo* (Mantua, 1934).

55 R. Signorini, 'Two Notes from Mantua: A Dog Named Rubino', *Journal of the Warburg and Courtauld Institutes* 41 (1978), pp. 317–20. The epitaphs follow the conventional form for canine epitaphs. Rubino's epitaph is: 'RUBINUS CATVLVS / LONGO ET FIDO AMORE PROBATVS DOMINO / SENIO CONFECTVS SERVATA STIRPE HIC IACEO / HOC ME HONORE SEPVLCHRI / HERVS DIGNATVS EST.' Bellina's epitaph is the following, affirming that the charming and pretty little dog was the best and unfortunately died while giving birth: 'BELLINÆ / CANVM FLOSCVLO BELLISSIMO SVAVISSIMO / IN DOMINI DOMVSQ. DELICIIS OLIM / HABITÆ / QVÆ PRIMO VENERIS CONGRESSV LVCINAM LÆVAM / EXPERTA / DIFFICVLTATE PARTVS INTERIIT / HEV BREVEM VOLVPTATEM LONGA MORTE PERSONLVENS'. Signorini also suggests that the large brown dog underneath Ludovico's chair in Mantegna's fresco in the Camera degli Sposi in the Ducal palace in Mantua is Rubino.

56 On Mario Equicola see S. Kolsky, *Mario Equicola: The Real Courtier* (Geneva, 1991).

57 ASMN AG, b. 2479 [28 November 1510]: 'Essendo manchato questi si il pouero Martino di bona memoria con vniuersal dolore della corte: lha dato ampla materia alli ingegni Mantovani di celebrarlo: Messer Mario di alto spirito fa le Exequie sue con honore in Pompa: ne credo cheL virtuoso calandra manchara di pietoso officio: vn vostro Seruitor di tenue vena ha fatto lo Epithaphio, Toccando dilla Nation, virtu, e condicion dil Morto: Et perche gli Interuiene Ribolin vostro, et Aura Delicie hereditarie dilla Gentil fratilla: non mi e parso Indecente di presentare questi trei Epigramme alla Signoria Vostra: qual so che per il suo Nobil ingegno non sol capiragli senza altro Interprete: ma anchora sapria megliorargli, et degnerassi di Legerli per spasso, in memoria de quelli suoi fideli corteggiani.' The letter is mentioned in Luzio and Renier, 'La coltura e le relazione letterarie di Isabella d'Este Gonzaga', and partially transcribed and modernized in Cottafavi, 'Cani e gatti alla Corte dei Gonzaga'.

58 Mateo Bandello, *Novelle*, ed. G. G. Ferrero (Turin, 1974), p. 282. Bandello's *Novelle* are popular tales of a highly secular nature, although their author was nominally a member of the Dominican order. For a brief biography see *Dizionario biografico degli Italiani* (Rome, 1960–), pp. 667–73.

59 ASMN AG, b. 2482, nos. 115 and 116 [30 August 1511]: 'Ho heri laltro accadeti qui una grande disgratia: che essendo andata la Ilustrissima madama uostra madre a casa di Bagni per uistare la moglie del Conte Bacarino da Canossa paiolata: et uolendose parttire sua Excellentia Aura et la Mamia cagnoline de sua signoria se appizonno insieme per essere stata grande inimicicia tra loro per amore del cane de Alfonso et ritrouandose su un poggiolo in capo de la scala alto da terra forsi uintidua braza la pouea bella Aura cadde da esso poggiolo su la salicata de la corte, et subito morite. con tanto dolore de Madama che non se potria dire: lo puote ben imaginare ogniuno che sa lo amore che la le portaua: et quanto meritamente per essere stata la pui bella et pui piacuole cagnolina che fosse mai. sua signoria fu ueduta piangere quella sera a tauola: et mai la non ne parla che la non sospira, La Isabella piageua come se le fosse mortu sua madre et non se puo anchora ben consolare. non posso gia negare che anche io non habbi giettata qualeche lachrima. Madama subito fece dare una cassetta de piombo: et ui lha fatta ponere entro: et credo la tenira cosi fin che la se possi mettere in una bella sepoltura alla casa noua de unguria che sua Excelentia fa fare de la quale hoggi sua signoria ua a mettere de sua mano la prima pietra a xx hore per calculo astrologico. Fra tanto se attendera a fare acrsi et Epit. per la nobile Aura. Il uostro Zaphyro ha perduto una gentil compagna. Signore la notte seguente il giorno infelice de la crudel morte de Aura fu un malissimo tempo qui …'

60 The elegy that Calandra mentions composing for Aura is probably the one found under his name in a manuscript that collected many of the compositions dedicated to the dog (ASMN AG, Serie Autografi, cassata

no. 10, file no. 356, fol. 3r). Calandra also wrote a long literary work titled 'Aura' that is now lost; the title suggests that this may have had the Marquise's dog as its subject but there no further evidence to confirm this. See Luzio and Renier, 'La coltura e le relazione letterarie di Isabella d'Este Gonzaga', *Giornale storico della letterature italiana*, pp. 49–54.

61 For Guarino see *Dizionario biografico degli Italiani*, pp. 333–4. I cannot pinpoint with certainty his identity of the other scholar, called 'Messer C'. He could be either Girolamo Cusatro or Celio Calcagnini, since we know that these two Ferrarese scholars sent elegies. The epitaphs they composed were possibly sent with Bernardino's letter, as Isabella thanks him on their part in her reply.

62 ASMN AG, b. 1243, no. 188 [25 September 1511]: 'IlLustrissima Madama: hauendome scripto Messer Mario de la dolce Cagnolina de vostra signoria che era morta e chio uedesse farli Componere a quisti modi qualche Epitaphio, ne parlai cum alcuni donde me hano dato Li duo introclus, cioe per panizato e lo azaiolo quali se raccomandano ala S. V. assaj excusandosse se non sono de la dostima che Lei meretaria de hauere. IL Guarino et Messer C cho mi da promesso de darmi mehor Loro li fuoi, quali hauueti ge li remett*ere* …'

63 ASMN AG, b. 2996, libro 29, no. 59r [30 September 1511]: 'Gli Epitaphij de la nostra Aura che ci haueti mandati ni sono stati gratissimi et ni ringratiareti gli compositor in nome nostro et se altri se ne faranno ne piacera che ci gli mandati …' Cf. 'Varietà archivistiche e bibliografiche CCLXXXIX. Necrologie di una cagnuola marchionale', *Il Bibliofilo* 9:4 (1888–9), p. 56.

64 ASMN AG, b. 2996, libro 29, no. 82 [10 January 1512]: 'Hauemo receeuti gli uostri uersi che ni hauete mandato de la nostra Aura quali ne sono stati gratissimi per esser dotti beli conformi al nostro gentil ingegno el tenemone molto honorata la nostra cagnola. Ve ne ringratiamo molto et a tutti gli nostri comodi ne offerimo.'

65 This letter is in Stazio Gadio's hand, although it is signed by Federico. Stazio Gaudio was Federico's tutor in Rome.

66 Beroaldo would later write an epitaph to Leo X's elephant Hanno when it died in 1516. Hanno's funeral rites would outshine those of a Mantuan court dog. Raphael painted a mural of the elephant next to an inscription of Beroaldo's epitaph near a Vatican gate. The entire case is recounted in S. A. Bedini. *The Pope's Elephant* (Manchester, 1997).

67 ASMN AG, b. 1894, no. 57 [25 January 1512]: 'Hauendo fatto Maestro Philippo beroaldo alcuni uersi in laude di Aura cagnolina di vostra signoria mi li ha dati acio che in suo nome li mandi a quella hauendo lui inteso da statio cheI fara piacer a vostra signoria Eperho qui alligati le li inuio che credo per quanto mi e detto, non le spiacecano, egli li ha fatto molto uoluntieri per far cosa grata a Vostra Excellentia mostrando di esserle gran seruitor: Quella adunche li acceptara, et legera con lieta fronte che

lamoreuole prompteza sua lo merita: spero ben di mandarle anchor de altri de diuersi poeti: …' A few lines of this letter and Stazio's letter to Isabella in April [ASMN AG, b. 860 no. 29] are quoted in A. Luzio, 'Federico Gonzago ostaggio alla corte di Giulio II', *Archivio della Real Società Romana di Storia Patria* 9 (1886), p. 536.

68 A dissenting view can be found in L. K. Regan, 'Ariosto's Threshold Patron: Isabella d'Este in the Orlando Furioso', *Modern Language Notes* 120:1 (2005), n. 30: 'One might take the proliferation of humanistic poetry in Latin in memory of a dog as amusing proof of the disingenuousness of much of the poetry produced by these courtiers to please their patrons.'

69 ASMN AG, b. 1894, no. 60, single folio, written in Federico Gonzaga's own hand [16 March 1512]: '… apresso *perche* uedo che *vostra signora* piglia piacer de uersi Fati *per* la cagnolina ho procurato di farmi componer de le aleri, ulera quelli dil Beroaldo, quali qui alligati serano che credo *non* le dispiacerano …'

70 ASMN AG, b. 2996, libro 30, no. 8 [28 March 1512]: 'Laudamoti anchora di liuersi che ni hai mandati, composti per la morte de la nostra cagnolino che Tutti sono belli: et elleganti: maxime la silua de quello messerm Blosio: volemo che ringracij, o, facci ringratiarlui et tutti gli altri da nostra parte cum gionta de quelle offerte ti pareranno conuenire …' Blosio's elegy for Aura is not included in the elegy collection for Aura and I have not been able to locate it in the Gonzaga archives. It does not appear in any published collections of his work.

71 ASMN AG, b. 860, no. 29 (in a folder titled 'Roma 1512 Stazio Gadio') [4 April 1512]: '… ad disnar seco messer Petro bembo, messer Philippo beroaldo, messer Marco cauallo quel che fece lo epigramma del cupidine di vostra Excellencia con tre altre persone uirtuose et docte et dal signor Federico furno honorati …'

72 Pietro Bembo, *Carmina* (Turin, 1990), p. 58, no. 37.

73 ASMN AG, b. 1894, no. 89 [25 July 1512]: 'Mandare a vostra Excellencia tutti tre li gatini che ho per messer Federico cataneo.'

74 ASMN AG, b. 2485 [14 August 1512]: 'IlLustrissimo signore mio Heri guinse messer Federico Cattanio tanto ben ueduto da ogniun ma principio da la IlLustrissima madama uostra madre quanto fosse possibile per el bon noncio del ben stare di vostra signoria Hon potrei scriuere con guanta allegreza Sua Excellentisma accetto el nobilissimo patre di vostra signoria la quale di essere certa che la non poteua mandare cosa che fosse pui grata per la belleza ne pui mirabile per la sua rarita di quel bello animalens. Fu forza che esso messer Federico differisse molto in longo a fare la sua ambassata fin che madamma se succiasse alquanto in mirare et andare quel animalino delicato: el quale fin qui non ha altra allogiamento che la manica e seno di sua Excellisima gli altri doni di vostra signoria sono ben stati grati ma per albora e per bon pezo non forno guardati estimandosi solamente la belleza di quello uiene ma el tempo loro: che come se fossero guinti pur adesso, se

mirano et laudano. Vno di gattini cioe il masebio non ha potuto guingere uiuo la gentiliza del piccolino recompensa el danno di quello Madonna gattina sta in la camera di madamma in delicie et feste di ogniuno per essere cosi piaccuolo. ma beato chi puo toccare el bellino. La pietra anticha e una bellisimma cosa et molto laudata da ogniuno. la signoria vostra lha anche honorata dun bello repositorio come lo animalino d'una bellissima gabia et il gentilissimo animo di quella e, stato molto laudata che in ogni cosa mosta splendideza et virtu. a coroneine et agnusdei sano state accettissima a madamma. insumma da la presentia di vostra signoria in fori quella non postua donni a sua Excellentissima cosa piu grata di questi presenti. de che la ringratia infinitamente. La signoria vostra non potrie credere la cura che madama parta continuamente che quel animalino repossi mollemente et mangi cose che gli piacia: ma non se sacia di basarlo et fisteggiarlo con le piu tenere paroletti del mondo. Lo amore de la sua Aura era niente appresso questo. la gli fa fare una lettica bellissima da allogiarlo: ma ui stara poco: per che uolo be io che lo allogianento suo ha esse ella istessa. La morte del gatino e stata per che santo famiglio di messer Mario amalo a Siena et iui resto: onde el gattino bisogno caualcare un cauallo da sua posta minato a mano …'

75 ADM AG, b. 1894, no. 96 [28 August 1512]: 'Grandissimo piacer ho receuuto che le siano sta grati li gatini che li ho mandati …'

76 ASMN AG, b. 2930, no. 51 [15 October 1526]: 'Mi e morta una Cagnolina di parto La quale uoressimo far sepelir in una bella sepoltura di Marmore con un epitaphio, pero uolemo che facciati dui dessegni che siano belli che li faremo far di Marmore, Et fatti essi dessegni mandatemli o, portatemeli uoi quanto piu presto poteti …' Cf. A. Bertolotti, 'Curiosità storiche mantovane: una magnifica tomba per una cagnetta', *Il Mendico* 4:18 (1884), p. 6. Cf. Cottafavi, 'Cani e gatti alla Corte dei Gonzaga', p. 10.

77 Ulisse Aldrovandi, *De quadripedibus digitatis viviparis libri tres et de quadrupedibus digitatis oviparis libri duo* (Bologna, 1637), p. 525. Viola's epitaph is the first: 'CATELLA VIOLA / LUCINAM INFAELICITER EXPERTA HIC SITA SVM / HOC LVSVS, HOC FIDES MERVIT MONVMENTVM / QUID MIRARE? / FIDES IPSA CANES COELI INCOLAS ACIT.' The only canine epitaph still extant in Mantua today is on a marble plaque in the hanging garden in the Ducal Palace for a seventeenth-century little dog called Oriana, which is in similar format to the earlier Mantuan epitaph: 'ORINAE CATELLAE COELESTI / CANICVLAE FORMA FIDE / IOCIS PRAEFERENDAE / MEMORIAE ERGO .P.' Oriana's tombstone is reproduced in Cottafavi, 'Cani e gatti alla Corte dei Gonzaga', p. 10. R. Signorini, 'Two Notes from Mantua: A Dog Named Rubino', p. 318, suggests that the anonymous canine tomb still extant in the Palazzo Te is Viola's tomb and reproduces it as pl. 46a.

78 The portrait is reproduced in C. Hope, *Titian* (London, 2003), p. 81, pl. 41. It is in marked contrast to Titian's portrait of Charles V (1536?, now in the

Museo del Prado, Madrid) in which the emperor is painted with a large hunting dog (p. 91, pl. 46).

79 Aldrovandi, *De animalibus quadrupedibus digitatis viviparis*, p. 524; Jan Papy, 'Lipsius and his Dogs: Humanist Tradition, Iconography and Rubens' Four Philosophers', *Journal of the Warburg and Courtauld Institutes* 62 (1999), p. 167.

80 J. B. Trapp, 'Petrarch's Inkstand and his Cat', in *Il passaggiere italiano: saggio sulle letterature di lingua inglese in onore di Sergio Rossi*, 1994, pp. 23–40. Trapp reproduces some manuscript illuminations depicting Petrarch in his study with cats, pp. 37–9.

3 Pet Welfare

1 Francesco Petrarch, *Petrarchae poëmata minora*, ed. D. Rossetti (Milan, 1829–34), vol. 3, p. 214, lines 160–1.

2 For further details on the papal menagerie, see Loisel, *Histoire des ménageries*. There are numerous references regarding food purchased for the lions and other exotica in the papal accounts in K. H. Schäfer, ed., *Vatikanische Quellen zur Geschichte der Päpstlichen Hof-und Finanzverwaltung, 1316–1378* (Rome, 1937).

3 Petrarch, *Petrarchae poëmata minora*, vol. 3, pp. 38–46.

4 Francesco Petrarch, *Le Familiari*, ed. V. Rossi (Florence, 1933–42), vol. 3, pp. 91–3. These included tales from Pliny the Elder and Solinus, such as the dog which threw himself into the Tiber to stay with the corpse of his executed master and how the dogs of Garamentes protected him when he was attacked.

5 Petrarch, *Le Familiari*, vol. 3, pp. 84–7.

6 Petrarch, *Le Familiari*, vol. 3, pp. 177–9.

7 Petrarch, *Le Familiari*, vol. 3, pp. 179–82.

8 Clement Marot, *Œuvres* (La Haye, 1731), vol. 3, p. 152: 'Sa maistresse, en un beau tableau / L'a fait paindre à Fontainbleau. / La Royne en sa couche parée / Luy a sa place préparée. / Et dort la petite follastre / Dessus la gorge d'allebastre / De sa dame, si doucement / Qu'on ne l'oit suffler nullement.'

9 J. Schiesari, '"Bitches and Queens": Pets and Perversion at the Court of France's Henri III', in *Renaissance Beasts: Of Animals, Humans and Other Wonderful Creatures*, ed. in E. Fudge (Urbana, IL, 2003), pp. 37–49.

10 P. L'Estoile, *Registre-journal de Henri III, roy de France et de Pologne 1574 à 1589* (Paris, 1837), p. 72. Schiesari, 'Bitches and Queens' is full of details on the king's eccentric petkeeping, such as giving the Order of the Holy Spirit to a man who presented him with two Turqués dogs (p. 38).

11 Agrippa d'Aubigné, *Histoire universelle*, ed. A. de Ruble, vol. 7 (Paris, 1893), p. 102. Cf. B. Boehrer, 'Introduction: The Animal Renaissance', in *A Cultural History of Animals in the Renaissance*, ed. B. Boehrer (Oxford and New York, 2007), p. 23, and Schiesari, 'Bitches and Queens', p. 39.

12 L'Estoile, *Registre-journal de Henri III*, p. 62. Cf. Franklin, *La Vie privée d'autrefois*, vol. 25, pp. 57–8.

13 Bartosiewicz, *Animals in the Urban Landscape in the Wake of the Middle Ages*, p. 61.

14 Geoffrey Chaucer, *The Canterbury Tales*, lines 146–7 (*The Riverside Chaucer*, p. 25). The next two lines (148–9) underline the Prioress's affection for her dogs ('But soore wept she if oon of hem were deed') and relate that her dogs were never physically disciplined ('Or if men smoot it with a yerde smerte').

15 C. M. Woolgar, *The Great Household in Late Medieval England* (London, 1999), p. 123.

16 J. M. Steadman, 'The Prioress' Dogs and Benedictine Discipline', *Modern Philology* 54:1 (1956), pp. 1–6; R. Rex, '*The Sins of Madame Eglentyne' and Other Essays on Chaucer* (London, 1995), pp. 95–169; H. A. Kelly, 'A Neo-Revisionist Looks at Chaucer's Nuns', *The Chaucer Review* 31:2 (1996), p. 121; M. L. Dutton, 'Chaucer's Two Nuns', in *Monasteries and Society in Medieval Britain*, ed. P. Thompson (Stamford, 1999), pp. 296–311, esp. p. 298.

17 Oxford, Magdalen College, Ms. Estate Paper 85/2 (Sept 1347–March 1348), printed in C. M. Woolgar, ed., *Household Accounts from Medieval England* (Oxford, 1992), vol. 1, p. 240.

18 Woolgar, *Household Accounts from Medieval England*, vol. 1, pp. 175–7, pp. 264–8; vol. 2, p. 526.

19 Ibid., vol. 1, p. 15; vol. 2, pp. 490, 493–4, 500, 526, 532.

20 Ibid., vol. 1, pp. 264–404, 416–17.

21 London, British Library, Add. Ms. 8877, edited in Turner, *Manners and Household Expenses of England*, pp. 8, 15, and 29. Cf. M. W. Labarge, *A Baronial Household of the Thirteenth Century* (London 1965), ch. 10.

22 Franklin, *La Vie privée d'autrefois*, vol. 25, p. 51 details an entry from one of the registers: '16 novembre 1547, à Anthoine Andrault, boulengier des petits chiens blancs, 30 escus'. Cf. *Magasin pittoresque* 42 (1874), p. 164.

23 *Mémoires et poésies de Jeanne d'Albret*, ed. Ruble (Paris, 1893), p. 35. Cf. Franklin, *La Vie privée d'autrefois*, vol. 24, p. 25.

24 Gray, 'Notes on Some Medieval Mystical, Magical and Moral Cats', p. 193; cf. Harvey, *A Medieval Oxfordshire Village, Cuxhom*.

25 Kelly, *Early Irish Farming*, p. 123.

26 Chaucer, *The Canterbury Tales*, Squire's Tale, lines 613–14 (*The Riverside Chaucer*, p. 175).

27 *The Complete Poems of John Skelton*, ed. Henderson, p. 294.

28 I am grateful to Dr Ivan Polancec for informing me of an entry in Rome, Archivio Segreto Vaticano, IE 302, fol. 34r. It notes for payment for two pounds of parrot's bird seed by Agapitus Melior, the papal apothecary, on 30 April 1364. For a discussion of the parrots (and other household pets) of another pope, John XXII, see H. Dienen, 'Die "Camera papagalli" im Palast des Papstes', *Archiv für Kulturgeschichte* 49 (1967), pp. 43–97.

29 Schäfer, ed., *Vatikanische Quellen zur Geschichte der päpstlichen Hof- und Finanzverwaltung*, vol. 6, pp. 48, 83, 129.

30 *The Goodman of Paris*, p. 199.

31 Richard of Durham, *The Lanercost Chronicle*, Maxwell, p. 37; cf. A. Gransden, *Historical Writing in England, 550–1307* (Ithaca, NY, 1974), p. 499.

32 Albertus Magnus, *On Animals*, p. 1463, which adds in n. 113, 'Oats would provide high dietary fiber and bulk in the dog's system.'

33 *Anecdotes historiques, légendes et apologues tirés du recueil inédit d'Étienne de Bourbon*, ed. A. Lecoy de La Marche (Paris, 1877), n. 191 (from Paris, Bibliothèque nationale de France, Ms. 15970).

34 See the entry 'Servire' in Bromyard's *Summa praedicantium*, p. 362. Cf. Owst, *Literature and Pulpit in Medieval England*, p. 327; I quote from Owst's translation. Bromyard mentions pets frequently but his criticism is not directed at the keeping of pets *per se*, rather at the ostentatious care lavished on them rather than the needy.

35 *Le Livre du Chevalier de la Tour Landry pour l'enseignement de ses filles*, ed. M. A. de Montaiglon (Paris, 1854), pp. 44–6. The translation here is based on the one in London, British Library, Ms. Harley 1764, and printed in *The Book of the Knight of La Tour-Landry*, ed. T. Wright (London, 1906), pp. 28–9.

36 C. Plummer, ed., *Vitae sanctorum Hiberniae* (Oxford, 1910). Medieval Irish monks had great fondness for cats, see the poem 'Pangur Bán' in Chapter 4 below, and McCormick, 'The Domesticated Cat in Early Christian and Medieval Ireland'.

37 R. Flower, *The Early Irish Tradition* (Oxford, 1947), pp. 26–7. Cf. Gray, 'Notes on Some Medieval Mystical, Magical and Moral Cats', p. 191.

38 Albertus Magnus, *On Animals*, pp. 1457–63. Albertus' hints on dog care in this text are derived from his earlier work on dogs, the *Practica canum*: see J. Loncke, *La Practica canum – le De Cane d'Albert Le Grand, l'art de soigner les chiens de chasse au Moyen Âge* (Nogent le Roi, 2007). A good overview of medieval texts on the care of hunting hounds, an extensive literature that is outside the remit of this book, is provided in B. van den

Abeele and J. Loncke, in *Inquirens subtilia diversa: Dietrich Lohrmann zum 65. Geburtstag*, ed. K. van Horst and L. Falkenstein (Aachen, 2002), pp. 281–96.

39 *The Master of Game*, pp. 105–22.

40 Albertus Magnus, *On Animals*, p. 1459–61.

41 *The Surgery of Henri de Mondeville*, vol. 2, trans. L. D. Rosenman, pp. 602–24.

42 H. Gaidoz, *Bibliotheca mythica: La Rage et St-Hubert* (Paris, 1887); A. Champollion-Figeac, *Louis et Charles Ducs D'Orléans: leur influence sur les arts, la littérature et l'esprit de leur siècle* (Geneva, 1980), p. 93.

43 S. Teuscher, 'Hunde am Fürstenhof: Köter und "edle Wind" als Medien sozialer Beziehungen vom 14. Bis 16. Jahrhundert', *Historische Anthropologie* 6 (1998), pp. 347–369, esp. p. 350.

44 Oxford, Bodleian Library, Ms. Douce 335, fol. 46v. Available on the Bodleian Library website.

45 London, British Library, Add. Ms. 42130, fol. 33r, reproduced in J. Backhouse, *The Luttrell Psalter* (London, 1989), p. 49.

46 John Lyly, *Endymion* (1588), ed. D. Bevington (Manchester, 1996), Act 2, scene 2, lines 147–50. The squirrel can also be seen as a heraldic symbol: the Lovell family had squirrels on their coat of arms. Nevertheless, the practice of keeping pet squirrels on chains was well established. The painting is dated to *c.* 1527.

47 London, British Museum, no. 00358545001. Available on the British Museum website.

48 The fragile nature of this object explains why there are few surviving examples. For leather dog collars see G. Egan, *The Medieval Household: Daily Living, c. 1150–c. 1450* (Woodbridge, 2010). The earliest examples at the Leeds Castle Dog Collar Museum date from the sixteenth century and are all large metal collars designed for guard dogs. More delicate metal collars that could have been used on pets in the collection date from the seventeenth century (and later). See *Four Centuries of Dog Collars at Leeds Castle* (Maidstone, 1991).

49 ASMN AG, b. 1438, nos. 351–2. Cf. Brown, *Isabella d'Este and Lorenzo da Pavia*, p. 246. The letter is dated 13 October 1498.

50 London, British Library, Add. Ms. 24686, fol. 13r.

51 See Kelly, *Early Irish Farming*, esp. pp. 120–2, and McCormick, 'The Domesticated Cat in Early Christian and Medieval Ireland'.

52 *Tristan with the Surviving Fragments of the Tristran of Thomas*, p. 256.

53 London, British Library, Add. Ms. 74236, p. 412. The manuscript is dated to *c.* 1400. Available on the British Library website.

54 Oxford, Bodleian Library, Ms. Lat. liturg., fol. 3r. Available on the Bodleian Library website.

55 Schäfer, *Vatikanische Quellen zur Geschichte der päpstlichen Hof- und Finanzverwaltung*, vol. 6, p. 297. The belief in the use of a little iron bar to discipline parrots dates back to classical antiquity, and it is mentioned in Albertus Magnus, *On Animals*, p. 1647.

56 The entire text of 'Speke Parrot' appears in *The Complete Poems of John Skelton*, ed. Henderson, pp. 288–307.

57 Oxford, Bodleian Library, Ms. Bodley 764, fol. 51r.

58 Alfonso X, *Cantigas de Santa Maria*, ed. Mettmann, no. 354.

59 J. Labarte, ed., *Inventaire du mobilier de Charles V* (Paris, 1879), nos. 1900 and 2797. Cf. Franklin, *La Vie privée d'autrefois*, vol. 20, pp. 290–3.

60 Gay, *Glossaire archéologique*, vol. 1, p. 607 (Compte royal de Guill. Brunel, fol. 65v). Cf. Franklin, *La Vie privée d'autrefois*, vol. 20, p. 324.

61 Franklin, *La Vie privée d'autrefois*, vol. 20, p. 325.

62 Gay, *Glossaire archéologique*, vol. 1, p. 324 (Argenterie de la reine, 4e cpte de J. Leblanc, fol. 141v).

63 A. J. V. Le Roux de Lincy, *Vie de la Reine Anne de Bretagne* (Paris, 1860), vol. 4, p. 55.

64 Le Roux de Lincy, *Anne de Bretagne*, vol. 4, p. 57. Cf. H. Carré, *Jeux, sports et divertissements des rois de France* (Paris, 1937), p. 121, and MacDonach, *Reigning Cats and Dogs*, p. 129.

65 Carré, *Jeux, sports et divertissements des rois de France*, p. 121; cf. MacDonach, *Reigning Cats and Dogs*, p. 129.

66 Franklin, *La Vie privée d'autrefois*, vol. 24, ch. 1, pp. 30, 31–3.

67 M. L. Incontri, *Il piccolo levriero italiano* (Florence 1956), p. 68, and G. R. Jesse, *History of the British Dog* (London, 1856), vol. 2, pp. 134–5.

68 London, British Library, Ms. Harley 4431, fol. 3r. Available on the British Library's website.

4 Living with Pets

1 London, British Library, Add. Ms. 18850, fol. 288v.

2 Brussels, Bibliothèque royale, Ms. 9967, fol. 39r. Cf. G. Dogaer, *Flemish Miniature Painting in the 15th and 16th Centuries* (Amsterdam, 1987).

3 The finished oil painting, dated to 1523, is currently in the Hermitage, St Petersburg. The image is reproduced in J. Bonnet, *Lorenzo Lotto* (Paris, 1996), p. 75. Since the man is holding a piece of paper with the inscription 'Homo numquam' ('man never') as he points to the squirrel, Bonnet interprets the squirrel as an animal that chases the female away when food

is scarce 'according to a medieval legend'. This is in direct contrast to the sentiments displayed by the man's paper. In the preparatory sketch by Lotto for the portrait, in pen and ink (now in the Rijksmuseum, Amsterdam) it is not clear whether the artist intended there to be squirrel or another little dog on the table. Cf. P. Humfrey, *Lorenzo Lotto* (New Haven and London, 1997), p. 72.

4 Now in the Prado, Madrid. Reproduced in M. Bussagli, *Bosch* (London, 1967).

5 The illumination is in London, British Library, Add. Ms. 35313, fol. 1v. The manuscript from the South Netherlands is dated to *c.* 1500 and it was illustrated by Gerard Horenbout.

6 Bourgain, *La Chaire française au XIIe siècle*, p. 12, n. 4, from an unpublished sermon (Paris, Bibliothèque nationale de France, Ms Lat. 14934, fol. 82r).

7 H. C. Moffatt, *Old Oxford Plate* (London, 1906), p. 66, pl. xxxiii.

8 *The Chronicle of Salimbene de Adam*, ed. L. Baird, G. Baglini and J. R. Kane (Binghamton, NY, 1986). The Latin text is in *Cronica fratris Salimbene de Adam*, ed. O. Holder-Egger, Monumenta Germaniae Historica, Scriptores, 32 (Hanover, 1826), p. 304d.

9 Heidelberg, Universitätbibliothek, Ms. Col. Pal. Germ. 848, fol. 64r. Available on the University of Heidelberg website.

10 Oxford, Bodleian Library, Ms. Douce 276, fol. 110br–v. Cf. N. Orme, *Medieval Children* (London, 2001), pp. 61–3.

11 Venice, Biblioteca Marciana, Ms. Cod. Marc. Lat. I. 99 (2138), fol. 2v. Reproduced in facsimile in *Breviario Grimani* (Milan, 1971), pl. 3.

12 *The Chronicle of Salimbene de Adam*, p. 182; *Cronica fratris Salimbene de Adam*, p. 191.

13 *The Chronicle of Salimbene de Adam*, p. 614.

14 Orme, *Education and Society in Medieval and Renaissance England*, pp. 80, 83, 85; N. Orme, 'The Culture of Children in Medieval England', *Past and Present* 148 (August 1995), p. 81; Orme, *Medieval Children*, pp. 68 and 137; Thompson, *A Descriptive Catalogue of Middle English Grammatical Texts*, p. 150; E. Relle, 'Some New Marginalia and poems by Gabriel Harvey', *Review of English Studies* 23 (1972), 401–16. The Oxford English Dictionary defines a clog as 'a block or lump tied to anything for use or ornament; e.g. to a key to prevent its being lost'.

15 London, British Library, Ms. Harley 1002, fol. 72r. The text quoted from Orme, 'The Culture of Children in Medieval England', p. 81.

16 London, British Library, Add. Ms. 29433, fol. 20r.

17 The painting is in Santa Maria sopra Mercanti, Recanati. The image is reproduced in Bonnet, *Lorenzo Lotto*, p. 111.

18 F. Zeri, *La pittura in Italia: il Quattrocento* (Milan, 1997), II, p. 430, no. 605.

19 The fresco, *c.* 1320, in the San Francesco Basilica, Assisi, is reproduced in C. Frugoni, *Pietro and Ambrogio Lorenzetti* (Milan, 1993). Other notable images of animals present in the Last Supper are Stefano d'Antonio Vanni's fresco in Sant'Andrea in Cercina, *c.* 1434, which depicts three grey cats in the foreground; Jaime Huguet's painting, *c.* 1450–60, now in the Museu Nacional d'Art de Catalunya (Barcelona), which depicts a single cat under a bench; Domenico Ghirlandaio's fresco in Museo di San Marco, Florence, *c.* 1482 (lone cat in foreground): all are reproduced in *Ultima Cena* (London, 2005), pp. 62–3, 75, 84–5.

20 The fresco is by Giusto de' Menabuoi and reproduced in *Padua: Baptistery of the Cathedral* (Padua, 1994).

21 London, British Library, Add. Ms. 36684, fol. 79v.

22 Modena, Biblioteca Estense, Ms. Lat. 424 (V.G.11), fol. 1r. The manuscript is the Breviary of Ercole I d'Este (1502–4) and this folio is reproduced in G. Malacarne, *Sulla mensa del principe: alimentazione e banchetti alla corte dei Gonzaga* (Modena, 2000), p. 51.

23 *The Boke of Curtasye*, lines 87–8 and 105–7, in F. J. Furnivall, ed., *Early English Meals and Manners* (London, 1868). Also see Labarge, *A Baronial Household of the Thirteenth Century*, pp. 183–4; T. McLean, *The English at Play in the Middle Ages* (Windsor Forest, 1983), p. 139; and T. Wright, *A History of Domestic Manners and Sentiments in England During the Middle Ages* (London, 1862). The line 'ape teyge with a clogge' is a reference to the practice of tying monkeys to blocks of wood to train them.

24 Albertus Magnus, *On Animals*, p. 1457.

25 Musée Condé, Chantilly.

26 Furnivall, *Early English Meals and Manners*, p. 66.

27 E. C. Block, *Corpus of Medieval Misericords: Iberia* (Turnhout, 2004).

28 The painting is part of a series on the life of St Ursula, tempera on canvas, now in the Galleria dell'Academia, Venice. The preparatory sketch is likewise dated to 1495 and is in the Galleria degli Uffizi (Florence). Both are reproduced in J. Lauts, *Carpaccio* (London, 1962), pls. 22 and 23 respectively.

29 The fresco is around the tomb of Niccolò Brenzoni and is dated to 1426. It is reproduced in B. Berenson, *Italian Painters of the Renaissance* (Oxford, 1948), pl. 544.

30 John Gower, *Confessio amantis*, ed. R. A. Peck (Toronto, 1997), p. 207 (book 4, lines 1889–1991).

31 Dijon, Bibliothèque muncipale, Ms. 526. Cf. P. Ariès and G. Duby, ed., *A History of Private Life: Revelations of the Medieval World* (London, 1988), p. 146.

32 *Liber Exemplorum ad usum praedicantium*, ed. A. G. Little (Aberdeen, 1908), nos. 205a and 205b. Cf. Tubach, *Index Exemplorum*, p. 139, no. 1704.

33 A. Wesselski, *Märchen des Mittelalters* (Berlin, 1925), n. 26. Cf. Tubach, *Index Exemplorum*, p. 72, no. 893.

34 *The Register of St Augustine's Abbey Canterbury commonly called the Black Book*, ed. G. J. Turner and H. E. Salter, vol. 1 (Oxford, 1915), p. 283.

35 Johann Wier, *De praestigiis daemonum et incantationibus ac venificiis* (Basel, 1583), II, 5, pp. 165–6. L. Thorndike, *A History of Magic and Experimental Science*, vol. 5 (New York, 1941), pp. 136–7, cites other authors who claimed that Agrippa's pet dog was his familiar. Also see B. A. Woods, *The Devil in Dog Form: A Partial Type-Index of the Devil Legends* (Berkeley, CA, 1959).

36 *Chronicle of Adam Usk*, ed. and trans. C. Given-Wilson (Oxford, 1997), pp. 86–7. The story also appears in Froissart.

37 New York, Pierpont Morgan Library, Ms. 917, fol. 20v. The manuscript is dated to *c.* 1440 and is reproduced in facsimile in *The Hours of Catherine of Cleves*, ed. J. Plummer (New York, 1975).

38 Turin, Museo Civico, Ms. inv. n. 47, fol. 93v, an early fifteenth-century Hours of Milan. Reproduced in Meiss, *French Painting in the Time of Jean de Berry*, pl. 645.

39 Venice, Biblioteca Marciana, Ms. Cod. Marc. Lat. I. 99 (2138), fol. 593v. The breviary is from the Ghent-Bruges school and is reproduced in *Breviario Grimani*, pl. 70.

40 London, British Library, Ms. Royal 20 B.XX, fol. 86r.

41 Translated by R. Flowers, in *The Poem Book of the Gael*, ed. E. Hull (London, 1912)., pp. 132–3 (under the title 'The Student and his Cat').

42 London, British Museum, BM Ivories no. 1856,0623.105 (location: G42/dc6/no41). Cf. O. M. Dalton, *Catalogue of the Ivory Carvings of the Christian Era with Examples of Mohammedan Art and Carvings in Bone in the Department of British and Mediaeval Antiquities and Ethnography of the British Museum* (London, 1909), p. 374. London, Victoria and Albert Museum, Inv. A. 560-1910 (ivory of Paris manufacture, 1320–30). It is reproduced in P. Barnet, ed., *Images in Ivory: Precious Objects of the Gothic Age* (Princeton, 1997), pp. 222–3. Available on the Victoria and Albert Museum website. Other relevant fourteenth-century French ivories include a panel in the Stroganoff Collection (Rome) in which a lady sits with her falcon on one arm while patting a small dog (who is standing on his forelegs) with the other. In a panel in the Kaiser Friedrich Museum, Berlin, a man holds up a hawk while the lady holds a squirrel under her arm. A mirror back in the Martin Le Roy Collection (Paris) depicts a standing couple with the lady holding a small dog under her arm. In a similar mirror back in the British Museum a couple sit on a bench, and a bird is perched on the lady's hand.

43 Paris, Bibliothèque de l'Arsenal, Ms. 5072, fol. 71v. It is reproduced in M. Gousset, *Eden: le jardin medieval a travers l'enluminure, XIIIe–XVIe siecle* (Paris, 2001).

44 London, British Library, Ms. Royal 2B.VII, fol. 200v. Available on the British Library website.

45 London, British Library, Ms. Royal 14E III, fol. 146. Available on the British Library website.

46 G. L. Remnant, *Catalogue of Misericords in Great Britain* (Oxford, 1969), p. 50.

47 *Works of Sir David Lindsay*, vol. 1, pp. 55–90. Cf. McMunn, 'Parrots and Poets in Late Medieval Literature'.

48 London, British Library, Add. Ms. 24098, fols. 20v (construction of garden) and 21v (lovers in a garden). Both available on the British Library website.

49 Venice, Biblioteca Marciana, Ms. Cod. Marc. Lat. I. 99 (2138), fol. 4v. The image is reproduced in *Breviario Grimani*, pl. 7.

50 *La Chastelaine de Vergi*, ed. R. E. V. Stuip (The Hague and Paris, 1970). Cf. Chapter 6 for more details on the romance and see fig. 20.

51 This slightly abridged translation is from *Eustache Deschamps: Selected Poems*, ed. I. S. Laurie and D. M. Sinnreich Levi, trans. D. Curzon and J. Fiskin (New York and London, 2003), pp. 200–1, which also includes the Old French original.

52 Caius, *Of Englishe Dogges*, p. 21.

53 Franklin, *La Vie privée d'autrefois*, vol. 20, pp. 326–7.

54 Franklin, *La Vie privée d'autrefois*, vol. 24, ch. 1. p. 5.

55 London, British Library, Ms. Stowe 17, fol. 106r. The Maastricht Hours is dated to *c.* 1310–20.

56 Franco Sacchetti, *Opere*, ed. A. Borlenghi (Milan, 1957), *Novelle*, no. 47.

57 Cambridge, Fitzwilliam Museum, Ms. 1–200, fol. 58r. This folio is reproduced in S. Panayotova, *The Macclesfield Psalter: A Window into the World of Late Medieval England* (Cambridge, 2005).

58 Paris, Bibliothèque Nationale, Ms. Fr. 143, fol. 198v. Reproduced in M. Camille, *The Medieval Art of Love: Objects and Subjects of Desire* (New York, 1998), p. 72.

59 The painting by Vittore Carpaccio (1460–1526) is now in the Galleria dell'Accademia, Venice. The image is reproduced in Lauts, *Carpaccio*, p. 54.

60 The fresco, dated to *c.* 1427, is in the Brancacci Chapel, Santa Maria del Carmine, in Florence.

61 London, British Library, Add. Ms. 38126, fol. 145v. Dated to *c.* 1485–90, from Bruges. This folio is reproduced in Kren and McKendrick, *Illuminating the Renaissance*, p. 174.

62 Paris, Bibliothèque nationale de France, Ms. Fr. 9136, fol. 344r.

63 Cambridge, Trinity College Library, Ms. 0.1.20, fol. 265r. It is reproduced in Hunt, *The Medieval Surgery*, pp. 76–7.

64 *Cronica fratris Salimbene de Adam*, p. 146. For studies on wild animals in the legend of St Francis, see R. D. Sorrell, *St Francis of Assisi and Nature: Tradition and Innovation in Western Christian Attitudes towards the Environment* (Oxford, 1988) and E. A. Armstrong, *Saint Francis: Nature Mystic* (Los Angeles, 1976)

65 London, British Library, Ms. Stowe 17, fol. 35r. See *Medieval Cats*, p. 35.

66 London, British Library, Ms. Stowe 17, fol. 100r.

67 An example of such topsy-turvy behaviour in Ms. Stowe 17 appears in fol. 38r that depicts a friar playing bellows with a distaff while a nun dances. The manuscript is from the South Netherlands, *c.* 1310–20, and it was probably owned by a woman; fol. 19r depicts a patroness in grey robe with red cloak lined with vier, praying. Like many other books of hours, female ownership may explain the popularity of pets among the images. Other examples of pet dogs in Stowe 17: on fol. 29v a couple embrace while the lady's little fat dog looks up (fig. 18); on fol. 254v a very fat little white dog sits alone with red belled collar and bell.

68 Walter Map, *De nugis curialium*, ed. James, vol. 1, pp. 52–3 (i.17).

69 *Analecta sacri ordinis cisterciensis* 6 (1953), p. 26.

70 M. Thompson, *Cloister, Abbot and Precinct* (Stroud, 2001), p. 142.

71 A. H. Thompson, *Visitations of Religious Houses in the Diocese of Lincoln*, vol. 2 (London, 1969).

72 *Cartulaire de Notre Dame de Paris*, vol. 2 (Paris, 1850), p. 406.

73 From Migne, *Patrologia Latina*, vol. 185, col. 1144 (*Cistercian exordia*), trans. in G. G. Coulton, *Life in the Middle Ages* (Cambridge, 1930), pp. 22–4.

74 *Monasticon Anglicanum*, ed. W. Dugdale, vol. 2 (London, 1846), p. 619.

75 Cole Ms. 23, fol. 96, quoted in A. R. Goddard, 'Ickleton Church and Priory', *Proceedings of the Cambridge Antiquarian Society* 5 (Cambridge, 1904, published in 1907), 190.

76 York, Archiepiscopal Register, Greenfield, fols. 101b and 107b, quoted in *The Victoria History of the Counties of England: Yorkshire*, vol. 3, ed. W. Page (London, 1907–25), pp. 168 and 175.

77 Oxford, New College Ms., ff. 88a and 88b, cited and translated in G. C. Coulton, *Social Life in Britain from the Conquest to the Reformation* (Cambridge, 1918), p. 397 no. c.

78 Dresden, Sächsische Landes- und Universitätsbibliothek, Ms. L. 92 ('Ordinarius'). Cf. L. Eckenstein, *Women under Monasticism* (Cambridge, 1896), p. 415.

79 Odo Rigaldus, *Regestrum visitationum archiepiscopi Rothomagensis*, ed. T. Bonnin (Rouen, 1852), pp. 73, 305, 624, 94, 261, 295 and 602. Cf. *The Register of Eudes of Rouen*, trans., S. M. Brown (New York, 1964).

80 A. Jubien, *L'Abbesse Marie de Bretagne et la réforme de l'ordre de Fontevrault* (Angers-Paris, 1872), p. 156.

81 Kelly, 'A Neo-Revisionist Looks at Chaucer's Nuns', p. 121.

82 London, British Library, Add. Ms. 48978, fol. 47. The account book of Beaulieu Abbey is dated *c.* 1270 and the pen drawing in green ink appears in the top left margin. For an image, see Walker-Meikle, *Medieval Cats*, p. 4.

83 M. Wood, *The Medieval English House* (London, 1965), p. 27.

84 Historical Manuscripts Commission, Rep. IX, app. pt. I, p. 57. Cf. Power, *Medieval English Nunneries*, p. 307.

85 A. Jessop, *Visitations of the Diocese of Norwich, AD 1492–1532*, ed. A. Jessop (London, 1888), p. 191.

86 London, British Library, Ms. Cotton Cleopatra D. viii, fol. 109r–v. The manuscript is dated to the end of the fourteenth century. Cf. Ward, *Catalogue of Romances in the Department of Manuscripts in the British Museum*, vol. 1, pp. 200 and 249, and vol. 3, pp. 638–9.

87 *The Ancrene Riwle*, ed. and trans. M. B. Salu, Part VIII [External Rules] (London, 1955), p. 185.

88 N. Orme, *Exeter Cathedral: The First Thousand Years, 400–1500* (Exeter, 2009), p. 103 (image of cat-hole). For examples of some cathedral cats still *in situ*, see M. M. Howard, 'Dried Cats', *Man* 51 (1951), pp. 149–51.

89 Thompson, *Visitations of Religious Houses*, vol. 2, pp. 175–6 (20 January 1440).

90 Thompson, *Visitations of Religious Houses*, vol. 2, p. 185 (3 July 1440).

91 Newman, 'The "Cattes Tale": A Chaucer Apocryphon', p. 417; *A Revelation of Purgatory by an Unknown, Fifteenth Century Woman Visionary*, ed. M. P. Harley (Lewiston, NY, 1985), pp. 61 and 78. Harley gives the author as a nun from Nunnaminster and dates it to 1422.

92 *The Exempla or Illustrative Stories from the Sermones Vulgares of Jacques de Vitry*, p. 53, no. 194. Cf. J. Mielton, *Miracles de Nostre Dame* (London, 1885), p. 43, and Tubach, *Index Exemplorum*, p. 72, no. 887. The story also occurs in *La tabula exemplorum secundum ordinem alphabeti*, ed. J. T. Welter (Paris and Toulouse, 1926).

93 *Documents relating to the University and Colleges of Cambridge*, vol. 2 (London, 1852), p. 29. Cf. A. Cobban, *English University Life in the Middle Ages* (London, 1999), p. 203.

94 *Statutes of the Colleges of Oxford* (London, 1853), vol. 1, ch. 5, p. 48, and ch. 7, p. 44.

95 *Documents relating to Cambridge*, vol. 2, p. 542.

96 *Statutes of the Colleges of Oxford*, vol. 2, ch. 8, p. 42.

97 *Statutes of the Colleges of Oxford*, vol. 2, ch. 8, p. 68.

98 *Statutes of the Colleges of Oxford*, vol. 1, ch. 4, pp. 18–19. Cf. Cobban, *English University Life*, p. 204.

99 D. Lobineau, *Histoire de la ville de Paris*, vol. 3 (Paris, 1725), p. 39. For Heidelberg's 1453 statute see J. F. Hautz, *Geschichte der Universität Heidelberg*, vol. 2 (Mannheim, 1862–4), p. 393. Cf. H. Rashdall, *The Universities of Europe in the Middle Ages*, vol. 3 (Oxford, 1936), pp. 419 and 421.

5 Pets in Iconography

1 This chapter examines certain common iconographic motifs involving pets. For a general overview of medieval animal iconography, see F. Klingender, *Animals in Art and Thought to the End of the Middle Ages* (London, 1971); A. H. Collins, *Symbolism of Animals and Birds Represented in English Church Architecture* (New York, 1913); and V. H. Debidour, *Le Bestaire sculpté du Moyen Âge en France* (Paris, 1961).

2 This position summed up in P. Gathercole, *Animals in Medieval French Manuscript Illumination* (Lewiston, NY, 1995), p. 5.

3 H. W. Macklin, *Monumental Brasses: Portfolio Plates of the Monumental Brass Society* (London, 1953), no. 10. Similar individual brass of a lady appear on no. 70, depicting Lady Roos, *c.* 1390, with her small dog and no. 72, *c.* 1390, of an unknown lady from Holme Pierrepoint, Nottinghamshire, with a small dog half hidden in the hem of her gown.

4 Macklin, *Monumental Brasses*, no. 37.

5 Macklin, *Monumental Brasses*, no. 95. Other relevant plates are no. 69, Robert Albyn on a lion and wife, Margaret, with small dog, *c.* 1390; no. 71, a Northampton civilian and wife, he with a hound, she, with two little dogs; no. 74, John Curteys with hound and widow Aubrey with two little dogs, *c.* 1391; no. 78, Thomas de Topclyff, standing on a lion, his wife Mabel with a small dog on her robe, *c.*1291; no. 79, Thomas, Lord Berkeley, stands on a lion, while his wife Margaret has a small dog on her hem, *c.*1392; no. 94, a civilian from Tilbrook, Beds., on a hound, with his wife, who has small belled dog on her hem, *c.* 1400); no. 122, Sir Thomas Skelton, on a lion, with his wives Margaret and Katherine, both of whom have small little dogs on the hems of their gowns.

6 The joint tomb was formerly in the church of Saint-Pierre, Lille. There is an engraving in A. L. Millin de Grandmaison, *Antiquités nationales; ou, recueil de monuments pour servir à l'histoire de l'empire français* (Paris, 1790), vol. 5, pl. 4.

7 The effigy of Anne of Burgundy was part of a wall tomb commissioned by her brother, Phillip the Good of Burgundy in 1435–6 and is now in the Musée du Louvre (originally in the Celestine Church in Paris). See J. C. Smith, 'The Tomb of Anne of Burgundy, Duchess of Bedford, in the Musée du Louvre', *Gesta* 23:1 (1984), pp. 39–50 (the dogs are visible in Smith's fig. 1, which is a reproduction of the effigy).

8 For images of the tomb see A. M. Roberts, 'The Chronology and Political Significance of the Tomb of Mary of Burgundy', *The Art Bulletin* 71:3 (1989), pp. 376–400 (with plates), esp. p. 377. The Hours of Mary of Burgundy is Vienna, Österreichische Nationalbibliothek, Ms. 1857, fol. 14v. The manuscript, from Bruges, is dated to *c.* 1467–80; this illumination is reproduced in Dogaer, *Flemish Miniature Painting in the 15th and 16th Centuries*, pl. 14. The stained glass panel of Mary of Burgundy, *c.* 1496, is now in the Victoria and Albert Museum (Inv. no. C.439-1918).

9 'On Certain Rare Monumental Effigies', *Transactions of the Bristol and Gloucestershire Archaeological Association*, xxv (1902), p. 99. 'Terri' is a shortened form of 'terrier'.

10 Details of this effigy were supplied by Dr Malcolm Jones of the University of Sheffield.

11 C. Platt, *Abbeys of Yorkshire* (London, 1988); cf. C. Reeves, *Pleasures and Pastimes in Medieval England* (Stroud, 1995), p. 126.

12 Grössinger, *The World Upside-Down*, p. 135, pl. 196.

13 I have only examined in detail French and English personal seals in the collection of the British Library for this section, due the large number of seals extant in collections across Europe. There is considerable scope for future research into the presence of pets in seals elsewhere, in order to ascertain any regional variations or motifs. Animals that can be clearly identified as pets appear in approximately 5–10% of English and French personal seals of women examined.

14 London, British Library, Seal LXXVIII.61. W. de G. Birch, *Catalogue of Seals in the Department of Manuscripts in the British Museum* (London, 1892), vol. 2, p. 380 no. 6606.

15 London, British Library, Seal XCVI.90. Birch, *Catalogue*, vol. 5, p. 659, no. 19850.

16 London, British Library, Seal CXXIX.134. Birch, *Catalogue*, vol. 5, p. 639, no. 19811.

17 London, British Library, Seal LXXX. 18. Birch, *Catalogue*, vol. 2, p. 393, no. 6686.

18 London, British Library, Add. Ms. 23355. Birch, *Catalogue*, vol. 2, p. 375, no. 6577.

19 London, British Library, Seal LXXX.32. Birch, *Catalogue*, vol. 2, p. 394, no. 6691. The same seal is reproduced in the plate section of R. K. Ellis, *Catalogue of Seals in the Public Record Office: Personal Seals* (London, 1978), vol. 2, with accompaning text on p. 77 (reference P1805).

20 London, British Library, Add. Ms. 21451. Birch, *Catalogue*, vol. 2, pp. 394–5, no. 6692.

21 London, British Library, Ms. Harley 83 F.12. Birch, *Catalogue*, vol. 2, p. 388, no. 6658. Cf. P. Coss, *The Lady in Medieval England, 1000–1500* (Stroud, 1998), p. 38.

22 London, British Library, Seal CXXIX.44. Birch, *Catalogue*, vol. 5, p. 651 no. 19835.

23 London, British Library, Seal LXXX.14. Birch, *Catalogue*, vol. 5, p. 393, no. 6685.

24 London, British Library, Ms. Harley 58.C.5. Birch, *Catalogue*, vol. 2, p. 383 no. 6623. The inscription on the small anonymous seal reads VN✦BRACHET✦OV✦MOVN✦QVER✦EST. A 'brachet' is a small hound, frequently turned into a pet dog and owned by a lady, which makes this inscription an interesting puzzle.

25 London, British Library, Ms. Harley 4431, fol. 3r. The manuscript is a 'Collected Works of Christine de Pisan', dated to *c.* 1410–11. Available on the British Library website.

26 The illumination is in Nantes, Musée Dobrée, Ms. 17, fol. 1r. The manuscript is dated to *c.* 1505. Cf. Franklin, *La Vie privée d'autrefois*, vol. 24, p. 35.

27 Quoted from V. Dickenson, 'Meticulous Depiction: Animals in Art, 1400–1600', in *A Cultural History of Animals in the Renaissance*, ed. B. Boehrer (Oxford and New York, 2007), pp. 190–5.

28 The oil painting with the parrot is now in the Walker Art Gallery, Liverpool (accession no. WAG1308). The pastel portrait is now in the Musée Condé, Chantilly (inventory no. MN 44).

29 For an essay on female ownership of books of hours, see S. G. Bell, 'Medieval Women Book Owners: Arbiters of Lay Piety and Ambassadors of Culture', *Signs: Journal of Women in Culture and Society* 7:4 (1982), pp. 742–68.

30 This book of hours, from Amiens (France), is dated to *c.* 1280–90 and is now New York, Pierpont Morgan Library, Ms. M.729, fol. 232v. The full-page miniature is reproduced in R. S. Wieck, *Painted Prayers: The Book of Hours in Medieval and Renaissance Art* (New York, 1997), p. 11.

31 London, British Library, Add. Ms. 36684. The manuscript is of northern French production, possibly from Thérouanne, and is dated to *c.* 1330; the calendar section comprises Saint-Omer saints.

32 There are four illuminations of the lady owner praying in the presence of the pet dog, compared to two (fols. 43v and 46v) in which she prays alone.

33 The oil painting is dated to 1521, and is now in the Staatliche Museen, Berlin. The painting is believed to have been commissioned by the Tassi family in Bergamo and the woman has been identified as Elisabetta Rota, the wife of Domenico Tassi. The painting is reproduced in Humfrey, *Lorenzo Lotto*, p. 56, which also gives details of the sitter.

34 The manuscript, from Utrecht, is dated to *c.* 1440, and is now New York, Pierpont Morgan Library, Ms. M.917. It is reproduced in facsmile in *The Hours of Catherine of Cleves*, ed. Plummer, p. 160.

35 Vienna, Österreichische Nationalbibliothek, Ms. 1857, fol. 14v. The manuscript, from Bruges, is dated to *c.* 1467–80; this illumination is reproduced in Dogaer, *Flemish Miniature Painting in the 15th and 16th Centuries*, pl. 14.

36 Brussels Bibliothèque Royale, Ms. 9272–76, fol. 182r. The manuscript is dated to *c.* 1475–9. In an illumination of another manuscript owned by Margaret of York she kneels in front of the Risen Christ while the foreground a dog sleeps unaware of the significance of the scene: London, British Library, Add. Ms. 7970, fol. 1v. Both folios are reproduced in Kren and McKendrick, *Illuminating the Renaissance*, pp. 161 and 216.

37 Vienna, Österreichische Nationalbibliothek, Ms. 1897, fol. 243v. The manuscript, made in Ghent or Bruges, is dated to *c.* 1503. This illumination is reproduced in C. De Hamel, *A History of Illuminated Manuscripts* (London, 1994), pl. 148. The iconographic scheme is similar to an illumination in the Breviary of Eleanor of Portugal, as Eleanor prays to the Virgin alongside her dog in New York, Pierpont Morgan Library, Ms. 52, fol. 4. The manuscript, from Ghent, is dated to *c.* 1500–10. This folio is reproduced in Kren and McKendrick, *Illuminating the Renaissance*, p. 323.

38 For dogs and melancholy, see see C. F. Hefferman, 'That Dog Again: Melancholia Canina and Chaucer's Book of the Duchess', *Modern Philology* 84:2 (1986), pp. 185–90. Notable depictions of Melancholy accompanied by a canine companion are Durer's engraving 'Melancholia' (1514), reproduced in G. Bartrum, *German Renaissance Prints, 1490–1550* (London, 1995), pp. 46–8, no. 33, and Lucas Cranach the Elder's 'Melancholia' (1528, National Gallery of Scotland).

39 P. Reutersward, 'The Dog in the Humanist's Study', *Konsthistorisk tidskrift* 50 (1981), pp. 53–69. See Basil of Caesarea's Homelia IX.4 in *Homelies sur l'Hexaemeron*, ed. and trans. S. Giet (Paris, 1950), p. 501. On verbal imagery and the iconography of the dog, representing logic, dialectic, invention and imagination, see also K. J. Höltgen, 'Clever Dogs and Nimble Spaniels: On the Iconography of Logic, Invention, and Imagination', *Explorations in Renaissance Culture* 24 (1998), pp. 1–36. Reutersward also discusses the belief of canine supernatural awareness, observed previously in Lipsius's *laus canis* when he writes of *divinatio* power of dogs. Reutersward does not

deny that the depictions of dogs could also be representations of pets. His article is an superb source on iconography and symbolism on the scholar and his dog. For a general overview of canine symbolism, particularly in regard to the virtue of fidelity, see Rowland, *Animals with Human Faces*, pp. 58–66.

40 For the general symbolism of cats (association with heresy, the Devil, etc.), see Rowland, *Animals with Human Faces*, pp. 50–2, and K. H. Rogers, *The Cat and the Human Imagination: Feline Images from Bast to Garfield* (Ann Arbor, MI, 2001), pp. 45–8.

41 Darmstadt, Universitäts- und Landesbibliothek, Ms. Cod. 101, fol. 1v. The pose is very similar to the depiction of Petrarch in the Sala dei Giganti, Padua, from which it was probably copied. The latter is set in an open balcony while here the setting is a closed study. The dog adopts exactly the same position. The image is reproduced in T. E. Mommsen, 'Petrarch and the Decoration of the Sala Virorum Illustrium in Padua', *The Art Bulletin* 34:2 (1952), pl. 5.

42 Milan, Biblioteca Trivulaziana, Ms. 905, fol. 1v. The image is reproduced in Trapp, 'Petrarch's Inkstand and his Cat', p. 37, pl. 6.

43 The fresco is reproduced in Mommsen, 'Petrarch and the Decoration of the Sala Virorum Illustrium in Padua', pl. 3.

44 The fresco depicts 'St George drinking the poison' but includes portraits of many contemporary scholars. The detail of Petrarch in the fresco is reproduced in D. Bobisut and L. Gumiero Salomoni, *Altichiero da Zevio: Cappella di San Giacomo, Oratorio di San Giorgio* (Padua, 2002), p. 57.

45 London, British Library, Ms. Harley 3567, fol. 9r. Available on the British Library Illuminated Manuscripts Online Catalogue.

46 Reutersward, 'The Dog in the Humanist's Study', p. 55 reproduced this image (current whereabouts of manuscript unknown).

47 Reutersward, 'The Dog in the Humanist's Study', p. 55, reproduces this image and quotes the author's instructions to the artist. These include the inscription 'my dog' for the animal that appears in the engraving. The same article reproduces several images of scholars with dogs: e.g. fig. 12 is an engraving of the astronomer Tycho Brahe with his dog in his *Astronomiae instauratae mechanica* (1598).

48 San Marino, Huntingdon Library, Ms. HM 268, fol. 153. This illumination is reproduced in K. Scott, *Later Gothic Manuscripts* (London, 1996).

49 The painting is reproduced with further details in H. L. Roberts, 'St. Augustine in "St. Jerome's Study": Carpaccio's Painting and Its Legendary Source', *The Art Bulletin* 41:4 (1959), pp. 283–97.

50 Master of St Augustine (Bruges) 'Section of Scenes from the Life of St Augustine' (*c.* 1490) in the Metropolitan Museum of Art, Cloisters Collection, New York.

51 In the National Gallery, London, inv. NG1418. The image is reproduced in R. Weiss, 'Some Van Eyckian Illuminations from Italy', *Journal of the Warburg and Courtauld Institutes* 18 (1955), pl. a.

52 Hatfield House, Ms. Cecil Papers 324, fol. 4. The manuscript was illuminated by either Lucas or Susanna Horenbout in England and is dated to *c.* 1528–33. This folio is reproduced in Kren and McKendrick, *Illuminating the Renaissance*, p. 425.

53 London, British Library, Add. Ms. 35313 fol. 16r

6 Pets in Literature

1 The episode is described most extensively in Gottfried von Strassburg's thirteenth century Tristan. See the Middle High German original (with a modern German translation) in *Gottfried von Strassburg, Tristan*, ed. Rüdiger and Ranke, ch. 25, lines 15765–16402. An English prose translation can be found in *Tristan with the Surviving Fragments of the Tristran of Thomas*, pp. 249–56. The episode also occurs in the *Roman de Tristan par Thomas*, ed. J. Bedier (Paris, 1902–5), pp. 217–31. However, Gottfried's version is the only surviving one that has Isolde breaking the bell. A study of the two dogs in the Tristan romance (Petitcreiu and Tristan's hound Huidan) can be found in Gnaedinger, *Hiudan und Petitcreiu*.

2 *Tristan with the Surviving Fragments of the Tristran of Thomas*, p. 256.

3 H. Cooper, 'Magic that does not work', *Medicialia et Humanisiica* 7 (1976), pp. 131–46, esp. p. 14. Cooper remarks that this is possibly the only episode in medieval romance in which magic is destroyed on purpose.

4 This misericord is dated to *c.* 1370–80 and is reproduced in Grössinger, *The World Upside*, p. 148, pl. 222. Apart from the little dog in the waiting woman's arm, between the lovers in the carving there appears to be another dog, probably Huidan, Tristan's loyal hound.

5 This misericord is dated to *c.* 1380–90: Grössinger, *The World Upside*, p. 149, pl. 223. As is the case with the Lincoln cathedral misericord, the right supporter depicts a waiting women holding a small dog. Grössinger notes these two as the only known surviving Tristan and Isolde misericords in England.

6 The ivory casket, carved in Paris, is dated to *c.* 1325–50 and is now in the British Museum (Department of Medieval and Modern Europe 1856,6-23166). This casket is reproduced in Barnet, *Images in Ivory*, pp. 245–8, along with a similar ivory casket from the same period depicting the same scene from the Walters Art Gallery, Baltimore. Other ivory carvings of the same scene appear in R. S. Loomis, *Arthurian Legends in Medieval Art* (New York, 1938): pl. 122 (ivory casket, Metropolitan Museum of New York, 1999, almost identical to the British museum casket); pls. 123 (Vatican Library) and 124 (Musée de Cluny) are two ivory mirror cases

which have Isolde holding Petitcreiu. An ivory hair parter, pl. 125 (Museo Civico, Turin) has the lovers standing with Isolde tucking Petitcreiu under her arm. All these ivories are French, dating from 1325–40.

7 Munich, Bayerische Staatsbibliothek, Ms. Cgm 51, fol. 82v. See the facsimile *Tristan und Isolde: Faksimile-Ausgabe des Cgm 51 der Bayerischen Staatsbibliothek, München* (Stuttgart, 1979).

8 See A. Classen, 'The Dog in German Courtly Literature', pp. 78–82, on the two dogs in Gottfried von Strassburg's *Tristan*.

9 *Lancelot of the Laik and Sir Tristrem*, ed. A. Lupack (Kalamazoo, MI, 1997), lines 1693–5.

10 Guillaume Machaut, *Le Jugement dou roy de Behaigne*, ed. and trans. J. I. Wimsatt and W. W. Kibler (Athens, GA, 1988), pp. 62–3.

11 Geoffrey Chaucer, *The Book of the Duchess*, lines 387–96 (*The Riverside Chaucer*, p. 335). Cf. J. B. Friedman, 'The Dreamer, The Whelp, and Consolation in the Book of the Duchess', *The Chaucer Review* 3 (1969), pp. 145–62. On the dog and melancholy, see Hefferman, 'That Dog Again', pp. 185–90. The dog is not always seen as a docile and helpful beast, see B. Rowland, 'The Whelp in Chaucer's Book of the Duchess', *Neulogische Mitteilungen* 66 (1965), p. 150.

12 For the swan as a go-between the lovers see the lais of 'Milun' in *The Lais of Marie de France*, ed. and trans. K. Busby and G. S. Burgess (London, 1999), pp. 97–104.

13 Arnaut de Carcasses, *Las novas del papaguay* in *Les Troubadours*, ed. Lavaud and Nelli, vol. 2, pp. 214–35. Cf. Thiolier-Méjean, 'Le Motif du perroquet dans deux nouvelles d'oc'.

14 *Le Chevalier du Papegau*, ed. Heuckenkamp. Cf. McMunn, 'Parrots and Poets in Late Medieval Literature'.

15 The 'petit chienet' appears in the romance in *La Châtelaine de Vergi*, ed. J. Dufournet and L. Dulac (Paris, 1994), pp. 34, 60, 62, 82, 86, 88, 100, 102 (lines 33–5, 355–8, 379–83, 651–4, 715–18, 735–6, 879–82, 908–9).

16 Camille, *The Medieval Art of Love*, p. 102.

17 Ivory casket, Paris, *c.* 1325–50, British Museum Department of Medieval and Modern Europe 1892,0801.47. Another fourteenth-century French ivory casket that depicts the same Romance is in the Metropolitan Museum of New York (n. 17.190.177), in which the dog appears in every panel. Reproduced in Barnet, *Images in Ivory*, pp. 242–4.

18 Reproduced in J. Holdeweij, 'The Wearing of Significance Badges, Religious and Secular: The Social Meaning of a Medieval Pattern', in *Showing Status: Representations of Social Positions in the Late Middle Ages*, ed. W. Blockmans and A. Janse (Turnhout, 1999), p. 314. Dogs are not an unusual subject for medieval badges; Holdeweij reproduces (p. 309) the image of another lead-tin badge from fourteenth-century France in the

form of a dog with a decorated collar and with the motto: 'Bien aia qui me porte'.

19 Machaut, *Le Jugement dou roy de Behaigne*, ed. Wimsatt and Kibler, pp. 120–1.

20 The text of this tale is printed in E. Gorra, 'La novella della dama e dei tre papagalli', *Romania* 32 (1892), pp. 71–8; see also *Romania* 26, pp. 565–9 and 29, pp. 109–12. Literary antecedents and discussion can be found in L. W. Yoder, 'The Late Medieval Tale: The Example of "La Dame e les trois papegaulz"', *The French Review* 53:4 (1980), pp. 543–9.

21 The tapestries are now exhibited in the Musée nationale du Moyen Âge, Paris. Reproduced in Erlande-Brandenburg, *La Dame à la licorne* [without plate numbers].

22 Alberti's *Muscae encomium* is based on *Musca*, which in Alberti's time was accepted as written by Lucian, although there is doubt now regarding its attribution. Cf. A. H. Tomarken, *The Smile of Truth: The French Satirical Eulogy and its Antecedents* (Princeton, 1990), which discusses the genre of mock-encomium, from its classical origins, through the works of the Italian Neo-Latinists to members of the French Pléiade.

23 M. Jarzombek, *On Leon Battista Alberti, his Literary and Aesthetic Theories* (Cambridge., MA, 1989), p. 90. J. Gadol, *Leon Battista Alberti: Universal Man of the Early Renaissance* (Chicago, 1969), pp. 7 and 220.

24 See Tomarken, *The Smile of Truth*, p. 76. The author groups *Canis* along with all other animal mock-encomia although acknowledging that 'the praise of household pets is not of necessity comical', p. 76.

25 Leon Battista Alberti, *Apologhi ed elogi*, ed. Contarino, pp. 142–69, esp. pp. 144 and 168.

26 The epitaphs and elegies that I discuss are those that appear to refer clearly to a pet. Thus I am not examining certain dog poems in which the function of the dog is in doubt, such as Francisco Cameono's *Epitaphium Bandere*, which describes the dog as a 'venatrix' (hunter) or the Veronese John Cotta's *Epitaphium Canis* for a dog called Caparion which emphasizes the dog's qualities as a guard-dog rather than as a companion. See *Carmina illustrum poetarum Italorum* (Florence, 1719), vol. 3, pp. 115 and 496–7. For an overview of the genre of Renaissance epitaphs, see I. D. McFarlane, 'The Renaissance Epitaph', *The Modern Language Review* 81:4 (1986), pp. xxv–xxxv.

27 For example, in Cesare Orsini's 'Alla gatta uccisa' uses mixture of Latin, Italian and Latinized Italian (Italian with Latin declined endings). O. Targioni Tozzetti, ed., *Antologia della poesia italiana* (Livorno, 1916), p. 624.

28 Catullus's *Carmina* II and III (both regarding Lesbia's pet sparrow) were used as a model for pet elegies. Catullus was rediscovered in the early fourteenth century and his poems were widely imitated by Italian scholars and poets. A good survey is provided in Morrison, 'Catullus in

the Neo-Latin Poetry of France before 1550'. The most influential texts by other classical authors for the genre of animal elegies were Ovid's *Amores* (Book II.6 on Corinna's dead parrot), Statius's *Silvae* (Book II.4, on his friend Atedius Melior's dead parrot) and Martial's *Epigrams* (Book I.109, on Publius's little dog Issa). For a study on the first two, see J. S. Dietrich, 'Dead Parrots Society', *American Journal of Philology* 123:1 (2002), pp. 95–110. The *Planudean Anthology* was first printed in Florence in 1494. J. Hutton, *The Greek Anthology in Italy to the year 1800* (Ithaca, NY, 1935) traces the influence of the *Planudean Anthology* (and the later *Palatine Anthology*) on the works of Italian scholars. There are several sepulchral epitaphs (mainly Hellenistic) for animals (on dogs, tame patridges, etc.) that served as inspiration for scholars knowledgable in Greek when composing elegies. For numerous examples, see *The Greek Anthology*, ed. W. R. Paton (London, 1916–18), vol. 2, book VII.

29 The epitaph appears with slight variations in different manuscripts; see F. Rico, 'Perro(s) de Petrarca', in *Patio de letras/La rosa als llavis* (Barcelona, 1984), pp. 125–8. Rico attempts to associate 'Zabot' with the dog given to Petrarch by Cardinal Colonna, which apparently came from the Spanish royal court, but this seems unlikely from the emphasis Petrarch puts in Epistolae Metricae III 5 on the dog's large size, which does not concord with the description of little 'Zabot'. The naturalist Ulisse Aldrovandi seemed to have had his doubts on the epitaph's provenance, and gave a version of it as a 'Roman epitaph' in his *De quadripedibus digitatis viviparis* (Bologna, 1537), p. 525. This is the same version (which does not refer to 'Zabot' by name) that appears in K. Burdach, *Aus Petrarcas ältestem Schülerkreise* (Berlin, 1929).

30 'Varietà: Jacopo Corsi e il Tebaldeo', *Giornale storico della letteratura italiana* 17 (1891), pp. 395–6.

31 Nightingales are also a popular subject for elegies, as are parrots, following Ovid and Statius. An example of Catullan influence are to be found in epitaphs on his lady's sparrow by the early sixteenth-century French poet Nicholas Bourbon: see M. Morrison, 'Catullus in the Neo-Latin Poetry of France before 1550', *Bibliothèque d'Humanisme et Renaissance* 27 (1955), p. 379. Morrison emphasizes the influence of Catullan style (hendecasyllables and iambics) on many poets, with some mannerisms such as the frequent use of terms of endearment.

32 Aldrovandi, *De quadripedibus digitatis viviparis*, p. 524. The final hope of a new star imitates many classical epitaphs.

33 Aldrovandi, *De quadripedibus digitatis viviparis*, p. 524.

34 Aldrovandi, *De quadripedibus digitatis viviparis*, pp. 524–5.

35 Ercole Strozzi, *Carmina borgetti canis*, in *Carmina illustrum poetarum Italorum*, vol. 3, pp. 181–7.

36 The influence of the Greek Anthology in Navagero's work is discussed in Hutton, *The Greek Anthology in Italy to the year 1800*, pp. 189–92. Hutton,

however, does not discuss *In obitum Borgetti catuli*, which appears to be influenced mostly by Catullus's *Carmen III*. *Catullus: A Critical Edition*, ed. D. F. S. Thomson (Chapel Hill, NC, 1978), pp. 74–5.

37 Andre Navegero, *In obitum Borgetti catuli*, in *Carmina illustrum poetarum Italorum*, vol. 6, pp. 494–5. For the allusions to *Carmen III*, see *Catullus: A Critical Edition*, pp. 74–5. Navegero wrote another poem for Borgettus, *Dum volui domini*, reprinted in C. Spila and M. G. Critell, *Cani di pietra: l'epicedio canino nella poesia del Rinascimento* (Rome, 2002), pp. 48–9, which also includes (pp. 21–2) *Borgetti canis urna haec est*, a poem for Borgettus by Angelo Colocci (1474–1549).

38 Pietro Gherardo, *Epitaphium catellae*, in *Carmina illustrum poetarum Italorum*, vol. 5, p. 291.

39 Cesare Orsini, *Alla gatta uccisa*, in Targioni Tozzetti, *Antologia della poesia italiana*, p. 624.

40 The Pléiade was the group of sixteenth-century French writers associated with Pierre de Ronsard. For more on animal poems by members of the Pléiade, many of them not specficially related to recognizable pets, see H. Naïs, *Les Animaux dans la poésie française de la Renaissance* (Paris, 1961) and A. Lytton Sells, *Animal Poetry in French & English Literature & the Greek Tradition* (Bloomington, IN, 1955), pp. 56–75.

41 Francesco Coppetta Beccuti and Giovanni Guidiccioni, *Rime*, ed. E. Chiorboli (Bari, 1912), pp. 307–10.

42 Tomarken, *The Smile of Truth*, pp. 205–8.

43 Joachim du Bellay, *Diverses jeux rustiques*, ed. V. L. Saulnier (Lille and Geneva, 1947), pp. 104–10.

44 J. C. Scaliger, in *Caspar Dornavius, Amphitheatrum sapientiae Socraticae joco-seria joc est encomia et commentaria autorum* (Hanover, 1619), p. 529. Dornavius' book is a huge compedium of animal encomia, elegies and other poetical compositions among other subjects. It includes J. Moshaim's fifteenth-century long encomium on dogs and John Caius's work on English dogs, as well as many of the elegies discussed here (such as Navegero's epitaph to Borgettus). Other pet elegies not analysed here but that can be found in Dornavius are Johanne Plazzon Servallensi's *De catella mortua ad Sirum*; Jo. Joviano Pontano's *Elogiam canis*, and Joannis Posthii's *De obitum bellinae catellae*. Other pet elegies can be found in the individual collections of sixteenth-century scholars' works, for example, Aonio Paleario's composition for a little dog called Ursula (*De Ursulae catello mortuo*) in *Aonii Palearii Vervlani: Opera* (Jena, 1728), pp. 715–18.

45 Theodore Beza, in *Dornavius, Amphitheatrum sapientiae Socraticae*, p. 529.

46 Tomarken, *The Smile of Truth*, pp. 205–8.

47 Naïs, *Les Animaux dans la poésie française de la Renaissance*, p. 594. Ronsard had nicer things to say on dogs, see *ibid.*, p. 605.

48 *Les Œuvres de François Maynard*, ed. M. Leroy de Gomberville (Paris, 1646).

49 Justus Lipsius, *Epistolarum selectarum centuria miscellanea*, vol. 5 (Antwerp, 1605–7), p. 62; A. Miraeus, *Vita Iusti Lipsi sapientiae et litterarum antistitis* (Antwerp 1609), p. 62; and *Iusti Lipsi epistolae*, vol. 13, ed. J. Papy (Brussels, 2000), p. 65. Cf. Papy, 'Lipsius and his Dogs', p. 167.

50 Justus Lipsius, *Epistolicarum quaestionum libri V, in quis ad varios scriptores, pleraeque ad T. Livium, Notae* (Antwerp, 1577), p. 95. Cf. Papy, 'Lipsius and his Dogs', p. 172. I have been unable to find mention of any feline epitaphs or monuments in Celio Calcagnini's scholarly works or verse; the only pet elegy of his that seems to survive is one written for Isabella d'Este on the death of her dog Aura in 1511. Cf. A. Lazzari, *Un enciclopedico del secolo XVI: Celio Calcagnini* (Ferrara, 1936).

51 Sixtus Octavianus, *Phaselus Catulli, et ad eum quotquot exstant paroediae, cum annotationibus doctissimorum vivorum. Accesserunt alia quadam eiusdem generis* (Antwerp, 1579), pp. 33–4. Cf. Papy, 'Lipsius and his Dogs', p. 172, which furnishes a translation.

52 *Iusti Lipsi epistolae*, vol. 13, pp. 51–67. First published in Justus Lipsius, *Epistolarum centuriae ad Belgas* (Antwerp, 1602), I.44.

53 *Iusti Lipsi epistolae*, vol. 13, p. 55. They are similar to the canine virtues lauded by Rudbert von Mosham (1493–1543) in his *Encomium canis*: these were memory (*memoria*), aptitude (*docilitas*), sagacity (*sagacitas*) and loyalty (*fidelitas*), which could also apply to the scholar.

54 For example on faithfulness (*fides*), *Iusti Lipsi epistolae*, vol. 13, p. 62. Lipsius uses his dogs Mopsus and Mopsulus to exemplify cleverness, *ingenium* (*ibid.*, pp. 58 and 60 respectively).

55 *Iusti Lipsi epistolae*, vol. 13, p. 65. All these compositions were also published in Franciscus Sweertius, *Selectae Christiani orbis deliciae urbibus, temples, bibliothecis et aliunde* (Cologne, 1608), pp. 481–3, which includes a large collection of assorted canine elegies.

56 *Iusti Lipsi epistolae*, vol. 13, p. 64.

57 *Iusti Lipsi epistolae*, vol. 13, pp. 65–6.

58 *Iusti Lipsi epistolae*, vol. 13, p. 66.

59 As mentioned previously, Lipsius's biographer claimed Mopsus accompanied Lipsius when he was lecturing: Miraeus, *Vita Iusti Lipsi*, p. 62.

60 *Iusti Lipsi epistolae*, vol. 13, p. 66.

61 *Iusti Lipsi epistolae*, vol. 13, p. 66.

62 *Lipsius, Epistolarum centuriae ad Belgas*, III.89. Cf. Papy, 'Lipsius and his Dogs', p. 168.

63 *Lipsius, Epistolarum centuriae ad Belgas*, III.89. Cf. Papy, 'Lipsius and His Dogs', p. 168.

64 François Garasse, *La Doctrine curieuse des beaux esprits de ce temps, ou prétendus tels* (Paris, 1623), pp. 903–4 (VIII.17). Cf. Papy, 'Lipsius and his Dogs', p. 169.

65 Writing elegies for one's pet is a practice that has not disappeared completely in scholarly tomes even today. Two volumes of Alfred Franklin's monumental work *La Vie privée d'autrefois* (Paris, 1887–1902) which deal with animals (vols. 20 and 25) are dedicated to 'the memory of my dog Toby, my dear and faithful friend for fourteen years', while Nona C. Flores, the editor of the collection of essays *Animals in the Middle Ages* (London, 1996) writes in the preface that 'This collection is dedicated in memoriam to Homer, a dachshund 'of infinite jest, of most excellent fancy'.

66 Marguerite of Austria (1480–1530), daughter of Maximillian I, Holy Roman Emperor and Mary of Burgundy. Widowed (for the second time) on the death of her husband Philibert II, Duke of Savoy in 1504.

67 Thiolier-Méjean, 'Le Motif du perroquet dans deux nouvelles d'oc', p. 1358, n. 16. Cf. McMunn, 'Parrots and Poets in Late Medieval Literature', p. 71.

68 On parrots in classical literature, see Dietrich, 'Dead Parrots Society'.

69 Lemaire, *Les Épîtres de l'amant vert*, ed. Frappier, pp. 1–7 (lines 1–380). The first epistle ends with the four-line epitaph: 'Soubz ce tumbel, qui est ung dur conclave, / Git l'Amant Vert et le tresnoble esclave, / Dont le hault cueur, de vraye amour pure yvre, / Ne peut souffrir perdre sa dame, et vivre'. Cf. Tomarken, *The Smile of Truth*, pp. 200–1. Tomarken remarks that despite the use of a model, the work is not a parody but the author's sincere contribution for his patron.

70 Lemaire, *Les Épîtres de l'amant vert*, ed. Frappier, pp. 18–37 (lines 1–576).

71 The parrot is dying as writes the epistles, having been blown off a tree by a gust of wind. *Works of Sir David Lindsay*, ed. D. Hammer (Edinburgh, 1931–6), vol. 1, pp. 55–90. Cf. McMunn, 'Parrots and Poets in Late Medieval Literature', and J. Smith, *The French Backgrounds of Middle Scots Literature* (London and Edinburgh, 1934), pp. 135–6. On a final note on parrot poems, J. Ziolkowski, 'Tito Vespasiano Strozzi's "Ad psyttacum": A Renaissance Latin Poet Parrots the Past', *Harvard Library Bulletin* 35:2 (1987), pp. 139–49, points out the uniqueness of Strozzi's poem (to his dead mistress's parrot). Unlike all its classical antecedents on dead bird poems (Ovid, Catullus, Statius), Strozzi's poem is addressed to a living parrot, with a dead owner, a complete reversal of the usual role.

72 Pierre de Ronsard, *Œuvres complètes*, ed. P. Laumonier (Paris, 1914–75), vol. 14, pp. 110–14, and vol. 9, n. 17. Cf. P. Laumonier, *Ronsard, poète lyrique: étude historique et littéraire* (Paris, 1909), p. 265. Jean Passerat (1534–1602) was another Pléiade poet who wrote pet epigrams such as *Epitaphe du Barbichon de Madame de Villeroy* (for Barbichon the pet dog of Madeleine d'Aubespine) and *Ode funebre sur la mort d'un petit chien*, edited in *Les*

Poésies françaises de J. Passerat (Paris, 1880), vol. 2, pp. 114–15, 126–7. Amadis Jamyn (1538–92) also wrote a poem on Barbichon the dog, in which the dead pet addresses its mistress from the underworld, *Œuvres de Jamin* (Paris, 1577).

73 Du Bellay, *Diverse jeux rustiques*, ed. Saulnier, pp. 97–103 (lines quoted 85–7). Cf. Tomarken *The Smile of Truth*, p. 205. Apart from his canine and feline poems in French, Du Bellay wrote a charming Latin epigram on a good 'cuiusdam canis: Latratu fures excepi, mutus amantes / sic placui domino, sic placui dominae', in *Poemata*, fol. 48, Lib. IV (Tumuli). Printed in A. Perosa and J. Sparrow, eds., *Renaissance Latin Verse: An Anthology* (London, 1979), p. 40.

74 Both these elegies are edited in Torquato Tasso, *Poesia*, ed. F. Flora (Milan and Naples, 1952), p. 890.

75 *Le rime de Serafino di' Ciminelli dall'Aquila*, vol. 1, ed. M. Menghini (Bologna, 1984), pp. 125, 126 LXXXVIII.

76 See Bedini, *The Pope's Elephant*, which extensively details Hanno's career. For poems by various authors commerating the elephant's arrival, see pp. 60–2. Giovanni Battista Branconio, the privy papal chamberlain, wrote an account of the elephant and a fresco of Hanno appears in the Branconio's family chapel in San Silvestro in L'Aquila (Abruzzo).

77 ASMN AG, Serie Autografi, cassata no. 10, file no. 356. A few of the very numerous Aura poems are printed in Spila and Critell, *Cani di pietra*. These include poems by Antonio Tebeldeo, Gian Giacomo Calandra, Battista Scalona, Mario Equicola, Antonio Guarini, Galeazzo da Montichairi, Celio Calcagnini, Pietro Barignono and Antonio dell'Organo.

78 For background information on some of these scholars and their connections to the Mantuan court, see Luzio and Renier, 'La coltura e le relazioni letterarie di Isabella d'Este Gonzaga'. The scholars mentioned are Mario Equicola, Gian Calandra, Francesco Vigilio, Antonio Tebaldeo, Antonio dall'Organo, Alessandro Guarini, Niccolò Panizzato, Pietro Bembo, Girolamo Avogadro, Marcantonio Flaminio, Filippo Beroaldo and Gaultiero di San Vitale. However, there is no discussion of this particular manuscript.

79 In a neat Italic hand, Latin in thirty-six lines, from fols. 1r to fol. 2r. Carlo Agnelli was a Mantuan courtier who often represented the Gonzaga in Rome. See *Dizionario biografico degli Italiani*, pp. 416–17.

80 Spila and Critell, *Cani di pietri*, p. 25, prints the short epitaph by Calandra but not his other compositions in the manuscript.

81 Spila and Critell, *Cani di pietri*, pp. 39–40, prints the first poem but not the others by Equicola.

82 Spila and Critell, *Cani di pietri*, pp. 27–8, prints the first poem by not the others by Scalona.

Conclusion

1 Sorabji, *Animal Minds and Human Morals*; E. Fudge, R. Gilbert and S. Wiseman, eds. *At the Borders of the Human: Beasts, Bodies and Natural Philosophy in the Early Modern Period* (New York, 1999).

2 Thomas Aquinas, *Summa theologica* (Turin, 1922), vol. 3, pp. 149–50 (Pars II 2a 2ae, quaest. XXV, art. III). Fudge, *Perceiving Animals*, pp. 34–63, esp. pp. 38–40, notes that for many early modern writers concern about cruelty towards animals was not focused on the suffering of the animals themselves but rather on the belief that a person who is kind to an animal would be kind to a fellow human being as well.

✦ ✦
✦

Bibliography

Printed Primary Sources

Adam of Usk, *Chronicle of Adam Usk*, ed. and trans. C. Given-Wilson (Oxford, 1997)

Adelard of Bath, *De cura accipitrum* (Groningen, 1937)

—— *Conversations with his Nephew: On the Same and the Different, Questions on Natural Science, and on Birds*, ed. and trans. C. Burnett (Cambridge, 1998)

Agrippa d'Aubigné, *Histoire universelle*, ed. A. de Ruble, vol. 7 (Paris, 1893)

Alberti, Leon Battista, *Apologhi ed elogi*, ed. R. Contarino (Genoa, 1984)

Albertus Magnus, *De animalibus*, vol. 2 (Münster, 1916–20)

—— *On Animals*, ed. and trans. K. F. Kitchell, Jr., and I. M. Resnick (Baltimore, 1999)

Aldrovandi, Ulisse, *De quadripedibus digitatis viviparis libri tres et de quadrupedibus digitatis oviparis libri duo* (Bologna, 1637)

Alfonso X, *Cantigas de Santa Maria*, ed. W. Mettmann, 4 vols. (Coimbra, 1959–72)

The Ancrene Riwle, ed. and trans. M. B. Salu (London, 1955)

Arnaut de Carcasses, *Las novas del papagay*, in *Les Troubadours: le trésor poétique de l'Occitanie*, ed. R. Lavaud and R. Nelli, vol. 2 (Bruges, 1966)

Aubrey, John, *Aubrey's Brief Lives: Edited from the Original Manuscripts*, ed. O. Lawson Dick (London, 1949)

Baildon, W. P., ed., *Court Rolls of the Manor of Wakefield*, 2 vols. (Leeds, 1901)

Bandello, Mateo, *Novelle*, ed. G. G. Ferrero (Turin, 1974)

Barber, R., trans., *Bestiary* (Woodbridge, 1999)

Bartholomeus Anglicus, *On the Properties of Things*, trans. John Trevisa, ed. M. C. Seymour *et al.* (Oxford, 1975)

Basil of Caesarea, *Homelies sur l'Hexaemeron*, ed. and trans. S. Giet (Paris, 1950)

Bembo, Pietro, *Carmina* (Turin, 1990)

Breul, K., ed., *The Cambridge Songs: A Goliard's Song Book of the XIth Century* (Cambridge, 1915)

Breviario Grimani [facsimile] (Milan, 1971)

Bromyard, John, *Summa praedicantium* (Venice, 1586)

Caius, John, *Of Englishe Dogges: The Diversities, the Names, the Natures, and the Properties*, trans. A. Fleming (1578)

Carmina illustrum poetarum Italorum (Florence, 1717–26)

Cartulaire de Notre Dame de Paris, vol. 2 (Paris, 1850)

Catullus, *Catullus: A Critical Edition*, ed. D. F. S. Thomson (Chapel Hill, NC, 1978)

La Chastelaine de Vergi, ed. R. E. V. Stuip (The Hague and Paris, 1970)

La Châtelaine de Vergi, ed. J. Dufournet and L. Dulac (Paris, 1994)

Chaucer, Geoffrey, *The Riverside Chaucer*, ed. L. D. Benson (Boston, MA, 1987)

Le Chevalier du Papegau, ed. F. Heuckenkamp (Halle, 1896)

Clement of Alexandria, *Clement of Alexandria*, ed. G. W. Butterworth (London, 1919)

A Collection of Ordinances and Regulations for the Government of the Royal Household Made in Divers Reigns, from King Edward III to King William and Queen Mary: Also Receipts in Ancient Cookery (London, 1790)

Commynes, Philippe de, *Memoirs*, trans. M. Jones (London, 1972)

Coppetta Beccuti, Francesco, and Giovanni Guidiccioni, *Rime*, ed. E. Chiorboli (Bari, 1912)

Dall, M. K., *Court Roll of Chalgrave Manor: 1278–1313* (Streatley, 1950)

Deschamps, Eustache, *Selected Poems*, ed. I. S. Laurie and D. M. Sinnreich Levi, trans. D. Curzon and J. Fiskin (New York and London, 2003)

Dictionnaire étymologique de la langue françoise, ed. G. Ménage (Paris, 1750)

Documents relating to the University and Colleges of Cambridge, 2 vols. (London, 1852)

Dornavius, Caspar, *Amphitheatrum sapientiae Socraticae joco-seria joc est encomia et commentaria autorum* (Hanover, 1619)

Du Bellay, Joachim, *Diverse jeux rustiques*, ed. V. L. Saulnier (Lille and Geneva, 1947)

Étienne de Bourbon, *Anecdotes historiques, légendes et apologues tirés du recueil inédit d'Étienne de Bourbon*, ed. R. A. Lecoy de la Marche (Paris, 1877)

Flower, R., *The Early Irish Tradition* (Oxford, 1947)

Furnivall, F. J., ed., *Early English Meals and Manners* (London, 1868)

Gammer Gurton's Needle, ed. C. Whitworth (London, 1997)

Garasse, François, *La Doctrine curieuse des beaux esprits de ce temps, ou prétendus tels* (Paris, 1623)

Geoffrey de La Tour-Landry, *Le Livre du Chevalier de la Tour Landry pour l'enseignement de ses filles*, ed. M. A. de Montaiglon (Paris, 1854)

—— *The Book of the Knight of La Tour-Landry*, ed. T. A. Wright (London, 1906)

The Goodman of Paris, ed. and trans. E. Power (Woodbridge, 2006)

Gorra, E., 'La novella della dama e dei tre papagalli', *Romania* 32 (1892), pp. 71–8

Gottfried von Strassburg, *Tristan*, ed. K. von Rüdiger and F. von Ranke, vols. 1–3 (Stuttgart, 1998)

—— *Tristan with the Surviving Fragments of the Tristan of Thomas*, ed. and trans. A. T. Hatto (Harmondsworth, 1960)

Gower, John, *Confessio amantis*, ed. R. A. Peck (Toronto, 1997)

The Greek Anthology, ed. W. R. Paton (London, 1916–18)

Guichenon, S., *Histoire généalogique de la royale maison de Savoye* (Turin, 1778–80)

Hands, R., ed., *English Hawking and Hunting in The Boke of St Albans* (Oxford, 1975)

Henryson, R., *Fables* (Edinburgh, 1802)

Hildegard von Bingen, *Hildegard von Bingen's Physica: The Complete English Translation of her Classic Work on Health and Healing*, trans. P. Throop (Rochester, VT, 1998)

The Hours of Catherine of Cleves, ed. J. Plummer (New York, 1975)

Hull, E., ed., *The Poem Book of the Gael* (London, 1912)

Jacobus de Voragine, *Legenda aurea*, ed. Th. Graesse (Breslau, 1846)

—— *The Golden Legend*, ed. F. S. Ellis (London, 1931)

Jacques de Vitry, *The Exempla or Illustrative Stories from the Sermones Vulgares of Jacques de Vitry*, ed. T. F. Crane (London, 1890)

Jamyn, Amadis, *Œuvres de Jamin* (Paris, 1577)

Jeanne d'Albret, *Mémoires et poésies de Jeanne d'Albret*, ed. A. de Ruble (Paris, 1893)

Jenkins, D., *The Law of Hywel Dda: Law Texts from Medieval Wales* (Llandysul, 1986)

Kors, A. C., and E. Peters, ed., *Witchcraft in Europe, 400–1700: A Documentary History* (Philadelphia, 2001)

Labarte, J., ed., *Inventaire du mobilier de Charles V* (Paris, 1879)

Lambard, William, *Eirenarcha, or The Offices of the Justices of the Peace* (London, 1588)

Lancelot of the Laik and Sir Tristrem, ed. A. Lupack (Kalamazoo, MI, 1997)

Lemaire de Belges, Jean, *Les Épîtres de l'amant vert*, ed. J. Frappier (Lille and Geneva, 1948)

L'Estoile, P., *Registre-journal de Henri III, roy de France et de Pologne, 1574 à 1589* (Paris, 1837)

L'Estrange Ewen, C., ed., *Witch Hunting and Witch Trials* (London, 1971)

Liber exemplorum ad usum praedicantium, ed. A. G. Little (Aberdeen, 1908)

Lindsay, David, *Works of Sir David Lindsay*, ed. D. Hammer, vol. 1 (Edinburgh, 1931–6)

Lipsius, Justus, *Epistolicarum quaestionum libri V, in quis ad varios scriptores, pleraeque ad T. Livium, Notae* (Antwerp, 1577)

—— *Epistolarum centuriae ad Belgas* (Antwerp, 1602)

—— *Epistolarum selectarum centuria miscellanea*, vol. 5 (Antwerp, 1605–7)

—— *Iusti Lipsi Epistolae*, vol. 13, ed. J. Papy (Brussels, 2000)

Livre de la Taille pour l'an 1292 (Paris, 1837)

Loncke, J., *La Practica canum – le De cane d'Albert Le Grand, l'art de soigner les chiens de chasse au Moyen Âge* (Nogent le Roi, 2007)

Lyly, John, *Endymion*, ed. D. Bevington (Manchester, 1996)

Machaut, Guillaume, *Le Jugement dou roy de Behaigne*, ed. J. I. Wimsatt and W. W. Kibler (Athens, GA, 1988)

Magnus, Olaus, *Description of the Northern Peoples*, ed. P. G. Foote (London, 1996–8)

Marie de France, *Fables*, ed. and trans. H. Spiegel (Toronto, 1987)

—— *The Lais of Marie de France*, ed. and trans. K. Busby and G. S. Burgess (London, 1999)

Marot, Clement, *Œuvres* (Haye, 1731)

Martial, *Epigrams*, ed. D. R. Shackleton Bailey (London, 1993)

The Master of Game: The Oldest English Book on Hunting, ed. W. A. and F. Baillie-Grohman (London, 1904)

Maynard, François, *Les Œuvres de François Maynard*, ed. M. Leroy de Gomberville (Paris, 1646)

Le Menagier de Paris, ed. G. E. Brereton and J. M. Ferrier (Oxford, 1981)

Meyers, A. R., ed., *The Captivity of a Royal Witch: The Household Accounts of Queen Joan of Navarre, 1419–21* (Manchester, 1940)

Miraeus, A., *Vita Iusti Lipsi sapientiae et litterarum antistitis* (Antwerp, 1609)

Monasticon Anglicanum, ed. W. Dugdale, vol. 2 (London, 1846)

Mondeville, Henri de, *The Surgery of Henri de Mondeville*, vol. 2, trans. L. D. Rosenman (Philadelphia, 2001)

Neckam, Alexander, *De naturis rerum librum duo* (London, 1863)

Nicholas, N. H., ed., *Privy Purse Expenses of Elizabeth of York* (London, 1830)

Octavianus, Sixtus, *Phaselus Catulli, et ad eum quotquot exstant paroediae, cum annotationibus doctissimorum vivorum: accesserunt alia quadam eiusdem generis* (Antwerp, 1579)

Odo Rigaldus, *Regestrum visitationum archiepiscopi Rothomagensis*, ed. T. Bonnin (Rouen, 1852)

Paleario, Aonio, *Aonii Palearii Vervlani: Opera* (Jena, 1728)

—— *The Register of Eudes of Rouen*, trans., S. M. Brown (New York, 1964)

Parsons, J. C., ed., *The Court and Household of Eleanor of Castile in 1290: An Edition of British Library Additional Manuscript 35294* (Toronto, 1977)

Passerat, Jean, *Les Poésies françaises de J. Passerat* (Paris, 1880)

Perosa, A., and J. Sparrow, eds., *Renaissance Latin Verse: An Anthology* (London, 1979)

Petrarch, Francesco, *Le familiari*, ed. V. Rossi (Florence, 1933–42)

—— *Petrarchae poëmata minora*, ed. D. de Rossetti (Milan, 1829–34)

—— *Petrarch at Vaucluse: Letters in Verse and Prose*, ed. E. H. Wilkins (Chicago, 1955)

Phébus, Gaston, *Livre de chasse*, ed. G. Tilander (Karlshamm, 1971)

Pliny the Elder, *Natural History*, ed. J. Henderson and trans. W. H. S. Jones (Cambridge, MA, 1975)

Plummer, C., ed., *Vitae sanctorum Hiberniae* (Oxford, 1910)

Quaife, G. R., *Godly Zeal and Furious Rage: The Witch in Early Modern Europe* (Beckenham, 1987)

The Register of St Augustine's Abbey Canterbury Commonly Called the Black Book, ed. G. J. Turner, and H. E. Salter, vol. 1 (Oxford, 1915)

A Revelation of Purgatory by an Unknown, Fifteenth-Century Woman Visionary, ed. M. P. Harley (Lewiston, NY, 1985)

Richard of Durham, *The Lanercost Chronicle*, trans. H. Maxwell (Llanerch, 2001)

Roman de Tristan par Thomas, ed. J. Bedier (Paris, 1902–5)

Ronsard, Pierre de, *Œuvres complètes*, ed. P. Laumonier (Paris, 1914–75)

Rymer, Thomas, ed., *Foedera*, vol. 4 (The Hague, 1739–45)

Sacchetti, Franco, *Opere*, ed. A. Borlenghi (Milan, 1957)

—— *Il Trecentonovelle*, ed. E. Faccioli (Turin, 1970)

St Clare Byrne, M., ed., *Lisle Letters*, vol. 2 (London, 1985)

St Clare Byrne, M., and B. Boland, eds., *The Lisle Letters: An Abridgement* (Chicago, 1983)

Salimbene, *Cronica fratris Salimbene de Adam*, ed. O. Holder-Egger, Monumenta Germaniae Historica, Scriptores 32 (Hanover, 1826)

—— *The Chronicle of Salimbene de Adam*, ed. L. Baird, G. Baglini and J. R. Kane (Binghamton, NY, 1986)

Sanchez de Vercial, Clemente, *The Book of Tales by A.B.C.*, ed. and trans. J. E. Keller, L. Clark Keating, Eric M. Furr (New York, 1992)

Schäfer, K. H., ed., *Vatikanische Quellen zur Geschichte der Päpstlichen Hof- und Finanzverwaltung, 1316–1378* (Rome, 1937)

Scheler, M. A., ed., *Lexicographie latine du XIIe et du XIIIe siècle* (Leipzig, 1867)

Serafino dall'Aquila, *Le rime de Serafino di' Ciminelli dall'Aquila*, ed. M. Menghini (Bologna, 1984)

Skelton, John, *The Complete Poems of John Skelton*, ed. P. Henderson (London, 1948)

—— *The Complete Poems of John Skelton*, ed. J. Scattergood (New Haven, CT, 1983)

Statutes of the Colleges of Oxford (London, 1853)

Sweertius, Franciscus, *Selectae Christiani orbis deliciae urbibus, temples, bibliothecis et aliunde* (Cologne, 1608)

La tabula exemplorum secundum ordinem alphabeti, ed. J. T. Welter (Paris and Toulouse, 1926)

Tanner, N. P., ed., *Decrees of the Ecumenical Councils* (London, 1990)

Targioni Tozzetti, O., ed., *Antologia della poesia italiana* (Livorno, 1916)

Tasso, Torquato, *Poesia*, ed. F. Flora (Milan and Naples, 1952)

Testamenta Eboracensia, ed. J. Raine, III (London, 1865, for 1864)

Thomas Aquinas, *Summa theologica* (Turin, 1922)

—— *Summa contra gentiles* (Madrid, 1967)

Thomas de Cantimpré, *De natura rerum*, ed. W. de Gruyter (Berlin and New York, 1973)

Thompson, A. H., ed., *Visitations of Religious Houses in the Diocese of Lincoln*, vol. 2 (London, 1969)

Tristan und Isolde: Faksimile-Ausgabe des Cgm 51 der Bayerischen Staatsbibliothek, München (Stuttgart, 1979)

Turner, T. H., ed., *Manners and Household Expenses of England in the Thirteenth and Fifteenth Centuries* (London, 1841)

Vasari, Giorgio, *Le vite de' più eccellenti pittori scultori e archittettori nelle redazioni del 1550 e 1568*, ed. R. Bettarini (Florence, 1966–1987)

Bibliography

Visitations of the Diocese of Norwich, AD 1492–1532, ed. A. Jessop (London, 1888)

Walter Map, *De nugis curialium*, ed. and trans. M. R. James (Oxford, 1983)

Wier, Johann, *De praestigiis daemonum et incantationibus ac venificiis* (Basel, 1583)

Woolgar, C. M., ed., *Household Accounts from Medieval England* (Oxford, 1992)

Secondary Sources

Alexander, D., *Saints and Animals in the Middle Ages* (Woodbridge, 2008).

Anon., 'On Certain Rare Monumental Effigies', *Transactions of the Bristol and Gloucestershire Archaeological Association* 35 (1902), p. 99

—— 'Varietà: Jacopo Corsi e il Tebaldeo', *Giornale storico della letteratura italiana* 17 (1891), pp. 395–6

——'Varietà archivistiche e bibliografiche CCLXXXIX: necrologie di una cagnuola marchionale', *Il Bibliofilo* 9:4 (1888–9), p. 56

Ariès, P., and G. Duby, eds., *A History of Private Life: Revelations of the Medieval World* (London, 1998)

Armitage Robinson, J., *The Abbot's House at Westminster* (Cambridge, 1911)

Armstrong, E. A., *Saint Francis: Nature Mystic* (Los Angeles, 1976)

Backhouse, J., *The Luttrell Psalter* (London, 1989)

Barnet, P., ed., *Images in Ivory: Precious Objects of the Gothic Age* (Princeton, 1997)

Bartosiewicz, L., *Animals in the Urban Landscape in the Wake of the Middle Ages: A Case Study from Vác, Hungary* (Oxford, 1995), pp. 859–85

Bartrum, G., *German Renaissance Prints, 1490–1550* (London, 1995)

Bedini, S. A., *The Pope's Elephant* (Manchester, 1997)

Bell, S. G., 'Medieval Women Book Owners: Arbiters of Lay Piety and Ambassadors of Culture', *Signs: Journal of Women in Culture and Society* 7:4 (1982), pp. 742–68

Berenson, B., *Italian Painters of the Renaissance* (Oxford, 1948)

Bertolotti, A., 'Curiosità storiche mantovane: Una magnifica tomba per una cagnetta', *Il Mendico* 4:18 (1884), p. 6

——'Curiosità storiche mantovane: I gatti e la gatta della Marchesa di Mantova Isabella d'Este', *Il Mendico* 9:8 (1889), pp. 6–7

Birch, W. de G., *Catalogue of Seals in the Department of Manuscripts in the British Museum*, vols. 2 and 5 (London, 1892)

Block, E. C., *Corpus of Medieval Misericords: Iberia* (Turnhout, 2004)

Bobisut, D., and L. Gumiero Salomoni, *Altichiero da Zevio: Cappella di San Giacomo, Oratorio di San Giorgio* (Padua, 2002)

Bodson, L., *L'Animal de compagnie: ses rôles et leurs motivations au regard de l'histoire* (Liège, 1997)

Boehrer, B., ed., 'Introduction: The Animal Renaissance', in *A Cultural History of Animals in the Renaissance*, ed. B. Boehrer (Oxford and New York, 2007)

—— '" Men, Monkeys, Lap-dogs, Parrots, Perish All!"': Psittacine Articulacy in Early Modern Writing', *The Modern Language Quarterly* 59:2 (1998), pp. 171–93

—— *Parrot Culture: Our 2500-Year-Long Fascination with the World's Most Talkative Bird* (Philadelphia, 2004)

—— *Shakespeare among the Animals* (Basingstoke, 2002)

—— 'Shylock and the Rise of the Household Pet: Thinking Exclusion in the Merchant of Venice', *Shakespeare Quarterly* 50:2 (1999), pp. 152–70

Bonnet, J., *Lorenzo Lotto* (Paris, 1996)

Bourgain, L., *La Chaire française au XII siècle d'après les manuscripts* (Paris, 1879)

Bordier, H., ed., *Les Églises et monastères de Paris* (Paris, 1856)

Brown, C. M., *Isabella d'Este and Lorenzo da Pavia* (Geneva, 1982)

Burdach, K., *Aus Petrarcas ältestem Schülerkreise* (Berlin, 1929)

Bussagli, M., *Bosch* (London, 1967)

Camille, M., *The Medieval Art of Love: Objects and Subjects of Desire* (New York, 1998)

Carré, H., *Jeux, sports et divertissements des rois de France* (Paris, 1937)

Cartwright, J., *Isabella d'Este, Marchioness of Mantua, 1474–1539: A Study of the Renaissance* (London, 1903)

Champollion-Figeac, A., *Louis et Charles Ducs D'Orléans: leur influence sur les arts, la littérature et l'esprit de leur siècle* (Genève, 1980)

Classen, A., 'The Dog in German Courtly Literature: The Mystical, the Magical, and the Loyal Animal', in *Fauna and Flora in the Middle Ages: Studies of the Medieval Environment and its Impact on the Human Mind*, ed. S. Hartmann (Frankfurt, 2007), pp. 67–86

Clutton-Brock, J., *Domesticated Animals from Early Times* (London, 1981)

Cobban, A., *English University Life in the Middle Ages* (London, 1999)

Collins, A. H., *Symbolism of Animals and Birds Represented in English Church Architecture* (New York, 1913)

Cooper, H., 'Magic that does not Work', *Medievalia et Humanistica* 7 (1976), pp. 131–46

Coss, P., *The Lady in Medieval England, 1000–1500* (Stroud, 1998)

Cottafavi, C., 'Cani e gatti alla corte di Gonzaga', in *El Ceppo* (Mantua, 1934)

Coulton, G. G., *Social Life in Britain from the Conquest to the Reformation* (Cambridge, 1918)

—— *Life in the Middle Ages* (Cambridge, 1930)

Cummins, J., *The Hound and the Hawk: The Art of Medieval Hunting* (London, 2001)

Dalton, O. M., *Catalogue of the Ivory Carvings of the Christian Era with Examples of Mohammedan Art and Carvings in Bone in the Department of British and Mediaeval Antiquities and Ethnography of the British Museum* (London, 1909)

Davidson, L., 'The Use of Blanchete in Juan Ruiz's Fable of the Ass and the Lap-Dog', *Romance Philology* 33 (1979), pp. 154–60

Dawes, E, 'Pulling the Chestnuts out of the Fire', in *Animals and the Symbolic in Mediaeval Art and Literature*, ed. L. A. J. R. Houwen (Groningen, 1997), pp. 155–69

De Hamel, C., *A History of Illuminated Manuscripts* (London, 1994)

Debidour, V. H., *Le Bestaire sculpté du Moyen Âge en France* (Paris, 1961)

Delort, R., *Les Animaux ont une histoire* (Paris, 1993)

Dickenson, V., 'Meticulous Depiction: Animals in Art, 1400–1600', in *A Cultural History of Animals in the Renaissance*, ed. B. Boehrer (Oxford and New York, 2007), pp. 165–200

Dienen, H., 'Die "Camera papagalli" im Palast des Papstes', *Archiv für Kulturgeschichte* 49 (1967), pp. 43–97

Dietrich, J. S., 'Dead Parrots Society', *American Journal of Philology* 123:1 (2002), pp. 95–110

Dizionario biografico degli Italiani (Rome, 1960–)

Dogaer, G., *Flemish Miniature Painting in the 15th and 16th centuries* (Amsterdam, 1987)

Du Fresne de Beaucourt, G., *Histoire de Charles VII* (Paris, 1881)

Dutton, M. L., 'Chaucer's Two Nuns', in *Monasteries and Society in Medieval Britain*, ed. P. Thompson (Stamford, 1999), pp. 298–311

Eckenstein, L., *Women under Monasticism* (Cambridge, 1896)

Edwards, P., 'Domesticated Animals in Renaissance Europe', in *A Cultural History of Animals in the Renaissance*, ed. B. Boehrer (Oxford and New York 2007), pp. 75–94

—— *Horse and Man in Early Modern England* (London, 2007)

Egan, G., *The Medieval Household: Daily Living, c. 1150–c. 1450* (Woodbridge, 2010)

Ellis, R. K., *Catalogue of Seals in the Public Record Office: Personal Seals* (London, 1978)

Erlande-Brandenburg, A., *La Dame à la licorne* (Paris, 1978)

Farmer, D. H., *St Hugh of Lincoln* (Oxford, 1985)

Flores, N. C., ed., *Animals in the Middle Ages* (New York, 1996)

Four Centuries of Dog Collars at Leeds Castle (Maidstone, 1991)

Franklin, A., *La Vie privée d'autrefois: arts et métiers, modes, mœurs, usages des Parisiens du XII au XVIII siècle d'après des documents originaux ou inédits*, vols. 20 and 24 (Paris, 1897 and 1899)

Friedman, J. B.,'The Dreamer, The Whelp, and Consolation in the Book of the Duchess', *The Chaucer Review* 3 (1969), pp. 145–62

Frugoni, C., *Pietro and Ambrogio Lorenzetti* (Milan, 1993)

——*A Day in a Medieval City*, trans. W. McCuaig, (Chicago/London, 2005)

Fudge, E., *Perceiving Animals: Humans and Beasts in Early Modern English Culture* (Urbana, IL, 2000)

——, ed., *Renaissance Beasts: Of Animals, Humans and Other Wonderful Creatures* (Urbana, IL, 2003)

Fudge, E., R. Gilbert and S. Wiseman, eds., *At the Borders of the Human: Beasts, Bodies and Natural Philosophy in the Early Modern Period* (New York, 1999)

Gadol, J., *Leon Battista Alberti: Universal Man of the Early Renaissance* (Chicago, 1969)

Gaidoz, H., *Bibliotheca mythica: La Rage et St-Hubert* (Paris, 1887)

Gathercole, P., *Animals in Medieval French Manuscript Illumination* (Lewiston, NY, 1995)

Gay, V., *Glossaire archéologique du Moyen Âge et de la Renaissance*, 2 vols. (Paris, 1882–1928)

George, W., and B. Yapp, *Naming of the Beasts: Natural History in the Medieval Bestiary* (London, 1991)

Gnaedinger, L., *Hiudan und Petitcreiu: Gestalt und Figur des Hundes in der mittelalterlichen Tristandichtung* (Zurich, 1971)

Goddard, A. R.,'Ickleton Church and Priory', *Proceedings of the Cambridge Antiquarian Society* 5 (Cambridge, 1907, for 1904), p. 190

Gómez-Centurión, C.,'Chamber Animals at the Spanish Court during the Eighteenth Century', *The Court Historian* 16:1 (2011), pp. 43–65

Gousset, M., *Éden: le jardin médiéval à travers l'enluminure, XIIIe–XVIe siècle* (Paris, 2001)

Gransden, A., *Historical Writing in England, 550–1307* (Ithaca, NY, 1974)

Gray, D., 'Notes on Some Medieval Mystical, Magical and Moral Cats', in *Langland, the Mystics and the Medieval English Religious tradition: Essays in Honour of S. S. Hussey*, ed. H. Phillips (Cambridge, 1990), pp. 185–202

Grössinger, C., *The World Upside Down: English Misericords* (London, 1997)

Guichenon, S., ed., *Histoire généalogique de la royale maison de Savoye* (Turin, 1778–80)

Hanawalt, B. A., *The Ties that Bound: Peasant Families in Medieval England* (Oxford, 1986)

Harvey, P. D. A., *A Medieval Oxfordshire Village: Cuxhom, 1240 to 1400* (Oxford, 1965)

——'After Adam: Naming the Animals in the Middle Ages and Later' (unpublished paper)

Hautz, J. F., *Geschichte der Universität Heidelberg*, vol. 2 (Mannheim, 1862–4)

Hefferman, C. F., 'That Dog Again: Melancholia Canina and Chaucer's Book of the Duchess', *Modern Philology* 84:2 (1986), pp. 185–90

Herbert, J. A., *Catalogue of Romances in the Department of Manuscripts in the British Library*, vol. 3 (London, 1910)

Holdeweij, J., 'The Wearing of Significance Badges, Religious and Secular: The Social Meaning of a Medieval Pattern', in *Showing Status: Representations of Social Positions in the Late Middle Ages*, ed. W. Blockmans and A. Janse (Turnhout, 1999), pp. 307–28

Höltgen, K. J., 'Clever Dogs and Nimble Spaniels: On the Iconography of Logic, Invention, and Imagination', *Explorations in Renaissance Culture* 24 (1998), pp. 1–36

Hope, C., *Titian* (London, 2003)

Howard, M. M., 'Dried Cats', *Man* 51 (1951), pp. 149–51

Humfrey, P., *Lorenzo Lotto* (New Haven, CT, and New York, 1997)

Hunt, T., *The Medieval Surgery* (Woodbridge, 1992)

Hutchinson, R., *The Last Days of Henry VIII* (London, 2005)

Hutton, J., *The Greek Anthology in Italy to the Year 1800* (Ithaca, NY, 1935)

Incontri, M. L., *Il piccolo levriero italiano* (Florence, 1956)

Janson, H. W., *Apes and Ape Lore in the Middle Ages and Renaissance* (London, 1952)

Jarzombek, M., *On Leon Battista Alberti, his Literary and Aesthetic Theories* (Cambridge, MA, 1989)

Jesse, G. R., *History of the British Dog*, 2 vols. (London, 1856)

Jones, M., 'Animal Names' (unpublished paper)

M. H. Jones, 'Cats and Cat-skinning in Late Medieval Art and Life', in *Fauna and Flora in the Middle Ages: Studies of the Medieval Environment and its Impact on the Human Mind*, ed. S. Hartmann (Frankfurt, 2007), pp. 97–112

Jubien, A., *L'Abbesse Marie de Bretagne et la réforme de l'ordre de Fontevrault* (Angers and Paris, 1872)

Kelly, F., *Early Irish Farming: A Study Based Mainly on the Law-Texts of the 7th and 8th Centuries AD* (Dublin, 1997)

Kelly, H. A., 'A Neo-Revisionist Looks at Chaucer's Nuns', *The Chaucer Review* 31:2 (1996), pp. 116–36

Klingender, F., *Animals in Art and Thought to the End of the Middle Ages* (London, 1971)

Kolsky, S., *Mario Equicola: The Real Courtier* (Geneva, 1991)

Kors, A. C., and E. Peters, eds., *Witchcraft in Europe, 400–1700: A Documentary History* (Philadelphia, 2001)

Kren, T., and S. McKendrick, *Illuminating the Renaissance: The Triumph of Flemish Manuscript Painting in Europe* (London, 2003)

Labarge, M. W., *A Baronial Household of the Thirteenth Century* (London, 1965)

Laumonier, P., *Ronsard, poète lyrique: étude historique et littéraire* (Paris, 1909)

Lauts, J., *Carpaccio* (London, 1962)

Lazenby, F. D., 'Greek and Roman Household Pets', *The Classical Journal* 44:5 (1949), pp. 299–307

Lazzari, A., *Un enciclopedico del secolo XVI: Celio Calcagnini* (Ferrara, 1936)

Le Roux de Lincy, A. J. V., *Vie de la reine Anne de Bretagne* (Paris, 1860)

Lindsay, W. M., 'Bird-Names in Latin Glossaries', *Classical Philology* 13:1 (1918), pp. 1–22

Lipton, S., 'Jews, Heretics, and the Sign of the Cat in the Bible moralisée', *Word and Image* 8:4 (1992), pp. 362–77

Lobineau, D., *Histoire de la ville de Paris*, vol. 3 (Paris, 1725)

Loisel, G., *Histoire des menageries: de l'antiquité à nos jours* (Paris, 1912)

Loomis, R. S., *Arthurian Legends in Medieval Art* (New York, 1938)

Luzio, A., 'Federico Gonzago ostaggio alla corte di Giulio II', *Archivio della Real Società Romana di Storia Patria* 9 (1886)

Luzio, A., and R. Renier, 'La coltura e le relazione letterarie di Isabella d'Este Gonzaga', *Giornale storico della letteratura italiana* 35–8 (1899–1901)

Luzio, A., and P. Torelli, *L'Archivo Gonzaga a Mantova*, 2 vools. (Ostiglia and Verona, 1920–1)

Lytton Sells, A., *Animal Poetry in French & English Literature & the Greek Tradition* (Bloomington, IN, 1955)

MacDonach, K., *Reigning Cats and Dogs: A History of Pets at Court since the Renaissance* (London, 1999)

Macklin, H. W., *Monumental Brasses: Portfolio Plates of the Monumental Brass Society* (London, 1953)

Malacarne, G., *Sulla mensa del principe: alimentazione e banchetti alla corte dei Gonzaga* (Modena, 2000)

Maulde-La-Clavière, M. A. R. de, *Jeanne de France, Duchesse d'Orléans et de Berry* (Paris, 1883)

McCormick, F., 'The Domesticated Cat in Early Christian and Medieval Ireland', in *Keimelia: Studies in Medieval Archaeology and History in Memory of Tom Delaney*, ed. P. F. Wallace (Galway, 1988), pp. 218–28

McFarlane, I. D., 'The Renaissance Epitaph', *The Modern Language Review* 81:4 (1986), pp. xxv–xxxv

McLean, T., *The English at Play in the Middle Ages* (Windsor Forest, 1983)

McMunn, M. T., 'Parrots and Poets in Late Medieval Literature', *Anthrozoös* 12:2 (1999), pp. 68–75

Manning, A., and J. Serpell, eds., *Animals in Human Society: Changing Perceptions* (London, 1994)

Meiss, M., *French Painting in the Time of Jean de Berry: The Limbourgs and their Contemporaries* (London, 1974)

Menache, S., 'Dogs: God's Worst Enemies?', *Society and Animals* 5:1 (1997), pp. 23–44

——'Dogs and Human Beings: A Story of Friendship', *Society and Animals* 6:1 (1998), pp. 67–86

Mielton, J., *Miracles de Nostre Dame* (London, 1885)

Millin de Grandmaison, A. L., *Antiquités nationales; ou, recueil de monuments pour servir a l'histoire de l'empire français* (Paris, 1790)

Moessner, L., 'Dog – Man's Best Friend: A Study in Historical Lexicology', *English Historical Linguistics 1992 = Current Issues in Linguistic Theory* 113 (1992), pp. 208–18

Moffatt, H. C., *Old Oxford Plate* (London, 1906)

Mommsen, T. E., 'Petrarch and the Decoration of the Sala Virorum Illustrium in Padua', *The Art Bulletin* 34:2 (1952)

Moore, E. A., and L. M. Snyder, *Dogs and People in Social, Working, Economic or Symbolic Interaction* (Oxford, 2006)

Morrison, M., 'Catullus in the Neo-Latin Poetry of France before 1550', *Bibliothèque d'Humanisme et Renaisance* 17 (1955), pp. 365–94

Naïs, H., *Les Animaux dans la poésie française de la Renaissance* (Paris, 1961)

Newman, B., 'The "Cattes Tale": A Chaucer Apocryphon', *The Chaucer Review* 26:4 (1992), pp. 411–23

O'Connor, T. P., 'Pets and pests in medieval and Roman Britain', *Mammal Review* 22 (1992), pp. 107–13

Orme, N., 'The Culture of Children in Medieval England', *Past and Present* 148 (August 1995), pp. 48–88

—— *Education and Society in Medieval and Renaissance England* (London, 1989)

—— *Exeter Cathedral: The First Thousand Years, 400–1500* (Exeter, 2009), p. 103

—— *Medieval Children* (London, 2001)

Orth, M. D., 'Francis de Moulin and the Journal of Louise of Savoy', *Sixteenth Century Journal* 13:1 (1982), pp. 55–66

Owst, G. R., *Literature and Pulpit in Medieval England: A Neglected Chapter in the History of English Letters & of the English People* (Cambridge, 1933)

Padua: Baptistery of the Cathedral (Padua, 1994)

Page, W., ed., *The Victoria History of the Counties of Engand: Yorkshire*, vol. 3 (London, 1907–25)

Panayotova, S., *The Macclesfield Psalter: A Window into the World of Late Medieval England* (Cambridge, 2005)

Papy, J., 'Lipsius and his Dogs: Humanist Tradition, Iconography and Rubens's Four Philosophers', *Journal of the Warburg and Courtauld Institutes* 62 (1999), pp. 167–98

Pascua, E., 'From Forest to Farm and Town', in in *A Cultural History of Animals*, vol. 2: *In the Middle Ages*, ed. B. Resl (Oxford, 2007), pp. 81–102

Platt, C., *Abbeys of Yorkshire* (London, 1988)

—— *Medieval Southampton: The Port and Trading Community, AD 1000–1600* (London, 1973)

Power, E., *Medieval English Nunneries* (Cambridge, 1922)

Prestwich, M., *Plantagenet England, 1225–1360* (Oxford, 2005)

Préaux, J., 'De Culex de Virgile a son pastiche par Thierry de Saint-Thrond', in *Présence de Virgile: Actes du colloque* (Paris, 1978), pp. 195–208

Quaife, G. R., *Godly Zeal and Furious Rage: The Witch in Early Modern Europe* (Beckenham, 1987)

Rashdall, H., *The Universities of Europe in the Middle Ages*, vol. 3 (Oxford, 1936)

Reeves, C., *Pleasures and Pastimes in Medieval England* (Stroud, 1995)

Regan, L. K., 'Ariosto's Threshold Patron: Isabella d'Este in the Orlando Furioso', *Modern Language Notes* 120:1 (2005), pp. 50–69

Relle, E., 'Some New Marginalia and poems by Gabriel Harvey', *Review of English Studies* 23 (1972), pp. 401–16

Remnant, G. L., *Catalogue of Misericords in Great Britain* (Oxford, 1969)

Reuterswürd, P., 'The Dog in the Humanist's Study', *Konsthistorisk tidskrift* 50 (1981)

Rex, R., *'The Sins of Madame Eglentyne' and Other Essays on Chaucer* (London, 1995)

Rico, F., 'Perro(s) de Petraca', *Patio de Letras* 7 (1984)

Riedel, A., *The Animal Remains of Medieval Verona: An Archaeozoological and Paleoeconomical Study* (Verona, 1994)

Roberts, A. M., 'The Cronology and Political Significance of the Tomb of Mary of Burgundy', *The Art Bulletin* 71:3 (1989), pp. 376–400

Roberts, H. L., 'St. Augustine in "St. Jerome's Study": Carpaccio's Painting and its Legendary Source', *The Art Bulletin* 41:4 (1959), pp. 283–97

Rogers, K. M., *The Cat and the Human Imagination: Feline Images from Bast to Garfield* (Ann Arbor, MI, 1998)

Rowland, B., 'The Whelp in Chaucer's Book of the Duchess', *Neulogische Mitteilungen* 66 (1965), pp. 148–59

—— *Animals with Human Faces: A Guide to Animal Symbolism* (London, 1974)

Rubin, M., 'The Person in the Form: Medieval Challenges to Bodily "Order"', in *Framing Medieval Bodies*, ed. S. Kay and M. Rubin (Manchester, 1994), pp. 100–22

Salih, S., *Versions of Virginity in Late Medieval England* (Cambridge, 2001)

Salisbury, J. E., *The Beast Within: Animals in the Middle Ages* (London, 1994)

Salter, D., *Holy and Noble Beasts: Encounters with Animals in Medieval Literature* (Woodbridge, 2001)

Schibanoff, S., 'Taking Jane's Cue: Phyllyp Sparowe as a Primer for Women Readers', *PMLA* 101:5 (1986), pp. 832–47

Schiesari, J., '"Bitches and Queens": Pets and Perversion at the Court of France's Henri III', in *Renaissance Beasts: Of Animals, Humans and Other Wonderful Creatures*, ed. in E. Fudge (Urbana, IL, 2003), pp. 37–49

Schmitt, J.-C., *The Holy Greyhound: Guinefort, Healer of Children since the Thirteenth Century* (Cambridge and Paris, 1983)

Scott, K., *Later Gothic Manuscripts* (London, 1996)

Serpell, J. A., *In the Company of Animals* (Oxford, 1986)

——'Guardian Spirits or Demonic Pets: The Concept of the Witch's Familiar in Early Modern England, 1530–1712', in *The Animal/Human Boundary* (Rochester, NY, 2002), pp. 157–90

Signorini, R., 'Two Notes from Mantua: A Dog Named Rubino', *Journal of the Warburg and Courtauld Institutes* 41 (1978), pp. 317–20

Smets, A., 'L'Image ambiguë du chien à travers la littérature didactique latine et française (XIIe–XIVe siècles)', *Reinardus* 14 (2001), pp. 243–53

Smith, C., 'Dogs, Cats and Horses in the Scottish Medieval Town', *Proceedings of the Society of Antiquaries of Scotland* 128 (1998)

Smith, J., *The French Backgrounds of Middle Scots Literature* (London and Edinburgh, 1934)

Smith, J. C., 'The Tomb of Anne of Burgundy, Duchess of Bedford, in the Musée du Louvre', *Gesta* 23:1 (1984), pp. 39–50

Sobol, P. G., 'The Shadow of Reason: Explanations of Intelligent Animal Behaviour in the Thirteenth Century', *The Medieval World of Nature*, ed. J. Salisbury (New York, 1993), pp. 109–22

Sorabji, R., *Animal Minds and Human Morals: the Origins of the Western Debate* (Ithaca, NY, 1993)

Sorrell, R. D., *St Francis of Assisi and Nature: Tradition and Innovation in Western Christian Attitudes towards the Environment* (Oxford, 1988)

Spila, C., and M. G. Critell, *Cani di pietra: l'epicedio canino nella poesia del Rinascimento* (Rome, 2002)

Spitzer, L., 'On the Etymology of Pet', *Language* 26:4 (1950), pp. 533–8

Steadman, J. M., 'The Prioress' Dogs and Benedictine Discipline', *Modern Philology* 54:1 (1956), pp. 1–6

Teuscher, S., 'Hunde am Fürstenhof: Köter und "edle Wind" als Medien sozialer Beziehungen vom 14. Bis 16. Jahrhundert', *Historische Anthropologie* 6 (1998), pp. 347–69

Thiébaux, M., 'The Medieval Chase', *Speculum* 42: 2 (1967), pp. 260–74

Thiolier-Méjean, S., 'Le Motif du perroquet dans deux nouvelles d'oc', in *Miscellanea Mediaevalia*, ed. J. C. Faucon, A. Labbé and D. Quéruel (Paris, 1998), pp. 1355–75

Thomas, K., *Man and the Natural World: Changing Attitudes in England, 1500–1800* (Oxford, 1996)

Thomas, R., 'Perceptions Versus Reality: Changing Attitudes towards Pets in Medieval and Post-Medieval England', in *Just Skin and Bones? New Perspectives on Human–Animal Relations in the Historical Past*, ed. A. Pluskowski (Oxford, 2005), pp. 95–104

Thompson, D., *A Descriptive Catalogue of Middle English Grammatical Texts* (New York and London, 1979)

Thompson, M., *Cloister, Abbot and Precinct* (Stroud, 2001)

Thorndike, L., *A History of Magic and Experimental Science*, vol. 5 (New York, 1941)

Tilley, M. A., 'Martyrs, Monks, Insects and Animals', *The Medieval World of Nature: A Book of Essays*, ed. in J. E. Salisbury (New York, 1993), pp. 93–107

Tomarken, A. H., *The Smile of Truth: The French Satirical Eulogy and its Antecedents* (Princeton, 1990)

Toynbee, J. M. C., *Animals in Roman Life and Art* (Baltimore, 1996)

Trapp, J. B., 'Petrarch's Inkstand and his Cat', in *Il passaggiere italiano: saggio sulle letterature di lingua inglese in onore di Sergio Rossi*, ed. R. S. Crivelli and L. Sampietro (Rome, 1994)

Tubach, C., *Index Exemplorum: A Handbook of Medieval Religious Tales* (Helsinki, 1969)

Ultima Cena (London, 2005)

Vale, M., *The Princely Court: Medieval Courts and Culture in North-West Europe, 1270–1380* (Oxford, 2001)

Vallet de Viriville, A., *Histoire de Charles VII* (Paris, 1862–5)

Van den Abeele, B., and J. Loncke, 'Les Traités médievaux sur le soin des chiens: une littérature technique méconnue', in *Inquirens subtilia et diversa: Dietrich Lohrmann zum 65. Geburtstag*, ed. K. van Horst and L. Falkenstein (Aachen, 2002), pp. 281–96

Waddell, H., *Beasts and Saints* (London, 1953)

Walker-Meikle, K., *Medieval Cats* (London, 2011)

Ward, H. L., *Catalogue of Romances in the Department of Manuscripts in the British Library* (London, 1883)

Weiss, R., 'Some Van Eyckian Illuminations from Italy', *Journal of the Warburg and Courtauld Institutes* 18 (1955), pp. 319–21

Wesselski, A., *Märchen des Mittelalters* (Berlin, 1925)

Wieck, R. S., *Painted Prayers: The Book of Hours in Medieval and Renaissance Art* (New York, 1997)

Wood, M., *The Medieval English House* (London, 1965)

Woods, B. A., 'The Devil in Dog Form', *Western Folklore* 13:4 (1954), pp. 229–35

—— *The Devil in Dog Form: A Partial Type-Index of the Devil Legends* (Berkeley, CA, 1959)

Woolgar, C. M., *The Great Household in Late Medieval England* (London, 1999)

Wright, T., *A History of Domestic Manners and Sentiments in England During the Middle Ages* (London, 1862)

Yapp, W. B., 'Birds in Captivity in the Middle Ages', *Archives of Natural History* 10:3 (1982), pp. 479–500

—— *Birds in Medieval Manuscripts* (London, 1981)

Yoder, L. W., 'The Late Medieval Tale: The Example of "La Dame e les trois papegaulz"', *The French Review* 53:4 (1980), pp. 543–9

Zeri, F., *La pittura in Italia: il Quattrocento* (Milan, 1997)

Ziolkowski, J. M., 'Literary Genre and Animal Symbolism', in *Animals and the Symbolic in Mediaeval Art and Literature*, ed. L. A. J. R. Houwen (Groningen, 1997), pp. 1–23

—— *Talking Animals: Medieval Latin Beast Poetry, 750–1150* (Philadelphia, 1993)

—— 'Tito Vespasiano Strozzi's "Ad psyttacum": A Renaissance Latin Poet Parrots the Past', *Harvard Library Bulletin* 35:2 (1987), pp. 139–49

Websites

Bodleian Library, Oxford: http://bodley30.bodley.ox.ac.uk:8180/luna/servlet/

British Library: http://www.bl.uk/catalogues/illuminatedmanuscripts/welcome.htm

British Museum, London: http://www.britishmuseum.org/research/search_the_collection_database.aspx

Koninklijke Bibliotheek, The Hague http://www.kb.nl/manuscripts/

Kongelige Bibliotek, Copenhagen: http://www.kb.dk/permalink/2006/manus/221/eng/

Medieval Animal Data-Network: http://www.imareal.oeaw.ac.at/animalwiki2/index.php/Main_Page

Victoria and Albert Museum, London: http://collections.vam.ac.uk

Walker Art Gallery, Liverpool: http://www.liverpoolmuseums.org.uk.

✦ ✦

✦

Index

✦ ✦
✦